What's
TRUE
About
YOU

life

What's
TRUE
About
YOU

7 Steps to Move Beyond Your Painful Past
and Manifest Your Brightest Future

Katherine Woodward Thomas

Penguin Life

VIKING
An imprint of Penguin Random House LLC
1745 Broadway, New York, NY 10019
penguinrandomhouse.com

A Penguin Life Book

VIKING is a registered trademark of Penguin Random House LLC.

Grateful acknowledgment is made for permission to reprint the following:

Excerpt from "Lesson 21: Release Ceremony" from *Calling in "The One"
Revised and Expanded: 7 Weeks to Attract the Love of Your Life* by Katherine
Woodward Thomas, copyright © 2005, 2021 by Katherine Woodward Thomas.
Used by permission of Harmony Books, an imprint of Random House,
a division of Penguin Random House LLC. All rights reserved.

Excerpt from "Introduction" from *The Cancer Journals* by Audre Lorde,
copyright © 1980 by Audre Lorde. Used by permission of Penguin Classics,
an imprint of Penguin Publishing Group, a division of Penguin
Random House LLC. All rights reserved.

Designed by Nerylsa Dijol

LIBRARY OF CONGRESS CONTROL NUMBER: 2025032508
ISBN 9780593994405 (hardcover)
ISBN 9780593994412 (ebook)

Printed in the United States of America
1st Printing

The authorized representative in the EU for product safety
and compliance is Penguin Random House Ireland, Morrison Chambers,
32 Nassau Street, Dublin D02 YH68, Ireland, https://eu-contact.penguin.ie.

To my mother,
Sandra Woodward Pullman,
who woke up with me

Contents

Introduction

My Story

~

Above all, be the heroine of your life, not the victim.

—NORA EPHRON

My library, much like yours, is filled with books that begin with the story of the author's past. Yet if I began my book in the same way, I'd risk you knowing only the bruised and broken version of me, which is not knowing me much at all. For it's not my past that defines me but my inspiring and intriguing possible future. A future that's endlessly recalibrating and redefining who I am and who I feel called to become. An urgent and compelling drive that something *more* is wanting to happen, both *to* me and *through* me.

It's not that my past isn't interesting. It would make an excellent, if not somewhat heart-wrenching, novel. Starting with my young and beautiful mother, who'd dress me up like a doll to show me off to friends while unconsciously re-creating the harsh, rejecting relationship she'd had with her own critical mother. My handsome, reckless father who abandoned my mother and me to eventually marry a woman who refused to allow me into their home, casting me as "the other woman" at the tender age of eight. A fifth-grade teacher who for some inexplicable reason made it her mission to stamp out any impulse I had toward leadership and creativity. Such that by the end of my school year with her, I was a shell of a girl. Totally off track to live a life of meaning and purpose. A stepfather who'd hold court deep into the night, drinking beer after beer, reminding me again and again that I'd never amount to anything. While I, so hungry for any semblance of parental attention at the highly impressionable age of fifteen, would sit there absorbing his poisonous perspective for hours. The past and all of its sordid stories and cavernous wounds does have its seductive pull. It's no wonder we can so easily get lost in the telling and retelling over and over again of these high-stakes dramas. Forever analyzing and agonizing over every little detail of the injustices and insults endured at a time when we had little defense against such an onslaught of bad behavior.

Yet as compelling as all of this is, isn't my story at least a little like your own? Don't far too many of us suffer the slings and arrows of being born into unhappy, unfair, unjust situations that brand us with untruthful, toxic, identity-based beliefs like "I'm not good enough," "I'm invisible," or "I'm not safe"? Haven't most of us crafted counterfeit identities in response to these disappointing experiences that put us at risk of living ineffective and unfulfilling lives? Where we fall short of blossoming into the brilliant beings we were born to become?

Even those of us who grew up in "good enough" homes of relative safety and support will often wrestle with a pervasive, undermining sorrow of having never received what we might have needed to know how worthy we are of taking up space in this world. To know beyond a shadow of a doubt, with conviction, that we are loved and lovable exactly as we are. That we came here to contribute gifts that are uniquely ours to give. That we are powerful beyond measure and supported by *all of life* to realize our dreams and destinies.

Secretly, we grieve. The gap between the lives we are living and the lives we intuitively feel we *could* and *should* be living seems so cavernous. And so we dutifully trudge through the wreckage of the past, anxiously trying to understand why we are the way we are. Who is to blame for the brokenness we feel deep down inside? What happened back then that handicapped us with these habitual insecurities

Most of us are suffering from some degree of identity theft.

—ALONZO KING

and self-doubts? As though understanding what happened—where, when, and with whom—were the keys to our freedom. If only he'd loved me more. If only she'd wanted me. If only God had kept me safe. If only she had, or he hadn't . . . you fill in the blank.

I know this path well. I spent over two decades desperately trying to close that uncompromising chasm. Fighting against the quicksand of pervasive low self-esteem that had me chronically, mindlessly overgiving to try to prove my value; as though I had to continually earn the right to exist. Or habitually self-abandoning, frantically trying to convince those with little love to give to please, please love me. Or my tenacious self-destructive tendencies like late-night binge eating, or worse, smoking, which I indulged in off and on well into my fifties. Desperate to get to the bottom of whatever was driving such dysfunctional behavior, I racked up years of "working on myself" as I faithfully attended weekly psychotherapy sessions, group therapy, various twelve-step programs, silent meditation retreats, healing workshops—anything and everything I could think of to *once and for all be rid of the unyielding evidence of past relational traumas* that continued to haunt me in the present. So determined was I to overcome it all that eventually I ended up becoming a licensed psychotherapist myself, helping others get to the bottom of whatever had happened to them that made them who they are today.

Yet fortunately, at some point, I became . . . well, *bored* might actually be the right word for it. Sick and tired of continually defining myself according to the immaturity, mistakes, and misdeeds of others who were either too weak, too selfish, too immature, or simply too damaged themselves to have done it any differently. Weary of introducing myself to yet one more kindhearted, empathetically attuned psychotherapist by dragging out the well-worn narrative of victimization, neglect, abandonment, and sorrow. As though the source of my current pain was a difficult past and not how profoundly out of integrity I was with who I actually am, and the positive, possible future I was here to fulfill.

At some point, I began questioning the ways I was working on myself. Like a fish who is suddenly aware of water, I began wondering if perhaps spending all of this time attending to my lonely past might actually be reinforcing the "I'm alone and no one wants me" narrative that had lodged in the center of my solar plexus as a child. Recognizing that story as a sort of home-base perspective I was defaulting to in the aftermath of any and all disappointments, I noticed that no matter how many insights I had about that, or how many used-up tissues lay crumpled on the couch, that narrative was decidedly fixed. It never really budged, no matter how much I understood who did what to me. And here's the real problem: Whenever I was interpreting what was happening through the lens of that perspective, I tended to respond in ways that created even more evidence for that story, chronically validating it and dooming me to never really be free.

> The source of my pain wasn't a difficult past, but how out of integrity I was with who I actually am, and the future I was here to fulfill.

My first book, *Calling in "The One,"* was initially published in 2004, and introduced a teaching that helps people transform their love lives from the inside out. A core principle of this work is taking radical responsibility for ourselves as the source of our experiences and giving up seeing things from a victimized perspective. It's not a denial of the complexities of life or the fact that many of the things we have to deal with are not at all our fault. Rather, it's a place to stand that gives us access to the power we need to transform deeply rooted patterns we may previously have felt powerless to change. As someone who aspires to hold myself accountable to walk my talk, I was confronted with the need to apply my own teaching fairly soon after the book was published.

I was a first-time author being published by a major publishing house. To say I was nervous was an understatement. I'd poured my heart and soul into this book. To me, it

What do sad people have in common?
It seems they have all built
a shrine to the past and often go there
and do a strange wail and worship.
What is the beginning of happiness?
It is to stop being so religious like that.

—HAFIZ, TRANSLATED BY DANIEL LADINSKY

was like giving birth to a child. And all of the things we want for our children, I wanted for this book; I yearned for it to find its rightful place in the world and to become all that it had the potential to be.

Imagine my disappointment, then, when the church I'd gone to for well over a decade failed to give me a book signing upon its release. This was a church that had thousands of members. A signing would have given the book a fair shot at being a success right out of the gate. For months leading up to the publication date I called the main office, leaving multiple messages, assuming they'd be happy to celebrate my accomplishment. As the weeks rolled by, however, with no return call, I became more and more indignant. How could they do this to me? I'd fully expected this signing to happen and had even included it in my book proposal. Deeply confused by this unexpected lack of response, I collapsed into the disappointment of it and left the church altogether.

Now, I had a story about this and it was nasty. In addition to the sting of my old familiar narrative of not being wanted *yet again*, I was also righteously convinced that the church was a mess; completely out of integrity and disorganized. That the people running the organization were incompetent at best. That the minister had lost control of his congregation and had become too self-important to see what was happening. I mean, this story went on and on, and it totally justified my withdrawal from the community. Why wouldn't I leave when all of this nonsense was going on over there? This is what I mean by "seeing things from a victimized perspective." It doesn't occur to us that we're feeling victimized. It occurs to us that we're *right* about this! This is just how it is!

I'm sure I would have left it at that had I not just put a book out into the world whose main premise was personal responsibility. So as a practice— and I mean, just as a practice—I decided to apply non-victimization to this experience. Taking out my journal, I began writing, asking myself, *IF I was responsible in any way for what went down, what might my part have been?* (Notice the emphasis on the word *if*.) Now, they say that one should never ask a question they don't really want to hear the answer to, and boy, did I get an earful.

Here is what I discovered when I finally got off it enough to inquire into my own responsibility for what happened. For years I'd considered myself to be a shy person. Shy to the point where it was hard for me to meet new people and look them in the eye when we spoke. So even though I'd spent ten years attending services at this church, the truth was, I rarely talked to anyone. When I did, I tended to underpresent myself by speaking softly and looking down at the ground. You have to understand, this was a church in Los Angeles, California—land of the aspiring and accomplished performer. The church was filled with glorious peacock personalities, many of them proudly parading in the parking lot both before and after services, delighted for the chance to meet and greet the other glorious peacocks in the flock. I felt as though I paled in comparison, and most of the time would shrink inside myself when attempting to socialize. I was so uncomfortable that for years I defended against my own feelings of insecurity by arriving five minutes after services began, slipping silently into the back row, and leaving five minutes before services ended. Thereby never really giving myself the opportunity to truly become a part of the community by forming authentic connections with like-minded others.

As embarrassing as this is to admit, I'm also not the best of students. Truthfully, I tend to prefer listening to my own thoughts over the thoughts of others and can become quite distracted by the latest musings going on inside my head from whatever might be happening around me. This often makes it hard for me to focus my attention on what others might be trying to offer me. So even though the church was a known learning center that offered a beehive of classes and workshops each day of the week, in all of my time as a member, I'd never once taken a class.

Hmm . . . maybe I was onto something here.

Digging deeper, I also had to acknowledge that in all those years, I'd never once served on any church committee. Nor had I made any significant financial contribution. Nor had I volunteered for any of the wonderful programs they offered to clean up the beaches, feed people living on the streets, visit the sick, adopt an elderly congregant, mentor orphans, or befriend those who are incarcerated.

You get the picture.

Once I began looking through the lens of seeing myself as the source of my experience, I was shamefaced to admit that what had happened was completely on me. I had re-created my deepest wounding from childhood of not belonging; of being on the outside looking in, forever alone and unwanted.

Now at that point, I could have begun analyzing why I had behaved this way, as I'd done for years, having been in and out of therapy for well over a decade. It wasn't hard to connect the dots. I could have easily explained my behavior by pointing to how I'd never felt wanted as a child. Or to how inferior I felt compared with my glamorous and beautiful mother. Or maybe it was the social awkwardness I felt at the start of each school year when having to make new friends yet again, having moved nearly every year throughout my childhood. In the face of all of this insight, I might have gone back to the drawing board, rolled up my shirtsleeves to do another round of healing work on past hurts, because clearly, I was not yet sufficiently sorted out.

Yet this time, I did something different. I asked myself what beliefs I was operating from that would have me show up in such self-defeating ways, skipping the story and heading straight for self-responsibility.

Looking to understand myself as the source of this disappointing experience, I closed my eyes and took a deep breath. I looked for where in my body I held the unpleasant feelings of social shame that would so quickly take over whenever I tried making an authentic connection. Once I found the feelings in my body, I looked for the underlying assumptions that were informing them. Having spent years talking about my past, I had clear cognitive ideas of what my beliefs were and had been dealing with them as "issues" for just as long—my low self-esteem, my codependence, and my sabotaging love-

> I asked myself what beliefs I was operating from that would have me show up in such self-defeating ways, skipping the story and heading straight for self-responsibility.

avoidance patterns that were chronically insistent, in spite of the fact that I longed to have love in my life. Yet in all this time, I'd never actually let my body speak for itself by inviting it to name the core assumptions I was holding in my belly.

Without trying to fix or change anything, I simply looked to accurately name the covert inner dialogue I'd been mindlessly relating to as truth. Though it took a while to decipher, little by little I was able to put the feelings into language that told a story about who I am and what was (or in this case wasn't) possible for me. *I don't belong anywhere or to anyone. Others belong to each other, but I'm not invited to the party. I will always be on the outside looking in.* I took a deep breath and asked how old the part of me was that first felt this way. I heard a faint whisper within. *Eight*, came the answer.

Eight. That was right after my mother's divorce from her second husband. A tall man named Herb who was an alcoholic and who made it clear he didn't like children. Eight. I'd just started a new school and was awkwardly trying to make friends. Eight. The year my father got remarried to a woman who agreed to tie the knot on the condition that I not be a part of their family. Eight. The year I became a "latchkey kid," and came home each day to an empty house, to eat saltine crackers while parked in front of the television for hours, waiting for my mom to come home. Eight. The time one of my grandmothers almost died from an aneurysm and I lost contact with the other—the one I loved most, who'd patiently taught me to tell time when I was four, and who was now part of the past due to the ugly divorce between my parents. Eight.

Not my best year.

By this time, I'm crying in my notebook. "Snot running down my face" kind of crying. "Splotches on the page, making the ink run all over the page" kind of crying. But I'm not crying because I feel sad about the past. I'm crying because I can see that the decisions I'd made about myself— that I didn't belong, that I wasn't wanted, that I was somehow inferior to others—were all so unfair. I'm crying because I can see that inside of these assumptions, I'd chronically shown up in ways that had re-created the agonizing experience of never belonging anywhere, over and over again.

I'm crying because I see I'd been relating to that little eight-year-old's story as though it were real. God made the mountains, God made the sun, and God made Little Kathi to not belong anywhere or to anyone. I'm crying because I know beyond a shadow of a doubt that it was never true, not even for one millisecond, and because I have so much compassion for that little girl who somehow breathed it into her heart and soul that she would always be on the outside of any community she tried to join and never be invited to the party.

And intuitively, without thinking about it, I suddenly became big, fierce, and brave. I imagined scooping her up into my strong, protective arms and looking into her sad little eyes, and I literally shouted out loud, "Sweetheart, you belong to me! I've got you, angel. I love you! And you don't just belong to me, you belong to the whole world! You're here to help people heal. You are here as mother to the world. You are a voice of love, hope, and truth, and the world needs you!" By then my tears had turned to laughter at the sheer power of this moment as I unselfconsciously and wholeheartedly proclaimed my *true self*.

Spontaneously, I came up with this *power statement*:

I am mother to the world.

Everyone belongs to me and I belong to them!

Initiating a long overdue adjustment in my own consciousness, I woke myself up from the trance of the lies I'd created as a child, and which had been driving me to show up in ways that literally enrolled others into that story, covertly pulling on them to validate it again and again. Standing in the deeper truth of myself as someone who belonged to

The displacement of the false by the true is the essence of the healing of all things visible and invisible.
—DAVID R. HAWKINS

everyone and they to me, I immediately began looking for new ways of relating that might generate a different experience. One by one, I began listing these new ways of relating in my journal.

→ Look people in the eye when you speak with them.
→ Arrive five minutes early and leave five minutes (or more) after an event ends.
→ Participate. Sit in the front row and raise your hand.
→ Volunteer to help. Do service in all communities you join.
→ Make visible the gifts and contributions you have to offer others.
→ Be the one to throw the party.

Now, as remedial as these actions may sound to you, to me they were radical. These ways of relating were completely outside of who I knew myself to be. Yet I was determined. The following weekend I strapped my four-year-old daughter into her car seat and off we went to church, arriving five minutes *before* services began. After dropping her at Sunday school, I walked into the sanctuary, deliberately looking people straight in the eye and smiling, as awkward as that felt. And believe you me, it felt weird to show up this way. Like I was playing a part in a play and was not myself at all. I found a spot up front and quickly discovered during pre-service announcements that the children's choir was looking for new members.

A few days later, my daughter and I walked hand in hand into the big warehouse where the children's choir rehearsed each week. Joining the other moms and dads in the parents' room as the kids started singing, I felt the self-consciousness of being a newcomer. I knew no one in the room, and they all seemed to know one another. I felt my face flush as I was invited to stand and introduce myself. A few moments later, the assistant director stood up with a clipboard and began reading off volunteer positions that needed to be filled. First on her list was the celebration committee. Now, I had no idea what the celebration committee was, but I was determined to break my pattern of not belonging. So up shot my hand. It was the only hand that went up in that room full of people. And that's how I ended up becoming the *head* of the celebration committee, which consisted of one person. Me.

The following week, when I arrived, the parents' room was alive with excitement, with everyone wildly animated, talking and laughing all at once. Apparently, the White House had called. The Obamas had heard about the children and wanted them to come sing for them. Suddenly, in the midst of the mayhem, I remember. *Oh! I'm head of the celebration committee! And this is cause for celebration!* So I stand up on a chair to get everyone's attention and announce I'm throwing a What to Wear to the White House party. Off the top of my head, I start rattling off all the things we're going to do to celebrate this momentous occasion. We'll all wear red, white, and blue; we'll barbecue by the pool (so bring your bathing suits!); and we'll play all sorts of fun games together. The parents love this.

In the tradition of two steps forward, one step back, the following week, I'm five minutes late to rehearsal, which means I'm the last parent to arrive. Walking into the room, everyone suddenly stops talking and turns toward the door, smiling and waving. And I do a double take and look backward to see who they're waving at. Completely clueless that they are actually waving at *me*. Welcoming *me* into the room. As though I actually *belong* in that room and to these people.

You have to understand how drastic a change this was for me. I was in my mid-forties and this was *the first time in my entire life* that a room full of people not only acknowledged my arrival but also happily and enthusiastically welcomed me into the room.

Sniff, sniff.

It's the little moments that matter. Particularly when it comes to outgrowing who you've known yourself to be. Turns out that the celebration committee was actually about observing each kid's birthday with a balloon. Who knew? And at that point, who cared? I stumbled through the post without ever getting a handle on exactly what was expected of me and was absurdly imperfect at doing the job. But perfection didn't matter, as I became a valued member of that group of good-hearted people.

I long, as does every human being, to be at home wherever I find myself.
—MAYA ANGELOU

The mirroring I received that day from that room full of parents did more to evolve my broken sense of belonging than a decade's worth of analyzing why I was the way I was. Beliefs are relational, and "self" is not a solo phenomenon. Beliefs are initially formed in relationship with others, and they must be *transformed* in relationship with others as well. Particularly beliefs as vital as the ones we hold about who we are and where we fit into this world. Insight is insufficient to graduate us from habitually painful patterns born from an impaired sense of self.

Several months later, I ran into the minister of the church at our local gym. I decided to tell him what had happened and why I'd left the church for a time, making sure to tell the story from a place of profound self-responsibility. He listened intently before saying, "You know, I never understood why you didn't do a signing when your book came out. I specifically instructed my assistant to make sure that happened." Upon which I thought, *Wow. Look how powerful our stories about ourselves are.* Recognizing that my old story had somehow managed to eclipse the minister's best intentions.

As Werner Erhard said, "Understanding is the booby prize." The real prize is waking up from the trance of an identity formed in response to past relational trauma. Awakening to a new, more *true* sense of self, and learning to show up in ways reflective of this truth. To stop enrolling others into an old, toxic narrative by unconsciously setting them up to validate it.

I felt as if I'd discovered gold. Perhaps I had. For there's little evidence in my life today of that recurring nightmare of not belonging. Before this, I'd been plagued with a kind of phantom pain of some elusive future I was here to fulfill, yet which forever seemed out of reach. I felt as though I were walking through life wearing clothes two sizes too small, and in colors that were totally wrong for me. As though I should be draped in maroon-red, flowing silk, yet was perpetually wrapped up in a medium-brown polyester. *Trapped* in a medium-brown polyester was more like it.

While I tried to make the best of whatever situation I was in, deep down I was confused and a little depressed by how "off" my life was. I yearned to belong to the smart, fun, creative crowd who were up to some-

Don't look for your
dreams to come true.
Look to be true to your dreams.
—MICHAEL B. BECKWITH

thing meaningful in the world, and this hunger drove me to keep shadowboxing with a past that seemed to have so cruelly set me up to fall short of my dreams and desires. It was not until I discovered the practices I share in this book that I was able to manifest the life I had so longed to be living for many, many years.

By owning myself as the source of my patterns, correcting my consciousness, and developing new ways of relating that were more aligned with the truth of who I am, and the future I'm inspired to create, I have virtually disappeared that old story. Rather than looking backward to forever try to heal my past, I needed to listen for the future that was calling me and actively grow myself in the direction of my dreams—plugging up the holes of the missing development left over from a challenging childhood. In so doing, the experience of being on the outside looking in, with all of its accompanying feelings of frustration, invisibility, and social shyness, soon became a mere memory of how life used to be.

How to Use This Book

Given how psychologically sophisticated we are these days, many of us know exactly what happened to us back then that has made us who we are today. We are well aware of the toxic beliefs we formed in response to old traumas that somehow seared themselves into the center of our souls. Beliefs that now show up as crippling self-doubt, chronic underlying anxiety, or shame-based inner narratives that are forever pulling on us to shy away from life. Yet as helpful as it is to be cognizant of how the past is now bleeding into the present, awareness is not an awakening, and insight alone won't get us to the promised land. We must cultivate a capacity to wake ourselves up when we fall into the ditch and consciously align both our identity and our behaviors with the bright futures we are here to create.

For over twenty years, I've been developing a deeply transformative process that can untether you from unwanted patterns born from false beliefs that may have plagued you for years. Having had the honor of leading tens of thousands of people through this process in my in-person and online learning communities, I'm happy to say that when you apply all I offer in these pages to your own life, you will become unrecognizable within a relatively short period of time. Although your inner experience will likely be that you feel more like yourself than you ever have before. Liberated from the limitations of your past and able to create your life outside of your old imprinting, you will begin to feel less victimized by what happened to you way back when and more capable of manifesting a life that feels lit up and alive with possibilities and potential.

Part one of this book will take you through a step-by-step process that has been carefully designed to help bridge the chasm between your life as you've known it to be and the life you're committed to creating. You can read and work through this portion of the book quickly or you can move through it slowly, savoring and working deeply with each step. Whether you move through it in seven days, seven weeks, or seven months is really up to you, and any time you devote will be time well spent. I also encourage you to bookmark the teachings and practices that feel especially relevant. In this way, you can return to them later to master their application in your own life.

As a licensed psychotherapist who worked in clinics and private practice for many years, I can attest that traditional therapy that's oriented around healing past trauma is invaluable and incredibly helpful. Yet if you find yourself frustrated by the years you've spent digging around in your past with nothing significantly changing, then this book is for you. I can confidently assert that if you do the program as it's offered in these pages, it will allow you to rapidly, radically transform any area of life that you're willing to stand for. And yes, I do mean any area—your love life (including self-love), finances, career, health, self-expression, friends, family, you name it. Wherever you've suffered and struggled the most—wherever you've felt the most stuck, resigned, and hopeless—this is the area I invite you to focus on as you move through the steps. By shifting the tide in this one area, you will discover your power to generate a life outside of your old story, which can then be applied to other areas of your life as well. Before moving into part two, I offer thoughts on how you might bring the work you've been engaging for yourself out into the world, to actively manifest greater happiness and abundance for all.

Part two of this book provides the True You Breakthrough Blueprint, a practical and easily understood atlas of the twenty-two most common identity-based beliefs that I call your *source fracture story*. That's the story you created about yourself and your relationship to others and to life in response to the original break in your sense of belonging—stories such as "I'm alone, everyone always leaves, and I can never get what I need from anyone," "I am invisible, others don't care about my feelings or needs, and it's dangerous to be seen," or "I don't matter, other people matter more than me and nothing I do or say ever really matters." These are the internal narratives that are at the heart of the frustrating patterns you're here to outgrow. The True You Breakthrough Blueprint will provide clarity on the very specific, habitual ways you have been showing up in relationship with yourself, others, and life that have unconsciously generated evidence for your source fracture story, and the exact steps you can take to graduate from doing so, such that you are finally free to generate your life outside of it. While you're welcome to refer to the blueprint in part two at any time during your journey, I encourage you to first engage the seven steps of the program in part one. The purpose of the blueprint is simply to *refine* what you are already discovering about yourself in part one and point your way to the growth needed to evolve beyond your old unwanted story of lack and limitation.

In closing, I provide information for therapists, counselors, and coaches on how you can begin to integrate the highly transformative future forward frameworks I introduce in this book into the work you're doing with clients.

Doing This Program with Others

If at all possible, I encourage you to gather a group of friends to go through the seven-step True You process together by forming a True You Intention Circle, to act as cheerleaders and accountability partners for one another. It helps to have others who care about us, and who are invested in our progress, right there with us to witness and inspire our journey. People we care about and admire, who can hold our intentions with and for us—particularly in the aftermath of a discouraging setback, obstacle, or delay, when we are most vulnerable to giving up or dimming down our dreams. In those moments, we carry one another, refusing to be enrolled into a lesser story of what's possible for one another. Remaining steadfast in our belief that what is being experienced is simply a clearing out, or an opportunity to grow into who we will need to be in order to manifest and sustain the vision we are standing for. While we are kind in the face of our friends' discouragement and offer compassion and understanding of how challenging the pathway toward realizing our highest potential can be, we also refuse to see them as anything less than what they are aspiring to become. This is true friendship. This is true love.

For guidance on how you can create a True You Intention Circle by gathering a group of your friends to do the program together, please go to katherinewoodwardthomas.com/trueyoubonuses.

If you have questions or need support, please contact us at support @katherinewoodwardthomas.com. We're here for you. We are standing with you, and for you, to become the person you intuitively know you are born to become, and to manifest the fulfilling life you came here to live, all in service to standing together to cocreate a more beautiful, healthy, and sustainable world for us all.

Now let's go manifest some miracles.

> *When we take people . . . merely as they are, we make them worse; when we treat them as if they were what they should be, we improve them as far as they can be improved.*
>
> —JOHANN WOLFGANG VON GOETHE, TRANSLATED BY THOMAS CARLYLE

Part One

7 STEPS OF
TRUE YOU

True You Premises

~

All of us are . . . discovering the nature of how powerful we are.
We are on a huge cosmic quest as we realize that we are participating
in the dynamic of creation. Every single thing we say and every single
thing we think sparks an act of creation. We are co-creating the
dynamic in which we live. That is the hugest mystical
revelation of our time, and it will reshape us.

—CAROLINE MYSS

The intention of this book is to awaken you to that which you already know.

In fact, you may have sensed much of what's written here for a while by now and reading it will simply validate your knowing. While some books are memoirs, this one might be considered a "rememboir"—writings to help you remember who you are and what it is you came here to create.

The book will help move you beyond who you assumed yourself to be in response to the wounds you experienced long, long ago. Hurts that somehow imprinted on you at the deepest level with unwanted beliefs and saddled you with the stubborn patterns you tend to struggle with in life today. It will help you not just *deal* with these old hurts but give you direct access to freedom beyond them. Awakening your power to make all of the wonderful things you want to happen in your life happen. Such that you're no longer on the outside looking in, just hoping, wishing, and praying for a miracle.

Ultimately, however, this book is not just about learning how to manifest everything you want in life . . . as much as it's about awakening to yourself as *a masterful manifester*—someone who's taken their rightful place as *a creator of life*, and not simply *a reactor to life*.

Which, for many of us, is a new way of being in relationship with life. A relationship where you have the spiritual strength, as well as the agency, to actively generate the future you desire. No matter how much evidence you've accumulated over the years that validates the story of your powerlessness.

> This book is about awakening to yourself as *a master manifester*—someone who has taken their rightful place as *a creator of life*, and not simply *a reactor to life*.

The assumptions laid out in the following pages are the foundational frameworks of the teachings included in this book. I invite you to take them on faith and not get too distracted by debate or philosophical differences. If this type of faith is uncomfortable or unfamiliar to you, I ask you to give it a try, at least for the duration of our journey together. Imagine that life is dynamic, and that you and I are the vehicles through which it is evolving. That the creative energies of life are calling us to consciously cocreate a bright and desirable future, in spite of how discouraging things may seem to be at the moment. We might call these creative energies God, Higher Power, the Universe, Spirit, or simply the Greater Field of Life, for all of us can admit we're not the only life-form here, no matter what your spiritual or religious beliefs. I'm inviting us to consider challenging the idea of God as some big parent in the sky who is holding all the power, while we weak mortals must resort to hoping, wishing, praying, and even begging for what we hope will or won't happen. Rather, I am inviting us to consider that the Universe is our partner in cocreating whatever future we have the courage to stand for. In other words, you'll want to begin relating to God, whoever or whatever God is for you, as your partner rather than your parent.

Though this book is finite, the practices it introduces are not. The premises below are meant to recalibrate how you are in relationship to life and to awaken you to the power you're holding to be proactive in co-creating the future of your life, and the future of our world.

Premise 1: The Future Is Fluid and Open to Our Influence and Intentions

To manifest what might be considered a miracle in an area where you've felt stuck in a loop of lack and limitation, you must have the courage—as well as *a touch of madness*—to declare a fruitful and fulfilling future in this very area. You must be brave enough to stand for a bright and beautiful future that both informs and initiates the growth necessary to manifest and sustain that possibility.

> You must be brave enough to stand for a bright future that informs and initiates the growth required to manifest and sustain that possibility.

You'll want to claim an inspired future that is big and bold enough to challenge your current identity, to recalibrate who you know yourself to be, and to kick-start you into a developmental mindset because it will immediately begin informing how you will now need to grow and change in order to fulfill that positive possibility.

Contrary to our tendencies to assume a fixed future—as though there were some Higher Being out there somewhere who's holding all the power to determine where we're going from here—we might consider that there is no future other than the one we ourselves actively stand for and generate. There are probabilities, of course. The karma of actions taken that have initiated movement in a particular direction. There may be long-term patterns at play or unhealthy habits that might predict what's coming next: personality preferences, tenacious tendencies, or ancient prophecies that haunt us late at night. In spite of all this, the future itself is up for grabs and easily swayed by the influence of our intentions to manifest what it is we are called and committed to creating.

Whether this is true or not is, of course, food for debate. However, I'm asking you to try this perspective on and to take it at face value, largely because it's the most powerful place to be standing in life.

> *It is not enough to*
> *believe in the future;*
> *we must believe*
> *the future in.*
> —ROBERT FROST

Premise 2: While Healing Is the Domain of the Past, Transformation Is the Domain of the *Future*

We have a collective assumption. One that has influenced the ways millions of us have been working on ourselves. We assume that once we've rummaged around in the past long enough to finally understand why we are the way we are, that we will somehow stumble upon our power to evolve beyond who we've known ourselves to be and be liberated to live the lives we long to be living.

While healing requires we look backward, transformation requires we lean in, listen for, and live into a *positive, possible future.* There's a time to grieve the pain of the past. To connect the dots between what happened way back then and the patterns we struggle with today. Yet for those of us who've been working on ourselves for a while now, the time of focusing solely on the past in order to change our lives for the better has now passed. At this point, you'll want to begin the jour-

> While healing requires we look backward, transformation requires we lean in, listen for, and live into a positive, possible future.

ney of actively growing yourself to become who you will need to be to manifest the miracles you're standing for.

Premise 3: Wherever You Are Centered at the Level of Identity Is Where You Are Generating Your Life From

By now, many of us know that what we focus on grows. And years of analyzing *who* did what to us *when*, *how* they did it, *why* they did it, *where* they did it, and how we *feel* about that has most likely served to solidify the self we formed in response to what we endured—which may be the absolute *worst* thing we could possibly do to try to get beyond it.

> Begin by actively growing into who you'll need to be to manifest the miracles you're standing for.

Identity drives creation. Wherever you are centered at the level of identity will determine your destiny. While most of us hold the equivalent of a PhD in our understanding of the nega-

> Identity drives creation.

tive impact our history has had upon our sense of self, few of us recognize our power to challenge and change the impaired identity–based narratives we formed about ourselves and our relationship to others and to life itself in response to past traumas.

I call it your source fracture story— your original attachment wounding. The break in your heart and spirit that lodged in your body as a self-defeating, shame-based sense of self that you are vulnerable to returning to and collapsing into when you feel disappointed, threatened, or scared *now*. If we allow ourselves to

> *The pain-body, which is the dark shadow cast by the ego . . . depends on your unconscious identification with it . . . if you don't face it, if you don't bring the light of your consciousness into the pain, you will be forced to relive it again and again.*
> —ECKHART TOLLE

> Redefine who
> you are according to
> the future you're called
> to create, rather than
> stay overly identified
> with the *traumatized
> self* you formed
> in response to
> past pain.

react from this perspective, we will inevitably create evidence for it.

To truly change your life, you will want to consciously redefine who you are according to the future you're called to create, rather than staying overly identified with the *traumatized self* you formed in response to past disappointments. In waking yourself up to a newer, truer sense of who you are, old self-defeating patterns organically start to disappear. They quickly become a mere memory of how things *used to be*, as you stop unconsciously showing up in ways that create further evidence for your outdated trauma-based story. When you are no longer swimming in the dirty waters of your old, pain-based story, you are finally liberated to create outside of it.

Premise 4: You Are the Source of Your Own Experience

By now, you may have volumes of evidence for your old story that's been keeping you stuck. You've been undervalued, not chosen, left behind, unrecognized, unsuccessful, or unloved one too many times—in spite of how hard you've worked on yourself, and how committed you've been to get beyond it. It's normal to feel victimized by our own consciousness, particularly when evidence of that story keeps showing up in the present. Most of us feel a little hopeless when it comes to overcoming the seemingly immovable imprinting of our past. Yet the key to accessing the power to evolve beyond it is to recognize that *you* are actually the source of all the evidence you've gathered through the years for this perspective.

Though it seems that all of the re-wounding experiences you've had over the years have just happened *to you,* they've actually happened *through you.* Through the choices you organically make, and the actions you organically take, when you are emotionally centered in your old story and overly identified with the self you formed in response to your old trauma. The specific and highly predictable habitual ways of relating, which clandestinely generate a cascade of evidence for this negative worldview.

The breakthrough happens when you become willing to take 100 percent responsibility for yourself as the source of your experience, letting go of blaming anyone else for why you are the way you are.

While what happened to you in the past is not your fault, the choices you chronically and mindlessly make in the present are now your responsibility to transform. No one else is coming to make this better for you. You are the only one who can disappear the unwanted residue of your past hurts.

> *When you reframe things, and*
> *you actually see the source within ourselves,*
> *all of a sudden, that's liberating because, guess what?*
> *If you're feeling that way because this guy did this*
> *or didn't do that, that makes you a victim . . .*
> *But if you see that you are the source,*
> *now, you're powerful.*
> —GABOR MATÉ

Premise 5: You Have a Significant Role to Play in Cocreating a Bright and Sustainable Future for Us All

You are not here just for you. You are an integral part of a vast matrix of life. How you show up and what you choose to give your love, time, and attention to matters. It matters not just to you and to your immediate friends and family. It matters to us all. *You* matter to us all.

At a time lacking in certainty, when we're suffering from a vast shortage of optimism and hope—where massive amounts of darkness and doom appear to be nipping at our heels each time we read the news—it's important to remember how fluid the future is, and how open it is to our input. To *your* input, in particular.

The light at the end of the tunnel is a mirror.
—NEAL ROGIN

In spite of how discouraged you may be, I ask you to suspend your judgment and assume that a bright and beautiful future is wanting to happen for us all. And that this positive, possible future needs all hands on deck. *Yours especially.* This is the context for this work, and it would be irresponsible not to mention it up front.

Let's also assume that we are to begin right where we are. With the urgent need that each of us feels to awaken our own ability to manifest the healthy, happy lives we long to be living. Because in order to take your rightful place in the world as someone whose gifts matter to the well-being of all, you must first know yourself as a *creator* of life, and not just as a survivor or a victim of circumstance. You must know yourself as someone who has the power to declare a vision that looks a little left of impossible and a whole lot unreasonable, and who then begins making choices to find their way to that beautiful bold future, one risky, wild, messy, magical step at a time.

Taking these premises at face value will be a stretch for some. Yet, as with most stretches, it will be well worth the effort. For embracing these foundational assumptions and adopting them as your own will immediately unleash a cascade of hope and inspiration—waking you up to the truth of who you are, and the power you're holding to manifest a life you love.

Step 1:
Claim a Positive,
Possible Future

~

May you have the courage to listen to the voice of desire
That disturbs you when you have settled for something safe.

—JOHN O'DONOHUE

L et's begin by turning toward the glorious, fiery hunger in your heart. The one that has you in its grip and won't let go with its chronic insistence that you be, do, and have *more*. It's bigger than hope. You're not just *hoping* to one day *maybe* manifest more love, abundance, happiness, health, and creativity. You're *yearning* for it *now*. Like its absence is burning a hole in your solar plexus, and each day you live without it is like being stuck on the wrong side of life.

It's not like you haven't been trying. You've probably been untangling the gnarly knot of your own psychology for a while by now, desperate to evolve beyond your unwanted patterns and clear the way for this golden phantom future to finally arrive. There are, of course, slivers of memories that make sense of your current dilemma. Things that happened long ago that seemed to set you up to pine after what you don't yet have.

You remember the dread you felt at the tender age of five as you listened to your father stumble home drunk after you'd gone to bed. Or the way you stopped breathing at the age of nine when you found your mother standing at the kitchen sink crying, recalling it as vividly as if it happened yesterday. Or that time your older brother teased you in front of your friends until your skin felt like it was on fire. Or when your sister got you into trouble for something she did, and rage welled up within you, causing you to do something you've never told anyone, not even your therapist. Perhaps it was the panic you felt as you wandered around lost for what seemed a very long time that day your aunt forgot you at the mall. Maybe these memories still make you feel the sting of shame. As though they somehow defined your value by stripping you of it.

Yet it's not what happened thirty or forty years ago that frustrates you the most. It's what happened thirty or forty minutes ago, when that ugly pattern repeated itself yet again, in spite of all you've done to try be rid of it. Someone left or didn't come through for you, even though they promised. Or you were once again lied to, rejected, misunderstood, or falsely accused. Or you found yourself all alone to try to figure things out, *again*. How is it that these things are still happening to you? And how is it that they still have the power to make you feel as though you're not good enough, not safe, not seen, not important, or so deeply alone in life?

We all have our tales to tell. Elaborate, often anguished accounts that describe in detail what happened when that made us who we are today. Narratives that explain how the painful, tenacious patterns that get in the way of realizing our dreams in life are not so much our fault as they are our inherited burden to bear. Stories that rationalize why the beautiful lives we yearn to be living stubbornly remain just out of reach, torturing us with what *should* be happening that *once again* isn't or with what *shouldn't* be happening that *once again*, unfortunately, is.

> Our inner work is compromised if we don't also include the positive, possible future we are here to create.

Surely, we think, we must only be a few more tear-filled therapy sessions away from getting to the bottom of whatever it is that's keeping us stuck. Maybe if we dig a bit deeper into the suffering we endured at the hands of our unconscious, unevolved families, we'll finally be empowered to create liberated, happy, healthy lives of love, success, recognition, and reward. Yet what if I told you that the ways we've been doing our inner work are compromised if we don't also include the positive, possible future we are called to create?

Healing Is the Domain of the Past

For years we've been rummaging through the past, assuming that in doing so, we'll somehow access the power we need to transform the present and unlock the possibilities of the future.

By now, however, many of us understand that what we focus on *grows*.

> What we focus on *grows*.

Though we've had great faith in leaving no stone from our childhoods unturned, digging through the dirty ditches of all the damage done—assuming this to be the Holy Grail of our healing—we must admit, it's only been somewhat helpful. Truth be told, most of us live with minor variations of the same disappointing themes year after year, in spite of spending hundreds, if not thousands, of hours and dollars diligently "working on ourselves."

Years of analyzing why we are the way we are, and paying attention again and again to the injuries we once endured, may have actually served to solidify the traumatized self we formed in response to our experience. Which may be the absolute *worst* thing we could possibly do to try to get beyond it. Because wherever we're centered at the level of identity—the "I am alone," "I'm bad," or the "I'm not safe" narrative that hijacks our bodies the moment we feel threatened or disappointed—is the "me" that is both interpreting what's

> Years of analyzing why we are the way we are, attending again and again to injuries once endured, may have served to solidify the traumatized self we formed in response to past experiences.

happening and spontaneously responding in ways that will unconsciously create evidence that validates this perspective. Causing us to unknowingly repeat the same frustrating patterns again and again. Finding ourselves once again in yet another codependent relationship, or once more being undervalued and underpaid or being constantly criticized by someone in a position of power. It seems like the pattern is simply happening *to* you, as though it's just your fate to be living this story, but it's actually happening *through* you. Through the choices you organically make and the actions you organically take when emotionally centered in that sense of self.

Healing your heart of past hurts and transforming your life in an area that has traditionally perplexed and pained you are two vastly different domains. It's not that your efforts to heal from a painful past don't matter. They do. Profoundly. Yet many of the hurts you suffered as an infant, child, adolescent, or early adult may always need your patience, love, and care. Particularly on certain days, like the anniversary of someone's passing or every fall when the leaves turn a particular shade of red. Maybe when you hear *that* song, the one that brings it all back again, as though it just happened five minutes ago and not fifty years ago. In that moment, you may just need to lovingly hold that younger, wounded part of yourself. The grief of being abandoned, unloved, unwanted, or unsafe is a valid grief. You have a right to feel sad about what you didn't get early on in life. What happened to you, as well as to many of us, was tragic and can never be undone. Yet it can be witnessed and loved from the part of you that's able to hold compassion for yourself. And allowed to carve wisdom, depth, and kindness into the center of who you are.

> It seems like the pattern is just happening *to* you, but actually it's happening *through* you— through the choices you organically make and the actions you organically take when centered in that sense of self.

Not all wounds can be fully healed. Some just need to be held with love. Healing is about coming home to your body, learning to regulate your nervous system, and finding your way to greater mental balance and emotional stability. It's about the tears of relief you might shed in recognizing that you've never been on the outside of love, even though you may have felt that way for years. It's the softening into a sense of

Despite the common misperception that psychological unpacking keeps you in your "story," I have seen many people get stuck by trying to bypass and transcendwhat needs to be faced with love.

—MIRANDA MACPHERSON

compassion not only for yourself, but perhaps also for your perpetrators, who likely were wounded in ways similar to how they wounded you. You might even allow these old hurts to break your heart open to a deeper level of compassion for others throughout the world who are also suffering with similar hurts in this very moment. All wounds come with golden gifts at their core, and those of us who are warriors of love and light will look for the ways we can now bless others because of what we once went through ourselves. As the great Carl Jung is purported to have once said, "I am not what happened to me. I am what I choose to become." I might also add, ". . . and the goodness I choose to create from the brokenness I once endured."

You've likely been connecting the dots for a while by now between what happened in your youth and how life goes for you today. Noticing the patterns, di-

> Not all wounds can be fully healed. Some just need to be held with love.

agnosing your issues, and discovering the impact of relational traumas you once suffered at the hands of those who were most likely too wounded themselves to have done it any differently. The work we've all been doing on ourselves to repair old hurts has been life altering. Our gratitude goes to the brilliant teachers who've been in the trenches for years, forging pathways to understand the impact past trauma has had on our lives and how it's been limiting what's possible for us to create. Yet recognizing the impact that past trauma has had on us is just one leg of the journey. It's not the destination itself. The destination we're aspiring to is the ability to create our lives outside of the story we made up about ourselves in response to whatever happened to us.

Transformation Is the Domain of the Future

The word *generate* shares the same root as the words *genesis* and *generation*. Essentially the prefix *gen* means to give birth to something, to initiate that which is new, to cause something that has never before existed. As much as your efforts to heal old trauma might *save* your life, if you're only looking backward, you're limiting your ability to actually *change* your life. Because changing your life has more to do with consciously generating an unprecedented future and developing new ways of relating that are consistent with the person you feel called to become than it does with analyzing the person you've known yourself to be.

I learned this myself only by grace. I, like many of us, suffered my share of soul-shattering relational traumas early on in life. I also endured the resulting shrapnel that showed up as seemingly immovable unhealthy patterns as an adult. Persistent underearning, as for years I barely made it paycheck to paycheck. A continual experience of being undervalued and underrecognized, feeling as though I were forever tap dancing in the desperate hope of finally being seen and valued for my talents. A chronic, compounded ache in my chest as one unworthy person after another found their way into my heart, my home, and my bed. All of this was made more discouraging by the urgent and compelling desire I felt to contribute healing, light, and love to the world. Yet for years, I saw no way to accomplish this dream. In spite of all I did to try to heal from my past traumas, I was continually derailed by a stream of unwanted, unwelcome circumstances and challenges that demanded my attention, as I put out one fire after another. No matter how hard I tried, I simply could not gain any traction in the direction of my dreams. I felt as though I were Alice in Wonderland, my gigantic arms and legs spilling out of the teeny, tiny house that was my small, little life. A life that could barely contain not just my creative impulses and noble ambitions, but also my huge frustrations and angst. In response, I did what most of us do. I trotted off to yet another therapist to try to do even *more* healing work on my past traumas, which so tenaciously kept showing up in my present, as consistently as the sun sets each day. I felt like Sisyphus forever rolling the huge boulder of my damaged psyche up a steep and incessant hill. Desperate to live a life of true purpose, abundance, happiness, and love.

Freedom finally came when I began to *disidentify* from the self I'd created in response to past wounding experiences and looked to discover a more accurate and empowering narrative of who I am and who I felt called to become.

> Freedom came when I disidentified with the self I created in response to past wounds, and looked to discover a more accurate narrative of who I am and who I felt called to become.

I'm not sure when it first dawned on me to take on the practice of standing for a positive, possible future to improve my life; to consciously identify with and start sourcing who I was being from the *possible self* of that future fulfilled. It was nowhere to be found in my years of doing personal psychotherapy. Nor could it be found in my many years of training to become a psychotherapist myself. Yet as a spiritual seeker, I'd also fed myself a steady stream of metaphysics, transformational technologies, and evolutionary theories, and they all seemed to cascade into an undeniable, gnawing sense that I was more than this endlessly frustrating story.

The seeds of my awakening can be traced back to when I was in my mid-thirties and training to become a marriage and family therapist. I'd just moved to California from New York for this very reason as, at the time, the epicenter of the new and emerging field of family therapy was Los Angeles. I'd made it into graduate school and was knee-deep in studying various theories of personality development when I began waking up in the middle of the night several times a week, as if startled out of sleep. Suddenly, I'd be wide awake and restless with an unlikely possibility. An undeniable feeling that made no sense at the time, given how socially awkward and shy I was. So introverted and insecure I could barely tolerate looking others in the eye, let alone speak with authority in a room full of people. Yet deep down I knew. One day, I would be speaking to thousands of people. How that might happen, I had no idea. My life was still a mess. I had been crawling out of the ditch of my traumatic childhood for well over two decades by then and still, I'd had no real success to speak of on either a personal or professional level. I was thirty-five and still doing all sorts of odd jobs to keep a roof over my head while endlessly sorting myself out. I was unhappily single in spite of wanting a relationship for years. And I was still trying to figure out what I wanted to be when I grew up. Yet even though this peculiar inner knowing made little sense to my rational mind, there was one thing I did know for sure. One emerging conviction that would soon become the stealthy, steady North Star that gave direction and meaning to my days.

If I was one day going to be speaking to thousands of people, I sure as hell better become someone who had something valuable to say.

That turned out to be one of my better decisions.

Pulled by a Possible Future

Thank God I had the wherewithal to not dismiss my intuitive knowing, like so many of us do. Instead, I harnessed it as an intention and began investing in it. I did so not by trying to run out to find fame and fortune, but by holding myself accountable to become a person who would be worthy of such a position of influence. A woman of integrity. A woman of depth and of wisdom. A person who was trustworthy with power. A woman who respected herself enough to take herself and her calling seriously. Living into that positive, possible future and becoming who I'd need to be to meet that date with destiny became my new North Star. I began practicing walking through the world from this center, as though running lines for a play I'd been cast in. Entering Starbucks each morning, I'd ask myself, *How would a world-class leader of love who is having a positive impact on thousands of people order her coffee?* And in spite of my shyness, I'd force myself to stand tall, look the barista straight in the eye, and in a measured, confident tone, declare that I'd like a grande Americano, please.

> *Create your future from your future, not your past.*
>
> —WERNER ERHARD

I began sourcing who I was being from the future and not the past as often as I could. My intention—to become a woman who had something valuable to say, and to try on the identity of someone who was already influencing thousands of people—became the catalyst that motivated me to grow in ways I never would have considered before. To take risks to be visible in spite of my shyness, largely because something so much larger than myself was now at stake. To say yes to things I might have wanted to say no to (and vice versa) and to stretch myself to show up in ways that were completely outside of my current identity. Ways of relating that felt foreign, and frankly, a bit uncomfortable. Not like anyone I'd known myself to be, and which required me to consciously lean in to learn new skills and capacities because I was determined to catch up to that vision.

> *. . . use imagination masterfully and not as an onlooker thinking of the end, but as a partaker thinking from the end.*
>
> —NEVILLE GODDARD

An Intention Is Different Than a Goal

As I define it, a goal is an assertion to realize a future that's the best foreseeable outcome given the resources you currently have available and the circumstances you're starting from. The Latin root of the word *intention* means to stretch out, or to extend. Therefore, an intention is a stretch to consciously cause a future that's a pattern interruption of the "you" you have known yourself to be. It's a commitment to extend yourself and start showing up in completely new and unfamiliar ways of relating that

Unless you consciously choose a different future, your past will decide it for you.
—ROD STRYKER

are outside of your comfort zone. Ways of relating that hold the potential to cause an unprecedented, unreasonable, and even irrational future that's not at all predictable when looking at your history, your circumstances, or the inadequate resources you currently have at your disposal. Once you gather your courage to claim this irrational and highly unreasonable future as your own, fasten your seat belt. Because life will immediately confront you with the need to let go of anything and everything inconsistent with this possibility, starting with the limited assumptions you've had about yourself. Suddenly, one opportunity after the other will come into your life that will require you to outgrow the "you" that you've always been and actively lean in to grow into a version of yourself that is capable of both manifesting and sustaining this positive, possible future.

An intention is the unreasonable assertion to create a positive, possible future that is completely outside of your current identity. It's not a passive process. Nor will it always feel like a safe one. In fact, it might even feel a little scary, as you'll intuitively be guided to take one bold, risky step after the other to find your way to a vibrant future that you have little evidence for at this point. Yet once you begin using your imagination to try on the "you" that you are called to become and start assertively walking through the world as though the circumstances of your life were already mirroring your new story, the externals of your life will begin organically transforming, as if by magic.

> An intention is the unreasonable assertion to manifest a positive, future that possible is completely outside of your current identity.

Transformation is about waking up to who you really are and redefining yourself according to the future you're called to create rather than staying overly identified with the *wounded self* you formed in response to past disappointments. In consciously shape-shifting your sense of identity, self-defeating patterns that validate the negative imprinting of your past will naturally begin to disappear and will soon become a mere memory of how things *used to be*, as you stop unconsciously showing up in ways that create further evidence for your outdated trauma-based story. For when you're no longer emotionally centered in a pain-based story, you are free to generate your life outside of it.

If you want a new outcome, you will have
to break the habit of being yourself,
and reinvent a new self.
—JOE DISPENZA

The Invitation on the Table

Most of the things we long for in life—true love, financial abundance, or a robust and rewarding social circle—have eluded us because they've been outside of our identity. If we did manage to create them somewhere along the way, out of sheer willpower and strength of character, it likely wasn't long before we found a way to mess it up, so that our lives soon returned to the more familiar and frustratingly small state we've been used to. The invitation now on the table is to gather your courage and set a radically unreasonable intention for a wildly happy and fulfilling future in an area of life that's been anything but.

> The invitation is to gather your courage, and set a radically unreasonable intention for a wildly fulfilling future in an area of life that's been anything but.

You'll want to stand for a future that immediately pulls you to redefine and recalibrate who you've known yourself to be, for the possibility of who you might become. A possibility that infuses you with the creative energy you'll need to start sourcing how you show up in life from the "you" of the future you're committed to causing. Actively striving to become this version of yourself is as essential as tending to the

Only as one is willing to give up [their] present identity, can [they] become that which [they desire] to be.

—NEVILLE GODDARD

traumas of your past, as without an inspiring vision to lean into and toil toward, you will forever be vulnerable to unconsciously re-creating your past, and will be left shadowboxing with a continual stream of evidence for the limited narrative of who you are and what is, or is not, possible for you in this lifetime.

Two social psychologists, Drs. Hazel Markus and Paula Nurius, coined the term "possible selves," which they used to describe the person we hope to become—the Gold Medal athlete, the Academy Award–winning actor, or the happily married mother of three. The term also describes the person we *fear* becoming—the former athlete who peaked in college, the out-of-work actor, or the now divorced, bitter, and overwhelmed single mother of three. Through their research, they were able to demonstrate that our future-self concepts hold significant emotional weight for all of us and play a considerable role in determining both our motivation, and our current behavior—the choices we make and the actions we take that are organic to the person we either hope to become, or fear becoming.

Most of us have spent a significant amount of time trying to understand the relationship between what happened to us in the past and the self-sabotaging ways we now show up in our present. Yet few of us have seriously considered that our habitual behaviors and choices are just as dictated by the commitments we make to our future, and perhaps even more so.

Pain pushes
until vision pulls.

—MICHAEL B. BECKWITH

Is It True or Is It Trauma?

Now, all of this sounds well and good, but you and I both know how hard it is to believe in the breakthrough when you've spent years accumulating evidence for an old story of non-possibility. Validating that you are somehow not enough to manifest the happy, purposeful, and successful life that you yearn to be living. In fact, it might even occur as somewhat insulting to the part of you that has suffered so acutely over the years to suggest that you could simply disappear deeply embedded and wildly painful patterns. Yet I'm going to suggest that if this describes you and begins to name the intensity of your own resistance and resignation, consider this: You are most likely relating to past hurts as the *truth* about you versus as simply a reflection of *traumas* once endured.

This question, "Is it true or is it trauma?," is vital, as most of us tend to believe everything we feel without question. Yet beliefs are not just random thoughts that pop into our heads, but are more like a cluster of emotions and energies that take over our bodies, hijacking our somatic selves in response to a disappointment, setback, or delay and weighing us down with a deep and foreboding sense of resignation that things will never change.

For now, I invite you to notice if this happens to you, and if it does, to develop the habit of disidentifying from that inner dialogue by becoming curious. Ask yourself, *How old is the part of me that is stuck in this story?* This simple question will allow you to start locating yourself outside of the traumatized self that has taken over your body and instead connect with the witness part of you. That witness part of you has access to wisdom, power, and perspective, and is able to observe what's happening within you with objectivity, compassion, and love.

Without needing to fix the old hurts that are informing the feelings in your body, do your best to simply find the part of you that has faith that you do, indeed, have access to the power you'll need to outgrow old narratives that were born of past wounds. That's the part of you that caused you to pick up this book. It might only be 1 or 2 percent of you at this moment. Yet when you find it, *stick your foot in the doorway of that opening!* For once you begin feeding your attention and love to *this* part of you, and begin looking for what's really *true* about you, you will discover how quickly you can outgrow your old story and activate your ability to evolve beyond it.

> We want to grow
> our ability to recognize
> the possibilities present
> with as much clarity as
> we recognize obstacles
> and evidence to
> the contrary.

We want to grow our ability to recognize the possibilities present with as much clarity as we see obstacles and evidence to the contrary. For most of us, this is a sorely undeveloped muscle that helps to wake ourselves up from what visionary writer Carter Phipps calls "the spell of solidity." Carter uses this term to describe our tendency to see situations, people, places, and things as fixed, static, and immovable. Yet I invite you to consider that we live in an open system. A system that is highly sensitive and responsive to our dynamic participation by way of our assertions, intentions, and inspired actions. As author Malcolm Gladwell puts it, "Look at the world around you. It may seem like an immovable, implacable place. It is not. With the slightest push—in just the right place—it can be tipped."

What might it look like to "tip" your life in a new direction by setting an unreasonable intention, and to break the spell of solidity as it lives in you?

All creation begins within. We must learn how to give language to our dreams, as our words generate reality. They're capable of initiating a beautiful and unpredictable future. Yet most of us squander our words because we use them just to describe our experience, and very often negatively—complaining rather than using them to generate a new possibility. So let's change that right now. Let's consider a personal pain point, an unwanted pattern that's caused you a substantial amount of disappointment in life. By now, you may have worn out the ears of a few therapists and friends with your sad story of hurt and betrayal. You may know your history backward and forward—exactly what happened, when, why, with whom, and where. Yet still the boulder hasn't budged. In spite of all you've done to try to get beyond it, that stubborn story of past wounding keeps popping up in your present like a frustrating game of whack-a-mole. It's here, in this place of chronic discouragement, that you now have the opportunity to manifest what might be considered a miracle.

*Imagination gives us the opportunity to envision
new possibilities—it is an essential launchpad for making
our hopes come true. It fires our creativity, relieves our
boredom, alleviates our pain,enhances our pleasure,
and enriches our most intimate relationships.*

—BESSEL VAN DER KOLK

Step 1 Practice: Setting Your Radically Unreasonable Intention

You may have more than one painful pattern you'd like to change—your romantic life, your finances, your health, your social circle, your creativity, or your career. The good news is, with the practices revealed in these pages, you can evolve them all. Yet for now, I encourage you to choose one area to work with first, and to move through the entire seven-step process presented in these pages with just that one intention in mind. This will give you a direct experience of the power you're holding to manifest an unreasonable and unprecedented miracle in any area of life that you have the courage to claim as your own.

*Don't tell me the story of your past.
Tell me the story of your future.*

—JOE DISPENZA

Read through the following practice two or three times before engaging in it, as it is a closed-eyes exercise where your primary attention is on yourself. If you prefer, you can download free audio and/or video of me guiding you through this practice at katherinewoodwardthomas.com/trueyoubonuses.

1. **Center yourself.**

   Close your eyes and take a deep breath, as though you could breathe all the way down into your hips.

   Move into a place of deep listening and receptivity.

   Drop your awareness down into your body.

   Notice all of the feelings and sensations in your body and let go of any tension that you find.

2. Identify one area you most desire to transform.

Ask yourself:

*Where have I been stuck in scarcity, frustration, or
fear that I yearn to transform into an experience
of fulfillment, freedom, love, and abundance?*

Choose an area of life that has held great suffering and heartache
for you; an area where you've suffered a lot of losses, perhaps because
you've habitually self-sabotaged, shot yourself in the foot, avoided going
for the gold, played too small, beat yourself up before you even got in
the game, or got in the game and then fell flat on your face, again, with
the same pattern. Go where life has been hard. Because that's the intention that will begin pulling on you to become the version of yourself
you need to be to manifest and sustain this positive possibility.

3. Vision the breakthrough as though it has already happened.

Let's have you discard any sense of resignation. Imagine yourself taking off any sense of non-possibility as easily as you might slip out of a
comfortable, well-worn old sweater. See yourself hanging resignation
up in the closet, closing the door, and feeling lighter and more free.

Now stretch your imagination to try on the possibility that a miracle
has already happened. See yourself putting on a colorful coat of possibility, a coat of blessings, a coat of miracles, where time has collapsed and
you are already experiencing this area of your life as happy and fulfilled.

Align with the overall goodness of life by imagining that the Universe
is on your side and inclined to give you everything you desire in this
area of your life. Allow yourself to feel nourished and satisfied as you let
your creativity soar.

Ask yourself:

What does it look like to be living the fulfillment of this future?

What does it feel like? Sound like? Taste like? Smell like?

In your mind's eye, allow yourself to play with slivers of images and sensations in your body by looking for glimpses of the possible future you desire. It might look like a sunset over the ocean or feel like someone's warm and comforting hand in yours. It might sound like wild applause as you stand on a stage or taste like fresh tomatoes picked from a field in Tuscany. It might smell like incense in India or the scent of your own sweat at a gym. Step into the positive, possible future you desire as though it were already happening, allowing yourself to "try on" the having of these experiences as though they were occurring right now, in real time.

4. **Try on the "you" of this future fulfilled.**

    Let's have you try on the possible self of this future fulfilled. Do your best to feel the feelings of personal pride, gratitude, safety, and joy you might be feeling in the experience of fulfillment.

    Ask yourself:

    > *Who am I in this future fulfilled and
    > what am I experiencing emotionally?*

    Notice who you are *being* in this future fulfilled. Imagine yourself moving through the world from this center. Notice how you are walking down the street, talking to your neighbor, or introducing yourself to a room full of people. Notice how you feel as you do so. Imagine, too, how differently you are relating to yourself—talking to yourself in encouraging, self-affirming ways, taking care of your body, setting healthy boundaries, and asking for what you want and need. Notice how easy it is to treat yourself with respect and kindness. Notice, too, how good you feel about expressing your authentic truth and inspiring others to support you to create what you're committed to creating. See yourself more openhearted, present, and available. More confident and clear. Feel the freedom and happiness that you have arrived at.

    Ask yourself:

Who am I for others?

Notice how differently others are responding to you. Imagine the love, respect, and appreciation in their eyes when they look at you.

5. **Set your unreasonable intention to find your way to this future.**

Now is the time to harness your desires and go for the gold! To take a powerful stand for the positive, possible future you yearn to be living, and not just the more predictable, smaller steps that may or may not eventually get you there.

For example, don't just set an intention to start dating nicer people. Set an intention to be joyfully engaged by your next birthday!

Don't just set an intention to reduce your debt. Set an intention to live in such abundance that you are empowered to step into your true vocation as a philanthropist of the arts by next year.

Be bold enough to put a date on your intention. By when will this happen? When you do, the immediacy of that possible future will begin informing the changes you'll need to make today in order for that to happen. If I know I'm running a marathon in six months, I'm more likely to go to the gym today than if I say I'm going to run a marathon someday.

Finish this sentence:

My intention is . . .

6. **Open yourself up to intuitive guidance.**

Turn toward the part of you that has access to wisdom beyond your years and begin listening for your own deeper knowing. Recognize that finding your way to this possible future will largely be an intuitive process, as you put one foot in front of the other to outgrow who you've known yourself to be and become the "you" of this future fulfilled.

Lean in and listen for the whisperings of wisdom at the center of your soul.

Ask life (God, the Universe, your Higher Power, etc.):

*What will I need to let go of and release from
my life in order to manifest this miracle?*

*How will I need to grow to prepare myself
to sustain this future once it appears?*

What is my next step to cocreate this positive, possible future?

After you ask yourself each of these questions, listen to your inner knowing. When you're finished listening, open your eyes and write everything down.

Take particular notice of the "next step" that popped into your awareness during the practice, as this is the part of the process that opens up cocreativity. You're not just hoping and praying for the future you desire, as though begging God to have mercy on you. You are anteing up by bravely making choices and taking actions that are generative of that positive possibility. We all hope for miracles. Yet in truth, miracles are cocreated. Only miracles that can happen *through* you can actually happen *to* you. *You* are the co–miracle maker. So don't hesitate. Act now on your guidance, even if you're afraid, or if what's coming to you to do doesn't make sense to your rational mind.

This is especially important for those of us used to overthinking everything we do before making a move. We can easily delay or even discard the impulses that come to us in the practice. Yet if you do this, you risk staying stuck in the quicksand of your past wounds. Remember, intuitive guidance is rarely a

> *With your desire defined, quietly go within and shut the door behind you. Lose yourself in your desire; feel yourself to be one with it; remain in this fixation until you have absorbed the life and name by claiming and feeling yourself to be and to have that which you desired. When you emerge from the hour of prayer you must do so conscious of being and possessing that which you heretofore desired.*
>
> —NEVILLE GODDARD

burning bush experience. Don't overthink it. Guidance shows up in many different forms—an out-of-the-box inspired idea, a quiet knowing in your body, or an odd and unexpected situation you suddenly find yourself in. One woman I know set her intention to manifest a beloved, a man who would one day become her husband. She soon met a man who was everything she'd been envisioning and more. Yet having been hurt many times in the past, she hesitated to open her heart to him. One day while driving, contemplating her dilemma, she stopped at a stop sign. The window of the passenger seat was open, and before she'd had the chance to drive away, a large man with wild hair and fiery eyes who looked like he'd been on the streets for a while stuck his head in the window, looked her in the eyes, and fiercely yelled, *"Well, what are you waiting for?"* She got the message. That evening she said yes to her suitor, and they recently celebrated their fifteenth wedding anniversary.

Most of us want to map it all out beforehand, to know *how* it will happen before we take the risk to move forward. Yet *how* it will happen is not nearly as important as *who you will need to be* to manifest and sustain your vision. When it comes to creating an unprecedented, unpredictable future, your focus needs to be on closing the chasm between who you know yourself to be and who you are coded to become. This is an intuitive process that relies heavily on alternative ways of knowing—the risky business of sticking your neck out and following your gut. Making radical new choices to show up in radically new ways that are outside of both your comfort zone and your current identity. Remembering that the journey of a thousand miles begins with the willingness to simply take the next step.

Learn to recognize when
something you hear triggers
a feeling of excitement deep within you—
that's your guidance system telling
you to pay attention.

—ANITA MOORJANI

Why Your Intention Matters

As inspiring as all of this is, I don't have to tell you how easy it is to give up when the going gets tough. In the face of an obstacle, setback, disappointment, or delay, we tend to see the hindrance as yet more evidence for why this whole thing was just a pipe dream. In these moments, we'll often choose the comfort of a cupcake over our commitment. To prepare ourselves for these inevitable moments, it's critical to know the why of your intention. Why does staying the course to become who you need to be to manifest and sustain your intention actually matter?

The first few years of my thought leader career, I felt as though I'd been shot out of a cannon. Almost overnight, I'd gone from being an unknown student of personal and spiritual development—really in an effort to try to find my way out of my own self-defeating and painful patterns in life—to suddenly sharing the stage with some of the most prolific teachers of our time. Even though I'd been preparing myself for this moment internally for years, nothing could have readied me for the terror I felt each time I walked onto a stage. I felt like a fraud standing next to other teachers whom I so greatly admired. And I was totally unprepared for the tidal wave of shame that would wash over me once I stepped off the stage, completely convinced I'd just humiliated myself beyond repair with whatever it was I'd just said, or more often, forgot to say. It was agony. As I intensely worked to expand my sense of self enough to tolerate the level of attention I was getting, what kept me going was my devotion to those whom I felt I was here to serve. Others who, like me, had received little support early on in life. Sponsorship that might have helped us to believe ourselves worthy and capable of creating the lives we felt called to create. The courage I needed to tolerate these growing pains came from my devotion to alleviating the suffering of others, and not from any personal desire for fame and fortune. Any hint of that lesser aspiration quickly faded once I started stepping onto those intimidating stages. In those moments, I would have been greatly relieved to simply open a small

*When I dare to be powerful,
to use my strength in the service of
my vision, then it becomes less
important whether
I am unafraid.*
—AUDRE LORDE

private practice and call it a day. I'm happy to say, some twenty-plus years later, that I no longer feel like a fraud. My identity has caught up with my life, and I find myself beyond grateful for the privileged position of being able to contribute in the ways I now get to do on a daily basis.

If you look at your history, you'll likely notice that when the going got tough—when you became triggered, felt threatened, unsafe, or too small; when you experienced a setback, felt unseen, unsupported, or insecure— you put your dream aside and started giving it less energy. Maybe you distracted yourself from moving forward by again giving your past more energy than your future, asking, *What's wrong with me? Why can't I be/ do/have this? Let me roll up my shirt sleeves to finally figure this out.* Going back to the comfort of standing on the sidelines earnestly analyzing why you are the way you are. As if understanding the origins of your short-comings has *ever* led you all the way home to the bright and brilliant future you are here to fulfill. Yet once we put our commitments into a larger context, where we recognize that what we're up to actually matters to others—our children, neighbors, and maybe even future generations— we're more apt to snap on our red capes and plow on through to the miracle that's waiting on the other side of the wall. It's only when standing for the larger why of our intentions that in those times when we're tempted to throw in the towel, we'll have the strength and stamina to stay the course.

That was certainly true for Dr. Jill Bolte Taylor, the bestselling author of *My Stroke of Insight*, which offers an inside look at her captivating journey of recovery from the massive stroke she experienced at the age of thirty-seven. A Harvard-trained neuroanatomist, Taylor found the opportunity to study the brain from the inside out to be a fascinating, if challenging, journey. The part of her brain that was damaged by the stroke was her left hemisphere. That's the side of the brain that controls reading, writing, language, and the logical, linear facts that make up our credentials and who we are in the world. She describes the nirvana she felt as that part of her brain went missing on the morning of her stroke. She became so lost in the euphoria of losing her left brain's ceaseless chatter that she almost succumbed to losing her life. As she was alone at the time of the stroke, it took her hours to figure out how to call for help, which she finally did, just in time.

The difficulties she endured on the road to recovery were compounded by her ambivalence about recovering at all, as she found herself reticent to renew the part of her brain that so easily makes us all a little miserable with its incessant tendencies to analyze and criticize everything and everyone. She was actually quite happy just floating around without all those pesky judgments getting in the way of her peace of mind. Yet, she says, "I became excited about what a difference my recovery could make in the lives of others—not just those who were recovering from a brain trauma, but everyone with a brain! I imagined the world filled with happy and peaceful people and I became motivated to endure the agony I would have to face in the name of recovery."

At the time Taylor had this thought, the people she was influencing were largely her family, friends, coworkers, and those associated with a nonprofit organization she was a spokesperson for. Yet she dreamed big. She expanded her circle of care to include all of us with a brain. This willingness to care about something larger than herself is what inspired her to keep pushing past the many limitations she was up against in relearning how to walk, talk, read, write, and do the other daily tasks we all take for granted. It took her eight years of dedicated struggle, much of it with the help of her mother, to either retrieve or relearn all she'd lost. Taylor is now one of the most recognized and beloved thought leaders of our time, with nearly thirty million and counting YouTube views of her TED Talk where she shares her hopeful and inspiring journey of recovering fully from a stroke.

Consider who *you* might bless in going for the gold in your life. Your family? Your community? All people everywhere with a brain? In standing for a positive, possible future, you're invited to expand your

> Expand your circle of care. Consider what's at stake for others in you creating your biggest, most fulfilling life.

circle of care. Consider what's at stake for others in you creating your biggest, most fulfilling life. I'm convinced that when we expand our circle of care beyond ourselves, we delight the Universe by offering ourselves up to be the vehicles of goodness, light, and love that are currently missing in our world. It's one thing to pray for healing, light, and love. It's another entirely to offer ourselves as the agents through which that goodness can happen.

In so doing, we tempt both benevolent ancestors and angels alike to fill our sails with the winds of synchronicity and magic to support our good efforts in astonishing and unexpected ways. For we are now up to what life is up to, and offering ourselves as partners in weaving greater goodness, light, and love in the world.

> It's one thing to pray for healing, light, and love. It's another entirely to offer yourself as the agent through which that goodness can happen.

Ask yourself:

What difference might it make in the lives of others if I were to realize my intention?

Who or what do I care about beyond myself that would motivate me to stay the course when the going gets tough?

In setting your unreasonable intention for a positive, possible future, consider these questions:

1. **What exactly are you committed to creating?** Be as specific as you can. Write it down and have the courage to speak it out loud, sharing it with a friend, counselor, or mentor you feel safe with, or with a trustworthy group of peers. People who have the consciousness to hold that pos-

sibility with you and for you, and who can see the fulfillment of your vision.

For example: *My intention is to become a number one* New York Times *bestselling author in the category of hardcover fiction.*

2. **By *when* will you have manifested your intention?** Putting your intention in a time frame adds urgency to the equation and pulls on you to get into action today to generate that possibility.

For example: *I will be on the bestseller list within three years from today.*

3. **How *might* this future happen *through* you and not just *to* you?** We can only make a strategic plan for a future that is predictable from where we're currently standing. If you set a goal to earn a PhD in counseling, you can make a list of all universities that offer that degree and begin applying. Yet standing for an unreasonable intention whose fulfillment is not predictable from where you are today will require a different system of creation. One where you learn to lean in and listen to your own intuitive guidance for your next steps and have the courage to take one step at a time. Some of the actions you'll be led to take will not make sense to your rational mind, or they will urge you to do things that are wildly inconvenient and unconventional. Be bold. Act on your gut knowing and follow the energy. Notice when your body feels a jolt of enthusiasm and excitement and take a risk to move in that direction. The more you do, the clearer and louder the voice within you will become. Finding your way to the future you're standing for will require both courage and a willingness to be unreasonable.

For example: *My intuition tells me to reserve a cabin in the woods and go there alone for the entire month of August, leaving my husband to care for our two teenagers while I write my book.*

4. ***Why* does this matter?** Be clear about what's at stake for others if you really take this on. Who else besides you will benefit from your tenacity and courage?

For example: *My daughters will see what it looks like when a woman believes in herself and invests in her potential. They will also see what it looks like when a man believes in his wife and supports her to give her gifts to the world. The story I am called to write holds a message of hope and healing for the world and will inspire thousands to begin speaking truth to power.*

The answer to these four questions will be essential to your success. *Yet the most important question to consider* is:

5. ***Who* are you in this future fulfilled?** If you're letting go of your identity as a "wanna be," and no longer relating to the "I'm not good enough" story as though it's true, then *who are you?* Not who you will be one day, but right now, today—someone who is worthy of receiving what you've had the courage to ask life for, and who is powerful enough to generate it. Because if you're still overly identified with the "you" you created in response to what happened to you long, long ago—the traumatized self that lives in your body like a knee-jerk reaction or an automatic . flight, fight, freeze, fawn, or flop response whenever you feel unsafe or threatened—then you'll not have sufficient power to generate the miracle you're standing for. So before writing a list of all the things you'll now need to *do* to make your intention happen, consider who you'll now need to *be* to make the fulfillment of your intention inevitable.

Once you've set your intention, you'll quickly want to memorize it. Powerful intentions change the course of our lives because they immediately begin influencing our choices and actions. For this reason, it's important to keep your intention short enough that you can repeat it to yourself when you come to a crossroads. Your vision may take up pages in your journal, yet your intention should only be one to three sentences long in order to bring clarity to each choice you make.

Fidelity to the future you're committed to creating becomes your primary focus as you use your intention to assess the pros and cons of each situation you're in. Does this choice bring you closer to this future or farther away from it? Learning to assess the consequences of each action you take is critical to finding your way to the future you desire.

POWERFUL INTENTIONS

1. **Are spoken in the affirmative.** It's more powerful to name what you're standing *for* rather than what you're against. Declare what you *do* want rather than what you don't.

2. **Recalibrate and redefine your identity.** Set an intention that challenges your current sense of self and recalibrates who you've known yourself to be. Your intention should inspire you to begin letting go of being overly identified with a smaller sense of self created in response to past trauma and help you to connect with the truth of your worthiness and power.

3. **Inform and transform how you show up.** Your intention should immediately begin pulling on you to let go of old ways of being that are sourced from a smaller sense of self and to point the way toward growth and development to become who you will need to be to fulfill that future. If you have the courage to put your intention in a time frame, do so, for that will create urgency that can inspire you to take the risks you will need to take to generate this possibility.

4. **Are clear and specific.** While it's noble to declare that you want to be a happier person, it's best to set intentions that are measurable. Ones whose fulfillment is not simply about a mood or a feeling that may be fluid but about a concrete and measurable outcome. Be as specific and detailed as you can. While you may have a big vision that has multiple stages to it, such as ending hunger throughout the world, make your intention concise, such as an intention to reduce child hunger by 1 percent in the United States within the next seven years.

5. **Are grounded in a meaningful why.** Knowing *why* this matters is critical to staying the course when the going gets tough. Have something *big* at stake, both for yourself and for others you care about.

BONUS: STEP 1 PRACTICE IN ACTION

What is my intention?

EXAMPLES:

→ My intention is to be in a happy, healthy, committed partnership with the great love of my life by my next birthday.

→ My intention is to become a philanthropist who generously gives away millions of dollars before my fiftieth birthday and still has more money than I need.

What does it look like, sound like, smell like, taste like, feel like to be living this future fulfilled?

EXAMPLES:

→ It looks like a table full of people I love smiling and raising their glasses to toast my engagement.

→ It sounds like tears of relief and gratitude from recipients of my generosity as I'm able to alleviate their suffering and provide hope for thousands.

Who am I in this future fulfilled?

EXAMPLES:

→ I am a wildly happy and satisfied betrothed who is madly in love with my amazing partner and who feels deeply respected and loved in return.

→ I am a benevolent leader of love, here to share my blessings with the world.

Who am I for others in this future fulfilled?

EXAMPLES:

→ I am answered prayer for my beloved.

→ I am the inspired and trustworthy leader they have been waiting for.

What will I need to give up or let go of to find my way to this future?

EXAMPLES:

→ I will stop assuming that I'm not good enough or attractive enough to attract "The One" whom I desire.

→ I will let go of sourcing my sense of safety by playing small.

How will I need to grow to prepare myself to receive this future?

EXAMPLES:

→ I need to develop my ability to self-soothe when I get upset so I can stop reacting in destructive ways that do damage to my relationships.

→ I need to get better at tolerating my own anxiety when saying no and disappointing others in order to stay true to my intention.

What's my next step?

EXAMPLES:

→ Let my friends and family know that I'm looking for a serious romantic partner and ask them to keep me in mind if they meet someone who seems like they'd be a potentially great match.

→ Hire an attorney to help me create structures for my new business.

Step 2:
Name Your
Source Fracture Story

~

Maybe every childhood is the terrain on which we try to
pinpoint how much we matter and how much we don't, a map
where we study the dimensions and the borders of our worth.

—EDITH EVA EGER

I t's an act of faith to declare a positive, possible future when you have little evidence that life could move in this direction, and a lot of evidence to the contrary. It's only natural, then, to hope that once you take this first courageous step, you'll immediately receive your reward. Yet it doesn't quite work that way.

What usually happens after we take this first big step is an equally big, or even bigger, breakdown. As the saying goes, destruction before creation. The structures that have been keeping your old story alive often have to crash and burn before the new, healthier ones you're standing for can emerge. Which means you'll want to be on the lookout for, and even welcome, rugs that are suddenly pulled out from beneath your feet, curtains that are ripped open to reveal the shocking truth of who Oz *really* is, or the blow of taking an inspired leap only to land face first in a dung heap.

When these letdowns occur, it's critical that you do your best to intercept any negative meaning you might automatically make of the disappointment. Interrupting the habitual interpretative lens of "See? *I'm not safe to dream big,*" or the shoulder-dropping resignation of *"I'm unworthy* to have what I want," or the sinking feeling in your gut of *"I'm powerless* to change my life in any meaningful way." You must notice the collapse as it's happening in your body and quickly move to mentor yourself to a more empowering perspective. Otherwise, you'll emotionally drop down into an old, false belief about yourself—your *false center*—and start to show up in ways that will unconsciously perpetuate your old, unwanted story by creating even more evidence for it.

> If you fail to notice the collapse as it's happening in your body and quickly move to mentor yourself to a more empowering perspective, you'll predictably start mindlessly showing up in ways that will perpetuate your old story by unconsciously creating even more evidence for it.

We can swim in the dirty waters of our false centers for years. Perhaps our whole lives, if left unchallenged. Doing our best to hide them by pretending to feel differently about ourselves than we actually do and ultimately producing a covert sense of inauthenticity and estrangement between ourselves and others. Or trying to fix them by endlessly analyzing why we are the way we are, as though desperate to scratch an itch in a place we can't ever quite reach. Or compensating for them by being driven to the extreme to have things be otherwise, like being obsessed with making a lot of money when we feel totally worthless inside.

I myself was driven to get rid of the shame-laced, pervasive, and persistent *source fracture story* that had taken root in my psyche at the age of fourteen of "I am inferior, others are better than me, and I can never do enough to prove my value." It was a story I created in reaction to my impossibly attractive mother whose Audrey Hepburn–like beauty and elegance was both unrivaled and unreachable. As my body was changing and I suddenly needed new clothes to accommodate my developing hips and breasts, I was no match for the tidal wave of shame that would wash over me whenever my mother would give a sideways glance at my thighs, which also seemed to be growing right alongside the rest of me. The ones I inherited from my "we never mention *his* name" father, who'd been banished from our family years before.

As I grew up, I tried hard to create a life worth living on top of that pesky little identity-based belief that had lodged in the center of my solar plexus. Yet after well more than a decade of psychotherapy, it seemed impossible to overcome. Inside of being emotionally enmeshed with that story, I couldn't help but do things like underpresent myself, overgive to try to prove my value, undercharge for my services, or assume the self-effacing role of handmaiden to those I admired and wanted to be friends with. All ways of relating that baited others to see me as less than them. As someone to like, but who clearly was not their equal in value. In this way, I created a continual stream of relational evidence for the story of my inferiority and lack of value, validating it over and over again, and making it all the harder to outgrow. It wasn't until I began noticing when that story hijacked my consciousness in response to even the smallest of triggers—someone I admired forgot my name, negated something I said, or walked into the room looking fabulous when I was feeling underdressed and self-conscious—that I finally located my power to overcome the humiliating habit of showing up as a lesser version of myself, and covertly convincing everyone in my life to treat me as such.

> Most of us assume "self" to be a solo phenomenon, yet beliefs are relational in nature.

While the majority of us assume "self" to be a solo phenomenon, the truth is that beliefs are relational in nature. Self-schemas such as "I am not good enough," "I am alone," or "I'm not safe" were initially formed in relationship to others and are now repetitively reinforced in our current relationships. As once again, someone who matters leaves, or abuse shows up in the dynamic, or here we are again, being criticized and spoken down to. It feels as though it's just our fate to be trapped in this story.

We fail to see ourselves as the authors of this unwanted narrative, blind to the specific ways we are mindlessly relating to others, pulling on them to behave in ways that generate further evidence for this story. In being unable to

Trauma is not the bad things that happen to you, but what happens inside you as a result of what happens to you.

—GABOR MATÉ

see our part clearly, we assume that this is simply happening *to* us once again, against our will. Until we name the underlying consciousness that is driving the distinct ways that the pattern is happening *through* us, and correct it at the core, we will forever feel locked into this unwanted identity simply because of how others tend to treat us.

No amount of insight, analysis, grief work, or even meditation is sufficient to withstand the tidal wave of relational evidence that most of us live with on a daily basis. Evidence that continually validates and reinforces the false trauma-informed narratives that we formed in response to past wounding. By now, you may have a fairly good idea of what your particular brand of bogus beliefs are that have been sabotaging your life in the area of your intention. Yet you might not know how to relate to the insidious lies that can so quickly capture and command your nervous system in order to wake yourself up from the trance. For the tender, younger part of you can be quick to interpret every disappointment, setback, obstacle, or delay as further evidence of your invisibility, your aloneness, your unworthiness, or your powerlessness to keep yourself safe.

As much as we all like to think of ourselves as mature adults, you and I both know that it's often the three-year-old within who's driving the car. Not a great plan if you're actually trying to get somewhere. While most of us know, at least intellectually, that we're not the stories we made up about ourselves in response to past trauma, the emotions we carry in our bodies will often tell a different story. In response to a disappointment,

A child who is struggling is not going to say, "This poor teacher simply does not understand . . . the impact of trauma on my ability to learn. He should be helping me to regulate, not conjugate." They say, "I must be dumb."

—DAN SIEGEL

or even the anticipation of one, we can quickly become enmeshed with a younger part of ourselves and begin sourcing how we behave from the emotions associated with that old, familiar story. When it happens, it *feels* true. It's *true* that "I'm not enough," or "not wanted," or "unworthy," or "unsafe" or "all alone in this world." Inside of being overly identified with that story, you'll quickly lose the thread of your intention and be swallowed by a swamp of resignation and non-possibility. Because on some level, you're right. When blended with, and generating life from, this false center, there is no possibility of manifesting a future brighter than the past. There can only be more of the same.

Connect with the Younger You

Few of us have learned how to cultivate a loving, trustworthy bond with the younger parts of us that are still stuck in stories born of a painful past. Certainly not in a way that would allow us to intercept and intercede on our own behalf in the moments they threaten to swallow us whole. We may have done some inner child work and made an effort to connect with these younger parts of ourselves. However, in those moments when old stories are activated, what we really need is to access our inner adult, or that which I call your *wise self.* We might also refer to this part of you as the *true you*, though you might be more familiar with the terms *adult self, higher self*—or even *Self* with a capital *S*. It's important to find the words that resonate for you to describe your own inner fairy godparent who is always trustworthy, wise, and kind. For it's this part of you that can see what's happening from a larger perspective and can bring maturity, depth, wisdom, and compassion into the room to comfort you and contain the runaway feelings of shame, alienation, fear, and unworthiness that the younger you is struggling with when you're triggered into old meaning.

Most of us are unaware of the profound need we have to cultivate a loving, mentoring relationship between our wise self and our wounded self, where the adult in us—the part of us devoted to Truth with a capital *T*—can compassionately and fiercely correct our own faulty perspectives

> Most of us are unaware of our need to cultivate a loving relationship between our wise self and our wounded self— where the adult in us compassionately corrects our own faulty perspectives with wisdom and love.

with profound levels of wisdom and love. If you've noticed, there is more than one of you here. The bestselling author of *No Bad Parts* and the founder of Internal Family Systems therapy (IFS therapy), Richard Schwartz, has done much to richly develop and popularize the "parts work" introduced by the late Virginia Satir, who is considered the mother of family therapy. She recognized that most of us have a cocktail of parts within us, many of them holding aspects of ourselves we don't particularly like or want. In response, we will often try to hide these aspects of ourselves and get into the habit of turning away from them in order to protect our self-image. Discovering how you can bring these lost, wounded parts of yourself into a loving relationship with the stronger, wiser part of you—the "you" that intuitively knows how to comfort a frightened child or the "you" that so easily extends kindness and wisdom to a friend in need is the "you" that can offer sponsorship and love to these lost parts of yourself. It is the mature, wise self within that can learn to hold, contain, and mentor the reactive younger parts that are seeing things through the lens of a source fracture story and filtering whatever is happening through a worldview formed in response to an initial break in belonging.

The primary task of childhood was to formulate a sense of who we are and where we fit into this world. This sense of self was formed inside of the dynamic between ourselves and our early caregivers. How our caregivers felt about us and tended to treat us registered in our newly forming psyches not as information about *them* but as information about *us*. If you had a single parent who was overworked and overwhelmed, you likely formed a belief that you're a burden and that your needs are too much for others to bear. If you were chronically neglected as a child, you may have formed a sense of yourself as all alone in this world and lowered your expectations that anyone would ever be there for you.

Unfortunately, at the time you were coming to such conclusions, there was no wise and loving adult nearby to intervene and intercept the meaning you were making of what was happening, which might have spared you decades of dysfunction and drama later in life. There was simply no one there to support you by explaining that whatever was happening, or not happening, wasn't about you at all. No caring adult was present to kindly correct the erroneous conclusions you were coming to. More likely, it was the adult in the room who was perpetrating the trauma.

When my client Cara was a young girl, she was awakened night after night to the sound of her parents fighting. Her father would inevitably be drunk as he stumbled into the house at two a.m., after a night out with his friends. Her mother would be waiting in the dark. As soon as he walked in the door, her mother would begin complaining loudly about how miserable she was being married to him and what a complete failure he was as a father and a husband. One night, her father came home and announced boastfully that he was leaving and moving hundreds of miles away. He'd been offered the chance to purchase a pub and he was taking it. Cara could barely breathe as she listened. She started shaking in her bed, terrified by the possibility of being left alone with her unhappy mother, who was without any means to support her and her two younger sisters. Even at the tender age of six, Cara knew they would be in deep trouble without her father. As bad as things were, she knew they could get much worse. As her father slammed the door of their bedroom shut, her mother sat crying alone at the kitchen table. Cara slipped out of bed and headed toward her. She wrapped her little arms around her mother's shoulders and whispered in her ear, "It's okay, Mama. Don't let him break up our family. We have to stay together, we have to." Over and over she said it until her mother calmed down and instructed her to go back to bed.

Two weeks later, the family moved hundreds of miles away to a small, run-down apartment above a pub that Cara's father had purchased. Yet the fighting continued each night for years. And each morning, Cara's angry mother would find a way to remind her "This is all your fault, you know." A heavy burden to bear for a young girl whose primary task in life was to form a healthy sense of self and discover where she belongs in the world. It's not a surprise that Cara grew up feeling overly responsible for other people's bad behavior. Bearing complete blame for any and all misunderstandings, mistakes, or misdeeds, and endlessly apologizing for things she hadn't done. It worked for others, as they never had to be accountable for their actions or make amends for the negative impact their choices may have had on others. Though she'd been in therapy for well over two decades, analyzing why she was the way she was, and had made the connection between her childhood experiences and the self-defeating, codependent ways she still behaved in her adult relationships, by the time we met, she was knee-deep in the unhealthy habit of harshly shaming and blaming herself for any and all of her relational challenges. Inside of the "I'm bad and it's all my fault" story, Cara chronically enabled others to behave badly as she let them off the hook for every little breakdown between them. Through naming her source fracture story and recognizing this impulse as coming from a younger, wounded part of herself, Cara was able to raise her expectations of others and communicate her unwillingness to continue mindlessly taking the blame for everything that went wrong. In doing so, she also liberated them to grow and mature, graduating everyone in her inner circle to a whole new level of mutuality, health, and well-being.

While most of us are psychologically sophisticated enough to label the residual symptoms of our old wounds as codependence, low self-esteem, or an anxious or avoidant attachment style, few of us know how to take the splinter out of our souls by naming and challenging the identity-based assumptions that are driving these maladaptive patterns. Identity-based beliefs can be difficult to name, as at the time they were created, there were often no words to describe what was happening. Perhaps you were just an infant left alone in the crib to cry for hours at a time, terrified that no one was coming to give you relief. Perhaps the shock of what happened was unacknowledged as someone you depended on just up and disappeared, and no one ever mentioned their name again. Maybe the wound was so pervasive, such as with chronic criticism or belittlement, that it simply became a part of life. Like water to a fish, insidious and all-encompassing. I mean, does a fish even know what water is?

Most of us have some recollection of an incident, or a series of incidents, that begin to explain the origins of the challenged sense of self we still struggle with today: a father who left, a mother who drank, a sibling who died, a bully who taunted. Yet often these stories have an even more stealthy start, as studies show that consciousness is formed as far back as in the womb. In their book *The Secret Life of the Unborn Child*, authors Thomas Verny and John Kelly share a story about a woman named Kristina. While born healthy, Kristina refused her mother's breast after birth, decisively turning her head away. At first her parents worried she might be sick. Yet shortly after, Kristina devoured a bottle of formula. The next day, Kristina again refused her mother's breast. In an attempt to understand what was happening, her doctor brought Kristina to another new mother and watched in amazement as she readily took to this stranger's breast. Finally, the doctor questioned Kristina's mother. "Why do you suppose [your daughter] is reacting this way?" he asked. She did not know. He pressed further. "Was there an illness during your pregnancy?" "No, none," the woman answered. Even more direct this time, he asked, "Did you want to get pregnant?" The woman looked at him, finally confessing, "No, I didn't. I wanted an abortion. My husband wanted the child. That's why I had her."

I suspect that from the womb, Kristina's source fracture story of "I'm not wanted, others will reject me, and there is no place for me in this world" was well established, and her self-protective mechanism of rejecting her mother as a preemptive strike against being rejected, firmly in place.

Tolerable disappointments early in life lead to the ability to self-soothe later in life. Yet unbearable disappointments, such as Kristina's, thwart this ability. Without becoming conscious of her tendency to default to and generate her relationships from this worldview, Kristina is in danger of suffering from a debilitating rejection sensitivity that could very well compromise her ability to bond with others in any meaningful way for the rest of her life. Perhaps she will learn to label herself as "love avoidant," as though describing something unchangeable about her, like her astrological sign or her skin color. She will be vulnerable to never quite getting it right when it comes to having intimate, count-on-able connections. After trying again and again to create a supportive social life, she may finally come to the sad conclusion that "she's just not good at relationships," and she will find ways to organize her life around this unfortunate "fact." Never quite seeing that inside of her perspective, she's developed a habit of dismissing others before they have the chance to dismiss her, which sets them up to reject her. Attempts at closeness will become just another unbearably painful re-wounding experience, and she will find ways to reject the part of herself that yearns for more.

Some speculate that we repeat self-defeating patterns because we're trying to heal. Yet I've never met anyone who said they felt renewed and invigorated by another re-wounding experience; one that ripped the scab off by duplicating the deepest hurts of a painful past. Usually, they feel even more resigned about not ever finding their way out of their unwanted story. It might be more accurate to say that we're repeating old patterns because we're missing specific skills and capacities that would allow us to do it any differently. Skills we might have learned organically had we grown up in a healthy home, with caregivers who were capable of loving us in the ways we needed to be loved. Skills such as encouraging self-talk in the face of failure, negotiating good boundaries, navigating conflict in a way that deepens love rather than destroys it, or speaking up in the moments it matters. Rather than meeting critical developmental milestones that would have prepared us to create healthy relationships with ourselves and others later in life, we instead became frozen in a fixed mindset that caused us to grasp at the straws of survival. Developing what I call *pseudo-safety strategies*, such as people-pleasing, rejecting others before they can reject us, or disappearing our needs to try to avoid abandonment. We never learned to navigate the world of relationships in ways that would have set us up to win, which left us ill-equipped to do anything other than duplicate, again and again, the patterns of our painful past.

The good news is that graduation from our unwanted patterns becomes possible once we learn to (1) notice when we've fallen into the ditch of a source fracture story, and (2) lovingly yet fiercely correct that perspective *before taking any action from that center.* Easier said than done. For the stumble into an old interpretive lens that begins to command our nervous system happens faster than an in-breath. Someone doesn't text us back right away, our boss says something critical, or we don't get asked out on a second date. In these moments, we need to *identify, intercept,* and *challenge* the automatic meaning we're making before we start unconsciously behaving in ways that generate further evidence for this worldview. Even the anticipation of disappointment might be enough to drop us down into an old familiar-yet-toxic narrative about who we are, how others feel about us, and what's possible, or not possible, for us in life and in love. What's the story you default to in response to a disappointment? Where do those feelings live in your body? How old is this part of you?

> What's the story you default to when you feel disappointed? Where do those feelings live in your body and how old is that part of you?

Beware the Pull of the Past

Over the years, I've noticed an odd conundrum. While many of us are a little tired of telling our tales of woe to yet another sympathetic soul, we may also secretly be a bit enthralled by the high-stakes drama of it all. We might even adamantly defend our right to be defined by all that we've endured, covertly insisting that we be witnessed, again and again, in the fullness of our anguish. As though we are wearing little badass badges of honor that both explain and excuse our own dysfunctional behavior in the here and now, and that give us a hall pass for why we are the way we are without being responsible for outgrowing this version of ourselves.

You can look back, babe,
But it's best not to stare.
—TOM PETTY

What happened to you in your past might be unbearably harsh and profoundly unfair. Being compassionately witnessed by people who care and tended to by those who are trained and capable of validating the shock and sorrow of it is critical to healing. What happens in the body and the brain in response to early childhood trauma is no small matter and is brilliantly explored by pioneering practitioners such as Bessel van der Kolk, Judith Herman, Richard Schwartz, Gabor Maté, Dan Siegel, Bruce Perry, Peter A. Levine, Janina Fisher, and others. Sit at the feet of these masters and discover how your own body is still impacted today by hurts and heartaches that happened long ago.

Yet I also want to caution us to beware the human tendency to fall in love with the stench of our own sad stories. Like a dog tenaciously sniffing for you-know-what or Lot's unfortunate wife, who was more fascinated with what was behind her than the possibilities of what lay ahead, we need not be so loyal as to continually turn our attentions to a disappointing, painful past. Rather than dwell too long in that house of horrors, we want to look around us to see if we can locate a doorway that can liberate us from this haunted home and seek a path that plants us firmly on a heroic journey beyond it. It's here that our pain becomes our purpose, and connects us more deeply with compassion, wisdom, strength, and hope. For these are the fruits of suffering.

The diagnosis of post-traumatic stress disorder (PTSD) is not solely reserved for returning soldiers of war or the victims of a crime. One does not have to have survived a war to be the walking wounded. If you were bullied, neglected, abandoned, or abused in your formative years, you, too, might identify as traumatized. Some

What I know for sure is that
everything that has happened to you,
was happening for you. And all
that time, in all of those moments,
you were building strength.
Strength times strength times
strength equals power.
What happened to you
can be your power.
—OPRAH WINFREY

traumas are more challenging to identify. Maybe you were habitually and mercilessly teased by an older sibling and your parents found it funny and failed to intervene. Maybe you felt that the real you was unacceptable and you needed to only be who your parents wanted you to be in order to be loved by them. Often, we dismiss our own early traumas as insignificant because we think that others had it so much worse. Yet you need not measure your trauma against the trauma of others. Your experience, and the unfortunate imprinting that has remained ever since, is valid and worthy of your love and attention. Nor is it a betrayal of your early caregivers to acknowledge their failure to give you what you might have needed in order to feel loved, safe, happy, and whole as you grew up. It happened, and you have a right to be sad about what you did not receive— unconditional love, protection, respect, mentoring, and sponsorship of your gifts and talents. We may want to give our caregivers the benefit of the doubt by suggesting they were doing their best. Yet is it true? Maybe. Maybe not. I mean, if everyone was doing their best we'd be living in a very different world. But for whatever reason, they did what they did, and they didn't do what they didn't do, and that impacted you. It's important to just give that to yourself.

However, the biggest problem most of us have now is not how mistreated we once were by our parents and other caregivers or teachers who mattered. Our biggest challenge is how we internalized those ways of relating to ourselves and now tend to treat ourselves in much the same way. For example, if the pattern in your childhood home was neglect, then you likely now struggle with a chronic pattern of self-neglect, the source of which may be a deeply embedded source fracture story of "I don't matter, others matter more than me and I am insignificant in this world." A narrative that lodged in your belly at the tender age of two, and which drives you to continually, unconsciously put the feelings and needs of others before your own, training those in your life today to mirror back to you that you're right—you don't actually matter. The remedy is not to get others to change. The remedy is to start relating to yourself with greater love and respect—as though you do matter. To cultivate the healthy habit of caring for your own feelings and needs before automatically caretaking the feelings and needs of others.

> *. . . our narrative self is sculpted*
> *from the . . . exchanges of energy and*
> *information with our caregivers, friends,*
> *teachers, and the larger culture in which we live.*
> *In these ways, we learn the story of who we*
> *come to narrate our self to be.*
> —DAN SIEGEL

Cultivate Self-Compassion

The relationship you have with yourself is *key* to outgrowing who you've known yourself to be, and you will make little progress until you are skillful in the art of self-compassion. Bestselling author Kristin Neff defines self-compassion "not as a way of judging ourselves positively . . . [but of] relating to ourselves kindly." According to Neff, self-compassion has three distinct components. The first is a practice of self-kindness versus the judgmental ways we often speak to ourselves. It's learning to befriend ourselves when we're hurting, much like we might show up for a friend in need. It's the ability to soothe and comfort ourselves when we're suffering. The second component is the practice of allowing life's disappointments to connect us more deeply with others, who also suffer in similar ways. Rather than allow our pain to separate us, we instead soften into the humbling recognition that we, too, are human. We, too, make mistakes. We are not exempt from hardship and the imperfections of life. While feelings of frustration, shame, and guilt usually cause us to feel even more isolated and alone in life, by surrendering to our shared humanity, we enhance a sense of belonging to all of life. The third and final component Neff distinguishes is a practice of mindfulness. Mindfulness is the ability to witness and welcome our own inner experience without needing to fix or change anything. It's turning toward and acknowledging our feelings, needs, and desires without becoming overly identified with them. To simply be with whatever is present without labeling it as good or bad.

These three ways of being with your own inner experience are foundational to recognizing and disidentifying from your source fracture story. They give us the ability to step outside of ourselves enough to begin to *name and tame* the inner conversation that has had us in its

> The relationship you have with yourself is *key* to outgrowing who you've known yourself to be, and you will make little progress until you are skillful in the art of self-compassion.

grip. They help us to wear our own automatic assumptions a bit more loosely, and to recognize our internal dialogues not as truth but as remnants of old trauma.

I want you to understand the cost of not seeing this clearly, for the stakes are high. Consider the value you are receiving by reading this book. I hope it's helping you to make sense of your struggles in a way that opens up the possibilities of your life. Yet it almost didn't make it into your hands as I myself was gripped by an "I'm not good enough" conversation as I struggled to get my ideas into a book proposal. I knew the teachings were powerful, but I did not quite believe myself capable of presenting them with enough wisdom and intelligence to do them justice. For four years I wrestled with writing a proposal worthy of the concepts I present herein. I even went so far as to book a two-week solitary writing retreat in the forests of Kaua'i, spending hours and hours alone and staring out the window at the wild foliage as I wrote, deleted, wrote, deleted, wrote, deleted. Still I somehow muscled through enough to finally have some semblance of a draft proposal to present to my agent. I knew it rambled in places, failed to go deep enough in others, and that a couple of the stories were a bit incoherent. Yet I

When we don't close off and let our hearts break, we discover our kinship with all beings.

—PEMA CHÖDRÖN

felt impatient to move things forward and I sent it off, hopeful she'd see beyond the imperfect way it was presented and think with me on how to best create the book. Now, my agent is not just my agent. She's also my good friend. Imagine then how hard it must have been for her to call me and confess that she just didn't get it, and that she was uninterested in representing the project. To say I was crushed was an understatement. I felt utterly humiliated and deflated. And I, of course, internalized her rejection as validation for my old, familiar "I'm inferior and not good enough" story.

Thankfully, I'm stubborn. So I stayed with it, sullenly taking the feedback she'd given and going back to the drawing board to solve the Rubik's Cube of this f%$#ing proposal. And that's when I got it. Here I was, writing a book about sourcing how you show up in the world from truth, not trauma, but I was emotionally anchored in the old, familiar *untrue* "I'm inferior" story *as I was working on it* and creating the manuscript from there. In spite of all I'd accomplished—the years I'd spent working with clients as a psychotherapist, the tens of thousands of students I'd had in my virtual and in-person classes, the thousands of coaches I'd trained in my methods, the two bestselling books I'd published—I still was assuming there were other teachers out there somewhere who were far more educated, intelligent, or equipped to present these ideas than I'd ever be. I was holding myself as less than those beloved teachers who seem to so easily pop onto the *New York Times* bestseller list, who are watched by hundreds of thousands on YouTube, and who join the ranks of the cream of the crop oracles . . . the ones that Oprah, queen of personal liberation, finds worthy of an interview. At that moment I realized I could not write a book about waking up to the truth of who you are from the lie of my old "I'm inferior and not good enough" source fracture story.

I put my computer down, closed my eyes, and took a deep breath. I extended unconditional self-compassion to the part of me holding that toxic narrative and spoke kindly yet firmly with my fourteen-year-old self, instructing her to step aside so the adult me—the part of me wise enough to recognize myself as worthy of presenting these teachings—could take charge of the project. I imagined myself in the future I was committed to creating, with the published book touching and transforming the lives of all those who needed it. I opened myself up to the possibility of being more visible in the world and took a stand for the impact for good that I longed to be having. At the end of that visioning, I felt a renewed sense of conviction and strength as it related to the book. The following day, my first book, *Calling in "The One,"* which had been out for nearly twenty years by then and had never once hit the top 100 on Amazon, shot up to number 63 in the rankings. Was it a coincidence? Or was it a sign from the Universe that something had indeed shifted and I was now on track and moving in the right direction? I took it as the latter.

Months later, after integrating the feedback and up-leveling the proposal significantly—writing now from the truth of my worthiness to be the one bringing forth this information—I called my friend, the agent who'd rejected the original proposal, for some advice. Now, I adore this woman, and I understand that a good part of healthy relatedness is granting someone the right to disappoint us in order to stay true to themselves. So I honored her no, and assumed I'd take the book elsewhere. Yet in that conversation, my enthusiasm for the True You work must have been contagious because she asked to revisit her decision. Several weeks later she happily took on the project, and went on to significantly contribute to the book you now hold in your hands.

> Wherever you are centered at the level of identity is where you are generating your life from.

Wherever we are centered at the level of identity is where we are generating life from. Many of us have been working hard to identify and release the old, toxic narratives that hold us back in life. Some of us are making heroic efforts to try to evolve beyond them—leaving no stone unturned in analyzing every little detail of what happened, making sincere efforts to forgive our perpetrators, using psychedelics, writing and reciting positive affirmations again and again, meditating for weeks on end . . . going to great lengths to try to disidentify from these inner lies in a way that leaves us free to create outside of them. Yet the most effective way to access your own agency to outgrow false beliefs is to get deeply related to the part of you still trapped in that story.

Witness Your Inner Experience with Love

I now invite you to go within, to discover how to witness your own inner experience with kindness and self-compassion. Few meditation practices take us deeper into our own humanity, focusing instead on transcending our inner experience. Yet in this practice, I encourage you to turn toward all that is happening within you with deep compassion. To witness yourself with objective kindness, or as poet Czesław Miłosz says, to look at yourself the way you'd look at "distant things." For once you've learned to hold the younger you from the part of you that has access to unconditional compassion, wisdom, and strength, you'll be capable of regulating yourself when you're triggered.

> The most effective way to outgrow false beliefs is to get deeply related to the part of you still trapped in that story.

Relating to yourself in this way might at first seem foreign, as I'm inviting you to speak to yourself as if you're talking to another person. Asking yourself questions like *What are you feeling?* or *What do you need?* as opposed to *What do I feel?* or *What do I need?* Studies show that speaking to ourselves in the third person, such as addressing ourselves with our own names—particularly when we are dysregulated—helps return us to a more balanced and calm emotional state. Bypass the need to try to figure everything out in your mind, which often increases rather than decreases anxiety. Since most of us tend to believe everything we feel, when we remember to self-soothe by speaking to ourselves either silently or gently out loud, we also help ourselves to disidentify from the traumatized self that's likely been activated. Because the part of you that's asking the question is not the same part of you that's in reaction. Getting your younger wounded self out of the driver's seat and safely buckled up

Emotions are not plans.
They don't solve problems or right
any wrongs. You can feel them . . .
but be careful about letting them
guide you.
Rage can be a dirty windshield.
Hurt is like a broken steering wheel.
Disappointment will only ride, sulking
and unhelpful,
in the back seat. If you don't do
something constructive
with them, they'll take you straight
into a ditch.

—MICHELLE OBAMA

in the back seat allows your mature wise self to be in charge of how you respond. This skill will be absolutely critical to master in order to succeed in manifesting and sustaining the miracles you are now standing for in life.

To live in alignment with the future you're standing for, you'll need to first learn the skill of regulating your very big and overwhelming emotions—especially those that feel historic in nature and reminiscent of hurts you've suffered in the past, as though they confirm your very worst fears. Rather than react from that part of yourself, you'll want to learn to step back and locate the part of you that can see what's happening more holistically and challenge the automatic meaning you find yourself making. In this way, you'll be capable of taking the right actions, and making choices that can keep you on track with the future you're committed to creating.

Step 2 Practice: Self-love Power Practice

This practice can be used in difficult moments when you feel triggered and/or simply as a kind and self-caring check-in that you make throughout your day. As preparation, I invite you to consider your intention. What's the one big breakthrough you're intending to cause? Once you've claimed that intention, see if you can name the unwanted pattern that's been showing up in this area of your life to date. For example, the minute you ask for what you want and need, others up and disappear. Or you never seem to advance professionally, as you watch others who are less deserving succeed. Or you somehow keep attracting alcoholics whom you end up caretaking. Or no matter how hard you try to save money, unexpected bills come in that wipe you out financially.

Ask yourself:

What disappointing pattern keeps happening again and again that makes me feel like it's just my fate to be living a lesser life?

Notice the emotions that come up as you name the pattern and take note of where and how you experience these feelings in your body. For example, as a tightening in your throat, a heaviness sitting on your heart, or as a tension smack in the middle of your solar plexus. Once you see this clearly, write down your intention, the pattern, and where in your body you feel the pattern. Then read through the following practice two or three times before engaging in it, as it is a closed-eyes exercise where your primary attention is on yourself. The goal of the exercise is to relate to yourself kindly and discover how to hold and contain your own inner experience from a deeper, wider center within.

If you prefer, you can download free audio and/or video of me guiding you through this practice at katherinewoodwardthomas.com/trueyoubonuses.

1. **Connect with your adult wise self and anchor this energy down into your body and beyond.**

   Let's begin by having you close your eyes and take a deep breath, as though you could breathe all the way down into your hips.

   Become aware of your adult wise self—the part of you that's resourceful, resilient, capable, and strong, and is already shining in another area of your life. This is the "you" that easily shows up as a successful professional, a powerful leader, a loving friend, and/or a wise and caring parent.

   Breathe the energy of your adult wise self down into your hips, down through your legs, out the bottoms of your feet, and down into the earth. From here, extend your energy out to the edges of the room and beyond.

   Treat yourself like someone you love.
   —GLENNON DOYLE

2. **Extend a sense of presence from your wise self to the wounded self in your body.**

   Imagine that the pattern is happening again right now. Notice where you're holding the feelings that come up for you around the pattern and put your hand on that part of your body.

   Staying identified with your wise self, extend a sense of deep presence and love to the part of you feeling these difficult feelings. Offer kindness and compassion to the wounded part of you that is struggling under the weight of these old and familiar feelings.

3. **Welcome and witness your feelings and needs.**

   From a place of deep listening and receptivity, ask yourself the following questions, welcoming whatever the response and mirroring it back with love.

   Ask yourself:

   Sweetheart, what are you feeling?*

   Listen for a response from your body and lovingly mirror it back by naming the feeling:

   I can see that you're feeling _____.

   Do this until all of your feelings have been named and witnessed with love.

   Note: If a feeling is particularly difficult and hard to hold, you can add a practice taken from Buddhism, called Tonglen. After mirroring back your response, "I can see that you're feeling _____," take a deep breath as though you could breathe that feeling straight into your heart. On the out-breath, offer a blessing to yourself and all beings ev-

   _____
   *If you're uncomfortable calling yourself "sweetheart," try speaking your own name kindly. If you had a nickname that you liked when you were younger, try addressing yourself by your own nickname in a loving and tender way.

erywhere who are also suffering with this very same feeling, in this very moment. Repeat until you're able to hold and contain the feeling without being overwhelmed by it.

Now shift your attention.

Ask yourself:

Sweetheart, what do you need?

Listen for the response and lovingly mirror it back by naming the need:

I can see that you need _____.

Ask several times until you've named and witnessed all of your needs with love.

Note: You may not be able to give yourself everything you need immediately. Yet validating your needs as worthy of your attention and love is often enough to relieve or lessen any suffering we may be experiencing at that moment.

Now that you have a way of accessing the part of you that can all too easily be triggered into an old narrative, it's time to put a name to your own personal source fracture story. You might already have a fixed idea about what your core identity-based beliefs are, particularly if you've been working on yourself for a while by now. You might have already come to the conclusion that your core belief is that you're not worthy of receiving what you want or that you're all alone in this world or that you're not safe to let others in. While your preconceived ideas might indeed end up being your source fracture story, it's important to remember that beliefs don't just live in our heads. They live in our somatic experience. When we're triggered, beliefs are activated in our bodies—

Do not fight against pain . . . irritation or jealousy. Embrace them . . . as though . . . embracing a little baby. Your anger is yourself, and you should not be violent toward it.

—THÍCH NHẤT HẠNH

our belly, our back, our hips, or our heart. These internal narratives then express as force fields of energy that envelop us, much like the *Peanuts* cartoon character Pig-Pen, whose own little sphere of messiness emanated from him everywhere he went. Eckhart Tolle calls this the "pain-body," and he describes it as "an energy field, almost like an entity, that has become temporarily lodged in your inner space."

Before doing the practice, it's also important to recognize that *turning toward* the "you" that you formed in response to past trauma is not the same thing as *collapsing into* that part of you and becoming what psychotherapist Richard Schwartz calls "blended" with your younger self. *Feeling your feelings* is very different from *holding and containing your feelings* from a deeper, wider center. I am asking you to do the latter. I am not asking that you revive the pain of your past. In fact, I caution you against it. If you find yourself collapsing into and feeling overwhelmed by old emotions associated with ancient trauma, simply open your eyes and ask yourself the question:

What's the best thing
about being my current age?

This question can help you find your way back to a more resourceful part of you, as it's critical that you stay identified with your wise self at all times in order for this practice to go well.

You may also find that you have more than one way of naming the story that's been causing you so much pain. In response to asking your body to put an "I am" or an "I am not" label to the feelings that come up when you're triggered, it's normal to find a cluster of false narratives that tumble out all at once—"I'm all alone in this world and no one will ever love me, and I'm not even worthy of doing this practice." If that happens, just stay with yourself long enough to notice which one of these "I am" statements is holding the biggest energy. Look for the one that brings tears to your eyes or that makes you feel a little sick to your stomach when you say it. As though that particular "I am" belief is foundational to all others. For example, if you unpack it further, you might discover the logic of the belief is that because you're all alone in this world, it's inevitable that no one will ever love you or find you worthy of love.

There's really no right or wrong answer to the question *What is the "I am" or "I am not" story that I'm assuming is true?* as your inner assumptions are subjective in nature. We're simply doing our best to give a name to the old, familiar feeling that has been simmering beneath the surface for as long as you can remember—your own personal version of Gilbert O'Sullivan's Grammy-nominated song "Alone Again (Naturally)." There's a reason his song was a worldwide hit and sold over two million copies. This tendency to collapse into a negative narrative at the level of identity is universal. We are all vulnerable to the lies that live within us and at risk of falling under their spell.

Usually, we do all we can to avoid giving this part of ourselves our full attention. Having done all we can to rid ourselves of these unwanted narratives, we fear going backward. As though naming it were somehow validating it as viable. Yet language serves as a container, and until we've given that cluster of old emotions a name, in the moments when it appears again, it will continue to hold power over us. The question becomes: Does it have you, or do you have it? Our goal is obviously the latter.

So, let's give it a go. To prepare yourself for the following practice, I invite you to again consider your intention, as well as the pattern that has chronically shown up instead. Prior to today, what conclusions, if any, have you already come to about the beliefs that are to blame for this pattern? It might be something like "I'm not good enough," "I'm not lovable," or "I'm too much." If you discover that you have any preconceived ideas about what your source fracture beliefs are, you might want to write them down and put them aside for now, as your body may be holding a different story than the one in your mind.

Also, I want to warn you that you could feel some difficult feelings as you do the practice, such as big fear, intense anger, or a cavernous sorrow.

If this happens, I suggest that you do the Self-love Power Practice, beginning on page 58, to help you hold and contain these feelings from a deeper center within you before moving forward to try to name the cluster of beliefs that are informing these feelings.

The most important tip I can offer is to monitor yourself. Make sure you don't become overly identified, or enmeshed, with the beliefs—the ones sitting in the center of your belly, or as a heaviness in your heart or a tightening of your shoulders and your throat. Stay centered and strongly anchored in your caring, mature wise self as you move through the practice, observing rather than collapsing into the story that your body is holding. If you can't manage to stay identified with your wise self, and find yourself slipping into becoming the story as opposed to observing the story, simply open your eyes and ask the question *What's the best thing about being my current age?* to reconnect with the part of you that has access to resources and resilience.

Step 2 Practice: Name Your Source Fracture Story

Read through the following practice two or three times before engaging in it, as it is a closed-eyes exercise where your primary attention is on yourself. If you prefer, you can download free audio and/or video of me guiding you through this practice at katherinewoodwardthomas.com /trueyoubonuses.

1. **Connect with your adult wise self and anchor your energy down into your body and beyond.**

   Let's begin by having you close your eyes again and take a deep breath as though you could breathe all the way down into your hips.

   Become aware of your adult wise self—the part of you that's resourceful, resilient, capable, and strong, and already shining in another area of your life. This is the "you" that easily shows up as a successful professional, a powerful leader, a loving friend, and/or a wise and caring parent.

Breathe the energy of your adult wise self down into your hips, down through your legs, out the bottoms of your feet, and down into the earth. From here, extend your energy out to the edges of the room and beyond.

2. **Imagine that your unwanted pattern is happening now and extend a sense of presence from your wise self to the wounded self in your body.**

   Aware of your intention, consider the pattern that normally shows up in this area of your life.

   In your mind's eye, imagine that the pattern is happening right now and notice where you feel the feelings associated with the pattern in your body.

   Ask yourself:

   Where do I feel it in my body when the pattern is happening?

   You may feel these feelings in more than one part of your body—your throat constricts, your heart drops, or your belly feels like someone just punched you. Find the lowest part of your body where these unpleasant feelings reside and lovingly place your hand there. Rather than try to get rid of them, simply welcome the feelings without judging or trying to fix or change them.

3. **Allow the feelings in your body to speak and tell their story.**

   Staying identified with your wise self, offer kindness and compassion to the wounded part of you that is struggling under the burden of these difficult yet familiar feelings. Look now to discover the meaning you automatically make of the pattern.

   Ask yourself:

   If I allow the feelings to speak for themselves,
   what might they say about who I am or who I am not?

For example: *I'm bad* or *I'm not safe.*

Ask yourself:

> *If I allow the feelings to speak for themselves,*
> *what might they say about how others feel*
> *about me and/or will behave toward me?*

For example: *Others will be mad at me* or *Others will hurt me.*

Ask yourself:

> *If I allow the feelings to speak for themselves,*
> *what might they say about my relationship with life?*

For example: *I will always be punished* or *It's dangerous to let someone get too close.*

4. **Identify the age of your wounded self.**

Now let's see if you can identify the age of this self in your body. This need not be accurate, but simply a felt sense you have about this younger part of you. You may or may not have a memory associated with the story. If you have more than one age, try to identify the age you were when you first came to these conclusions about yourself.

Ask yourself:

> *How old is this part of me still trapped in this story?*

5. **Identify how big and dense the energy of this story is.**

Observe the energy that's being held in this center. It might be a small, dense black hole in your heart or it could be a cold, hard cement wall that is surrounding you, three feet out from your body. Or it could take up the entire town you live in, like a vapor radiating from your body in each direction for miles.

Ask yourself:

How big is the energy being held in this center?

What color is it? How dense is it?

What is its texture?

6. Break state!

Once you've named your source fracture story, open your eyes and shake it out.

Ask yourself:

*What's the best thing about being my current age
compared with being me at the age of ___?*

Note: Look for the resources and strengths of your mature, resilient wise self.

Write down all that you discovered about the holistic narrative that becomes activated in your body in moments of stress. What is the "I am . . . /Others are . . . /Life is . . ." lens through which you suddenly start seeing the world? For example, *I am invisible, others don't care about me, it's dangerous to be seen.* Or *I'm not valuable, others are better than me, my life is worthless.* Or *I don't matter, others matter more than me, I am insignificant in this world.* Write down the age you were when you first came to these untrue conclusions and describe the energy of your own version of Pig-Pen's messy cloud.*

This, then, is your source fracture story. It's the old story of self that your body still holds deep down inside, like rings in a tree trunk. This

---

*If you need help in clarifying your source fracture story, feel free to peek at the True You Breakthrough Blueprint in part two. Yet I encourage you to stay with the steps of part one and only use part two to supplement what you are already discovering about yourself.

version of "you" has likely been creating frustrating patterns and nega-tively influencing the area(s) of life you've struggled with the most. Even more discouraging is that this "you" doesn't change simply because you now know where it comes from. What will allow for change is a shift in how you relate to this younger, tender you when it appears. Rather than ask what you can *do* to disappear the story, you must first discover the *who* of this center. In the moment you find yourself captivated by a false narrative, you must intercept the automatic meaning you are making by asking *Who do I believe I am right now, and what's really true?* You must look to articulate a more holistically informed and *true* narrative about who you are and what is or is not possible for you, claiming *the truth of who you are and who you came here to be* and waking yourself up from the trance of old trauma.

BONUS: STEP 2 PRACTICE IN ACTION

What is my intention?

EXAMPLES:

→ My intention is to double my income within the next six months.

→ My intention is to create a conscious-living community of friends who grow our own food and dine together each evening within one year from today.

What is the pattern that normally shows up in this area?

EXAMPLES:

→ I live hand to mouth and generate debt because I never have quite enough and my income stays the same no matter how hard I work.

→ I eat all of my meals alone because I'm fastidious about what I eat and I don't like the unhealthy restaurants my friends currently go to.

When the pattern happens, what do I make it mean about me?

EXAMPLES:

→ I am unworthy of receiving more money.

→ I am weird.

When the pattern happens, what do I make it mean about how others feel about and/or will behave toward me?

EXAMPLES:

→ Others need me to take care of them by offering my services for free or for less than they are worth.

→ Others don't get me.

When the pattern happens, what do I make it mean about my relationship with life?

EXAMPLES:

→ I'm only here to serve others.

→ There is no place for me in this world.

What age is the part of me trapped inside of this story?

EXAMPLES:

→ I'm six years old.

→ I'm twelve years old.

How big is the energy being held in this center?

EXAMPLES:

→ It radiates from my body about three feet out and is like a dark cloud that encapsulates me.

→ It's small and round like a black hole in the center of my heart.

What's the best thing about being your current age as compared with being you when you were _____ (the age of the self in your body)?

EXAMPLES:

→ I have spiritual beliefs that help me to trust that life is abundant and, as an adult, I know that what I have to offer is of great value.

→ I've come to appreciate that I'm so unique. I can acknowledge that my differences are actually my gifts, and that I can create things that don't yet exist because I see things so differently.

Step 3:
Wake Up to the
True You

You are free to choose the concept you will accept of yourself.
Therefore, you possess the power of intervention, the power
which enables you to alter the course of your future.
The process of rising from your present concept of
yourself to a higher concept of yourself is
the means of all true progress.

—NEVILLE GODDARD

When I was in the ninth grade, the students at my school were allowed to smoke between classes. The bell would ring and we'd shuffle out into the courtyard, one by one, until there was a pack of us huddling together for warmth as we lit up our Marlboros. We were the cool ones—the bad kids who lied to our parents and wore black leather jackets and low-hanging bell-bottoms. We drank sweet-tasting wine in the woods on the weekends, skipped classes to drink beer at the seedy bar across the street from school, and snuck out in the middle of the night to ride our bikes to parties, where we'd make out with people whose names we'd forget by the next day. To say I was on the wrong track might be an understatement.

It was around this time that I had an unlikely experience. I had little to do one weekend after a party I was hoping to attend, with the sole purpose of doing drugs for the first time, was canceled. When a friend invited me to her church that Sunday, I said yes out of sheer boredom. As we walked into the small white wooden chapel, we were led into a sunny room off to the right for Sunday school. Now, I'm fourteen and to me, Sunday school is for little kids. Already I'm too cool for the room. But I follow my friend and we find seats in the folding chairs set out in a circle. One by one the other teens lumber in and take their seats, until the circle is full with what appears to me to be a gathering of Goody Two-shoes. So there's me with my "I'm over this" attitude, and all of them leaning in and eager to hear whatever the Sunday school teacher—a woman aptly named Faith—has to tell them about Jesus. Within five minutes I'm wishing I was home in bed. But I stick it out, tolerating the twenty-one ways that Faith and the rest of the disciples are covertly trying to convert me to their point of view, which seems to come down to nine simple instructive words. That in order to be saved, "You must ask Jesus to come into your heart."

At the end of the hour, Faith announces that we will all close our eyes and go around the circle as each of us utters one prayerful sentence to end the meeting. When it's my turn, I find myself saying, without any premeditated intention to do so, "Jesus, please come into my heart." In that instant, I both felt and saw a golden yellow-orange light rush in through the top of my head and wash through my entire body like an electrified wave of love. I was so startled that my eyes shot open to see if anyone saw what just happened. I'd never heard of a spiritual awakening and was unaware that something like this was even possible. And while I was deeply confused as to the meaning of such an experience, there were three things I knew beyond a shadow of a doubt. The first was that there was a God—some force and field of life that was greater than me. The second was that this God loved me, and in a deeply personal and pervasive way. And the third was that God did not want me to continue down the precarious path that I was currently on. I credit that experience with saving my life, for clearly I was on the road to doing something stupid with potentially devastating consequences.

What opened up in that experience, which probably lasted no longer than three seconds, was a deep inner knowing that I was loved beyond measure. Before then, I didn't feel loved by anyone. Which of course didn't mean that no one loved me. Yet the experience of feeling seen, known, and held by love was new to me. This shift from an "I'm not loved" to an "I am loved" sense of self changed everything. While I still had a plethora of self-destructive patterns that I battled with for the next two decades, the inner conviction that I am loved by life was enough of a foundation for me to find my way. Such that I have been able to take all of the scary, shameful, and hurtful things that happened in my youth and weave them into the wisdom, kindness, and love that I now hope to offer others. This is the power of an embodied awakening to a new sense of self.

Historically, spontaneous awakenings to a new identity—to Self with a capital *S*—have largely been left to spiritual and religious circles, such as the one I was fortunate to visit that day. Yet the recent explosion of research into the use of psychedelics and plant medicine to help expand consciousness beyond the narrow confines of one's habitual egoic structure add to the ways that many of us are seeking to wake up to a new sense of self. In this way, the emerging field of psychedelics has much in common with the True You teachings, as both seek liberation beyond an overidentification with the traumatized self formed in response to a painful past.

> *Maybe the past is like an anchor*
> *holding us back. Maybe you have to*
> *let go of who you were to*
> *become who you will be.*
> —CARRIE IN *SEX AND THE CITY*

Beliefs Are Body Based

The invitation before you is to feel into who you are in the fulfillment of your desired future, and to experience that possibility like an awakening

True behavior change is identity change.
—JAMES CLEAR

that inspires you to grow into that version of your-self. If you've been stuck in the area of your inten-tion, ask yourself which self you've been sourcing yourself from. A younger, wounded, wannabe self? Or a future triumphant self? Then look to see what's missing by way of your own development that would equip you to live the life you came here to live. Because going for your dreams while emotionally centered in your old source fracture story—the "I'm not worthy enough" or "I'm too much" narrative born of past pain—will be insufficient to get you to the future you're now claiming as your own. To manifest your dream future, you must access the greater truth of who you are and feel it deeper than where your old story has been living in your body.

It's like waking up from a trance, and when you are able to do it, you become liberated to create your life outside of your old story. In other words, you finally have it and it no longer has you. For you are now stand-ing in the true you—a you that is holistically, somatically aligned with your value, your power, and your worthiness to create the future you're standing for, and you organically begin walking through the world as though it's just a matter of time before the external world catches up to reality.

Who you are being, and the energy you are centered in, is what's cre-ating your experience. If who you are *being* is out of alignment with all you are *doing* to try to make something happen, any progress you make toward a desired future will be slow. If you do manage to achieve your goal, you may not even enjoy it, because you'll likely struggle with feel-ings of being a fraud and with an anxiety that it will all disappear if you make one wrong move. If this is you, the problem is likely that where you are centered and sourcing yourself from is misaligned with the "having" of what you want for the long haul. Real change is sourced from where you are centered within yourself at the level of identity.

Most of us assume that it's by changing our thoughts that we can change our lives. Yet we have it backward. From a neurological perspec-tive, it's changing our *feelings*, and not our thoughts, that offers us the opportunity to truly transform. For it's our feelings that inform our thoughts and not the other way around. This is why affirmations so often fall flat when we're gripped by a shame-based emotion. You can tell yourself that life is good all you want, but if you *feel* confused, lost, and abandoned, then that's the part of you in charge.

> Affirmations fall flat when we're gripped by a shame-based emotion. You can tell yourself life is good all you want, but if you *feel* lost and abandoned, then that's the part of you in charge.

To wake yourself up to a deeper truth, you must notice where in your body you hold the emotions that so easily swallow you whole when you're triggered into an old story. In locating the place in your body that is so easily gripped by shame, sorrow, fear, or despair, you might also notice that there's a part of you that is already outside of it. The author of *The Untethered Soul*, Michael Alan Singer, reminds us that "When your mind is disturbed, don't ask, 'What do I do about this?' Instead ask, 'Who am I that notices this?' In time, you will come to realize that the center from which you watch disturbance cannot get disturbed." From this deeper, wider center—the part of you that is outside of the "you" that is triggered—look to observe what's happening in your body with curiosity, kindness, and compassion. Do your best to step back and un-blend from your feelings enough to notice the historic somatic sensations that accompany them. You might find a tense closing of your throat, a heaviness that feels as though it's crushing your heart, a tightening of your shoulder blades to guard against a stab in the back, or an unpleasant sick feeling churning in your solar plexus. False centers are body-based, and in order to wake yourself up to a greater truth, you must turn toward the "you" in your body and speak words of wisdom and truth directly to your somatic self.

The Japanese martial art of aikido is a path of personal transformation that examines who you are and how you relate to others. It is appreciated for its minimal use of force to overcome an opponent.

> *The body keeps the score.*
> —BESSEL VAN DER KOLK

Practitioners are taught to move from their *hara*, or lower part of their abdomen. The hara is considered the source of *ki*, or life force. When we speak words of wisdom and truth from our hara to the part of us anchored in the lie of a source fracture story, we need not force our way to a greater perspective. We simply need to take a breath and ask, "What am I assuming is true?" and challenge that perspective from a place in our bodies that is deeper and wider than where the lie has been living. In doing so, the part of us captivated by falsehood more easily softens and surrenders. For truth does indeed set us free.

Shift Centers

Waking up from the trance of old trauma is not a one-time, peak experience event. The story of self is a story that's been woven into the fabric of our lives so deeply, and is now so pervasive, that in order to create a life outside of that center, we must learn to differentiate the impaired sense of self from the wise, more mature true you—the calm, clear, cohesive self that lies at the core of who you are. Accessing this part of ourselves is easier said than done, particularly when we are triggered into an old story. In the brilliant book *The Myth of Normal*, written by Gabor Maté in collaboration with his son Daniel Maté, Gabor shares a compelling conversation he had with biologist Bruce Lipton. In explaining why we are so vulnerable to soaking up false information in our early years, Lipton says it's because delta brain waves, which predominate our first two years of life, are the brain's lowest frequency. After which we develop the capacity for theta brain waves, which dominate until the age of six. Because both delta and theta brain waves are highly vulnerable to and wide open to absorption, as though we are under the spell of hypnosis, we believe whatever messages we receive without question. It is only later, at roughly age seven or eight, that the logic associated with alpha and beta brain waves kicks in, and we are able to engage critical thinking. This is why the beliefs that lodged in our bodies when we're young are now so difficult to overcome, for they occur to us not as beliefs but as facts. The good news is, you can indeed wake up from the spell cast upon you by mastering the art of *shifting centers.* Learning to pull yourself up and out of the quicksand of a false center when you fall into it, so that you are able to stay the course and generate your life from the truth of your value, worthiness, and power. Growing your capacity to live from your *power center,* and securing a solid, sovereign sense of self as your *primary* internal home base.

To give you a glimpse of what it looks like when we intercept an initial primitive interpretation and look to discover what's happening from a more true and empowering perspective, I'll share a story with you. Several years ago, I flew to New York to take my father to the theater for his eightieth birthday. The two of us had actively been repairing our relationship for years by then, and in particular, the wounding that occurred when he'd given up parental rights when I was ten years old. His decision to do this, as well-meaning as it was at the time, left in me a cavernous wound that contributed to how lost I became as a teenager. It also had profoundly negative consequences that followed me well into adulthood, showing up most acutely in my relationships with men, who easily discarded me, much like I believed my father had. Through the many conversations my father and I had about this, as I desperately tried to "heal" this painful pattern, I'd come to understand that my father's second wife, a woman to whom he was still married, had always felt threatened by our relationship. It wasn't a logical reaction and she's not a bad person. But she did have a very primitive, possessive knee-jerk response to the fact that he'd been married before. One that had her behave in unsupportive, and even undermining, ways over the years. He recognized this as small-minded and immature of her, and he felt badly about it. He did his best to deal with her pettiness by meeting with me outside of their home—at a diner or a park—whenever I was in town. For years I felt like "the other woman," and tolerated this odd situation. On that particular day, however, as we walked toward the theater, it came up in our conversation. This time I shared something that I'd not confessed before. While I acknowledged we'd done a great job healing our relationship, I admitted to feeling sad that he never reclaimed me as his daughter by inviting me to be a part of his family, which would have required him to take a stand against his wife's wishes. As we squeezed past others to take our seats, he turned to me and said, somewhat matter-of-factly, "You're right, and I never will," and with that the theater went dark.

Frankly, he may as well have punched me in the stomach. For I immediately collapsed internally into an old familiar narrative of "I'm not good enough, men don't value me, and there's not enough love for me." Baiting me to shrink into myself and settle for less—not just with my father, but with men in general, which I'd done much of my adult life. Yet because I know and practice this work, I was able to intercept that interpretation, almost as though I could catch a fastball thrown furiously at me. Up came my inner baseball mitt as I said to myself in a fierce and powerful tone of voice worthy of a mother lioness, "Katherine, sweetheart, do not go there. That story is not the truth. You are a woman who is worthy of being honored with the position of daughter. Your father is a good man and he is proud of you. I don't know why he's responding this way, but it has nothing to do with you. Your father loves you with all his heart. There is more than enough love here for you." Ultimately, the power statement that calmed me down, and which I ended up repeating over and over in my mind to regulate myself, was:

I am a woman who is worthy
of being chosen, even if my father is not
choosing me at this moment.

Though I was still disturbed by his response, I was able to *not make it mean anything about me.* Nor did I come to any conclusions about him that may have limited our relationship. This is what it looks like to intercept false meaning in the moment it's being made. And this is what it takes to intervene on your own behalf in a way that wakes you up to truth and recalibrates your experience on a cellular level. This is what we all must learn to do if we hope to outgrow our identity-based beliefs and create a life that's no longer reflective of an old, toxic story.

Had I allowed myself to collapse and begin generating life from my old story of not being good enough to be chosen, I doubt I would have

When you meet that self that you no longer want to be, you have two choices . . . you can just stay there and be swallowed or you can move on. I choose to move on.
—VIOLA DAVIS

been ready to meet my partner, Michael, which happened just a few weeks later. Now, Michael is one of the most loving men I've ever known. When telling him of my father's unwillingness to reclaim me as his daughter, he leapt to his feet and swept me in his arms to declare, "I claim you!" It was a deeply joyful moment for us both! A few weeks after that, I was also able to have a heart-to-heart with my father about what he'd said. After I humbly acknowledged that he had the right to make the choices he was making, he felt safe enough to share his fear that reclaiming me as his daughter would cause a crisis in his marriage. In spite of his fear, by the end of that conversation, he actually offered to do an adult adoption. A gesture which, in and of itself, was enough to complete the situation for me, and one which I declined out of respect for his marriage. Since then, my father has found ways to include me more, recently inviting Michael and me to an awards ceremony where he was being honored. There we were—his wife and son (my half brother) and daughter-in-law and Michael and me—all of us together, laughing, eating, and celebrating like one big happy family. None of this would have happened had I allowed myself to collapse into my old source fracture story and shrink away from love, rather than stay generative of it.

Most of us know that we're vulnerable to being triggered and have been working hard to learn how to regulate our emotions in such moments before doing too much damage. When it happens, it's as though we've fallen down a rabbit hole of the past and are suddenly interpreting and responding to life through the lens of an old wound. For many of us, the dark crevices of negative meaning-making frames, and the unhealthy ways of relating that accompany them, have become unwanted companions on our journey through life. As much as you may now know what triggers you and why, you may have yet to graduate to a new and expanded Self—the "you" that is no longer at the mercy of old imprinting and, therefore, free to evolve beyond it.

The Need for Self-Sponsorship

You've probably noticed that there's more than one of you here. As Richard Schwartz tells us, each of us houses a multitude of parts, each one holding a unique way of interpreting the world. In the areas of life that come easily to you—where you feel confident and accomplished and trust your ability to manifest your desires—you likely had a plethora of positive experiences while growing up that gave you a sense of yourself as someone who's blessed in those areas. Maybe you aced all your tests in this subject, or your parents lovingly appreciated your exceptional talents, or the other kids always laughed at your jokes. This positive sponsorship gave you a preconscious identity of "I'm good at this, others value me, and I can handle whatever obstacles I encounter here," making it relatively effortless to see the possibilities present and create even more success in that area.

Where you may be struggling, however, is where you didn't receive positive feedback during your formative years. In fact, you may have received just the opposite—negative feedback. Maybe an older sibling chronically called you stupid, or your teacher scolded you each time you asserted leadership, or you had a parent who seemed irritated by your needs much of the time. Much like the old witch who casts an evil spell upon an innocent child, these acts may live like a curse that was placed upon you, a toxic form of sponsorship that, to this day, may still undermine your confidence and make it unsafe to take the necessary risks to grow in ways that would allow you to realize your intentions. Curses are salient in early relational trauma and live in the psyche as impostors of truth—leaving their mark as a perpetual lie that has coiled itself around your soul, habitually whispering deep within that you are unlovable, you are not wanted, or you are not good enough, no matter how much evidence you have created to the contrary. In fact, life can easily be experienced as an uphill climb as you try to compensate for this internal deficit, doing

May your heart never be haunted by ghost-structures of old damage.
—JOHN O'DONOHUE

all you can to prove to yourself and others that it's not true and going to great lengths to hide it from others, lest they, too, see it and reject you.

While children rely upon the blessings of others to come into the fullness of their being, we adults must cultivate the ability to bless ourselves with what might be considered a positive form of self-sponsorship. Learning to identify and challenge the toxic conversations that have habitually hijacked us into a lesser version of who we are, and to push back by actively claiming a greater truth. To develop the ability to notice when we're somatically centered in a false narrative and immediately look for the part of ourselves capable of speaking truth to the younger self being swallowed up by an old story.

Learning to push back and stand strong in the truth of your value and power in the face of failure and frustration is one of the most important things you will ever learn to do. For when somatically centered in an untrue story, failure is experienced as proof that your worst fear about yourself is valid, which then solidifies your impaired sense of self. This then has you narrow your life significantly. For you will shy away from taking the necessary risks to actualize your potential and choose a contraction into self-protection mode over self-expansion mode again and again. Anchored in the true you, however, you can better tolerate disappointments, setbacks, and delays, and therefore stay the course in the face of them. As unpleasant as they may be, the true you relates to them as valuable feedback that can help you get where you want to go. As the true you is centered in a preconscious conviction of your worthiness, value, and power, failure does not mean anything negative about you. It is simply the chance to refine your skills and grow your capacities.

Wake Yourself Up

Yet how can you wake yourself up when in the grip of a false narrative, seeing the world through the lens of an old wound? Most likely you know, intellectually anyway, that you're not the story you tell yourself—that you're crazy, too much, or unworthy of respect. Yet it doesn't feel that way in your body. Because most of us are overly identified with our feelings—particularly the soul-crushing ones of shame and humiliation. By now, it's almost second nature to fall into the trap of interpreting and reacting to life from that false center, and in ways that keep us stuck in old and tired patterns. Which is why many of us feel so victimized by our own consciousness and still struggle to forgive our parents for the imprinting we received because of the mistakes they made. It's bad enough that your mother undermined you, but now here you are, undermining yourself and creating relationships with those who follow suit. It's like trying to fight your way out of a straitjacket.

Rather than fix this story, what you want to do instead is look for the part of you that is already outside of it. Which sounds like a prescription to meditate eight hours a day for the next three years. Which might be a great way to go, if you can manage it. Yet waking up to the part of you that's holding a different perspective isn't always that hard. I learned this years ago while waiting tables in New York City. After a particularly busy shift, a group of us waitstaff gathered for drinks. At the time, I was a wannabe stage actor, and I was struggling. That afternoon I'd had a really disappointing audition, and I was feeling pretty down in the dumps. I started complaining to my friend Billy, who sat across from me. I told him that I thought it was all over for me, that I'd never make it in anything I tried to do. I began indulging in a dramatic monologue about how I wasn't good enough and would never amount to much in life. After several

When you start to rewrite the story of not-mattering, you start to find a new center. You remove yourself from other people's mirrors and begin speaking more fully from your own experience, your own knowing place.
—MICHELLE OBAMA

minutes of this, Billy must have gotten bored because he reached across the table, took my hand, looked into my eyes, and said, "I'm so glad you're facing this now, Katherine." To which I replied, completely indignant that he would say such a thing, "How dare you say that to me?" "Thank you," he said with a mischievous smile before turning to speak to one of the other waiters. That was a wake-up call for me along the lines of the scene in the movie *Moonstruck*, when Cher slaps Nicolas Cage across the face and yells, "Snap out of it!"

There's already a part of you holding a completely different narrative about your worthiness, value, and power than the one you automatically default to when disappointed or triggered. On the most basic level, it's the optimistic part of you that believes that by reading this book you could become who you sense, deep down, you were born to be. Maybe it's the part of you that's a seasoned spiritual practitioner who has access to an expanded, higher self. Perhaps it's the part that shows up as an inspiring, competent leader or a powerful and effective advocate for those less fortunate. Maybe you're an intelligent and valued employee with a reputation for excellence or you're an engaged and loving parent. Certainly, most of us know what it's like to show up as a good friend to offer wisdom and encouragement to a friend in need—the "you" that is wise, strong, mature, competent, and kind. And it is this "you" that the younger you desperately needs to connect with, particularly when drowning in a false narrative.

> There's already a part of you holding a completely different narrative about your worthiness, value, and power than the one you default to when disappointed or triggered.

Yet it's usually in those moments when we've dropped into a false center that the adult in us disappears. Much like it was when our original hurt happened—just when we needed a kind, loving adult the most, no one was there.

Here you are, all grown up, an adult who's just been triggered into experiencing the world through the lens of an old disempowering narrative.

Because your limbic system, also called your emotional brain, is now activated. Which happens to all of us, as neuroscientists tell us that this part of the brain doesn't ever really mature. And so you're back to being an embarrassed nine-year-old who just lost the spelling bee for the entire school. The meaning you're making is reminiscent of the meaning you made back then—some version of "I'm stupid, everyone else is smarter than me, and I can never get it right."

If back then, when the identity theft was occurring, a trustworthy adult had noticed what was happening, they might have intervened. Yet most likely, there was no wise and gentle mentor there to lovingly put their arms around you to tell you it was all okay. That everyone makes mistakes. That you're actually very smart and would one day grow up to do great things. Instead, you were alone with your humiliation and shame, and so it lodged in you like a damning truth, one that you've been dancing with ever since.

Speak Words of Wisdom to Your Wounded Self

If you look, you'll begin to see that whenever you're interpreting the world through the eyes of your wounded younger self, you tend to see things in an overly simplistic, absolute, and childlike way. That's because you initially created this worldview at a time when you developmentally lacked the cognitive capacity to see things from a more holistic and well-rounded perspective. You did not understand, at the tender age of four, that your mother's neglect was a symptom of her depression. Nor could you fathom that your father's rage was due to his addiction to alcohol. Instead, you made everything about *you*: your value, worthiness, and power—or, rather, the lack thereof. While no adult was available to tell you any differently at the time, the good news is *you're an adult now*. And your intelligent and mature wise self is more than capable of mentoring the wounded, younger part of you to a more empowering perspective; one that is objective, balanced, and discerning. For it's the wise self within who can set the distorted lens of shame aside and speak words of wisdom, kindness, and truth to the part of you trapped in the mud of false meaning-making frames.

Wisdom differs from knowledge, and most of us look for knowledge when we're lost. The egoic mind craves certainty and is preoccupied with questions like *When will it happen?*, *How will it happen?*, and *What do I need to do to make it happen?* Wisdom, however, asks more growth-oriented, expansive questions like *What lessons am I learning?* or *What would I need to surrender to be at peace with this situation as it is?* or *What is it costing me to give away my power to this person and what amends can I make to myself moving forward?* Knowledge wants the road map to get where it wants to go, but wisdom is more interested in becoming who you'd need to be to both manifest and sustain what you want.

> The wise self within can set the distorted lens of shame aside and speak words of wisdom and truth to the part of you trapped in the mud of false meaning-making frames.

By asking questions that inspire you to think contextually—not just *about* where you want to go but *from* that future and what it now requires of you—you can become masterful at using whatever life throws your way to become unstoppable in manifesting whatever it is you're committed to creating.

> By asking questions that inspire you to think contextually—not just *about* where you want to go but *from* that future and what it now requires of you—you become masterful at using whatever life throws your way to become unstoppable in manifesting what you're committed to creating.

By relating to breakdowns as though they were answered prayers, you can use them to deepen your faith in the goodness of life, hone your skills, grow your character, and cultivate your capacities.

Contrary to popular belief, wisdom does not come with age. Studies show that wisdom comes to those who actively seek it. Research also tells us that wisdom is developmentally available to us as early as adolescence. It's good to know that those of us over the age of thirteen have the ability to become wise people. So when you find yourself in a tough spot and notice that you're reactively interpreting life through an old lens, pause. Take no action from that center, lest you unconsciously perpetuate the very pattern you're so desperately trying to escape. Instead, look for the part of you that can consider your situation contextually, and from a more life-affirming perspective. The part of you that can process what's occurring with the goal of growth in mind. Allow this deeper, wiser part of you to take charge of how you respond. This internal leadership role is not a passive observance of whatever is happening but an active engagement in correcting misperceptions and mentoring the lost, hurt parts of you home to a more empowering worldview.

Ask yourself:

How might this be happening not just to me, but for me?

How might I recontextualize my problem by relating to the breakdown as a normal part of any meaningful transformative journey? Not just as something to tolerate, but as something to actually value and use to my advantage?

> *Fighting fear doesn't work . . .*
> *One has to focus on what is real.*
> *On the truth. When in darkness, don't fight it.*
> *You can't win. Just find the nearest switch, turn on the light.*
> —KAMAL RAVIKANT

The Power of a Good Power Statement

By now I hope it's becoming clear that the future you desire is not a place *to get to* but a place *to come from* as you begin walking through the world from the self of your future already fulfilled. Yet how can we get to a place where we feel the positive, possible self of our future burning bright in our bellies, just as vividly as we can smell chocolate chip cookies baking in the oven? What will initiate that expansive sense of optimistic anticipation that something *good* is about to happen, both *to* us and *through* us? Those of us who've wrestled with the tenacious internal perpetrator of shame know it's not always as easy as simply making a conscious decision to be a new you. As much as you might want to be a confident person instead of an insecure person, if you're emotionally blended with the part of you holding the story of being inferior to others, and if that narrative is enmeshed with deep and historic feelings of humiliation, then you probably lack the capacity to just override it at will. This is where power statements come in. A power statement is a conduit for a powerful truth that lies beyond the pain. An assertion of a fresh and empowering perspective that immediately begins to deconstruct the chokehold that a lie has had on your psyche, liberating you to suddenly see things anew. Like a bull's-eye that goes straight to the heart of it, a good power statement is like a truth bomb that wakes you up from an old falsehood in a way you can feel in your body, elevating you to a higher plane of awareness, and unleashing a sense of creativity and hope for a brighter future.

For years, my friend and colleague Leila Reyes felt called to write a book about the unusual yet very real and heartfelt healing she'd had with her father—a man who'd molested her after her mother abandoned their family when she was just eleven years old. Though she'd managed to stop the abuse soon after it started with a resounding no, she carried the scars of this appalling breach well into adulthood. Leila's recovery journey differed from many abuse survivors as, soon after her twenty-fourth birthday, she had the rare experience of her father confessing his sins with a heavy heart and deep humility; with his head bowed, he was able to express his genuine grief and shame, as well as a devotion to do whatever it took to repair their relationship. After understanding how much she blamed herself for the abuse—a common occurrence for survivors—he even went so far as to

> The future you desire is not a place *to get to* but a place *to come from* as you walk through the world from the self of your future already fulfilled.

gather a group of trusted family friends to his home in order to publicly admit the harm he'd done his daughter—his way of trying to shift the shame that Leila carried to himself.

When I met her, Leila had been working on herself for years to try to overcome the many ways she still felt impacted by the abuse. Leaning in together, Leila was able to see that in spite of all she'd done to try to heal, as well as her father's heartfelt good efforts, what tenaciously stayed with her was the meaning she'd made of it—the story she'd collapsed into at the time the abuse happened, and which had become a kind of internal home base; a shame-based sense of self that she operated out of so habitually in life that it had become a pervasive part of her personality. *I don't matter, others matter more than me, and nothing I do will ever make a difference in this world.* This disempowering narrative brought with it ways of relating that were organic to this center, and for years, Leila showed up small, deferential, and subservient in all of her relationships. Seamlessly tending to the dreams of others while dismissing and marginalizing her own. Sensitive and responsive to the feelings and needs of others while minimizing and ignoring her own. Inside of these ways of relating, Leila gained a reputation for being an amazing support person, and she found herself working tirelessly in the background for well-known authors who were launching successful books into the world, myself included. All the while secretly dreaming that maybe one day she would write her own.

It wasn't until I helped Leila to name the story in her body, and to start mentoring herself to a truer, more accurate perspective, that she was able to wake up from the trance. She first offered a heartfelt apology to her traumatized self for treating herself as though she didn't matter by chronically ignoring her own feelings and needs for all these years. She next apologized to herself for the many ways she'd trained others to ignore her feelings and needs, too, by failing to express them, an act that would have at least given them a chance to demonstrate that she did actually matter. She reassured herself that her feelings and needs did, indeed, matter, and vowed to begin treating herself as such. She then came up with this power statement, which immediately began to recalibrate how she showed up in life:

My feelings and needs matter.

They matter to me.

And it's appropriate for me to expect them to matter to anyone I let into my life in any meaningful way.

My actions have agency and matter in the grand scheme of things.

This then is how Leila woke up from the trance of old trauma and became liberated to start sourcing who she was from the bright future she felt called to fulfill. She was then able to turn the pain she'd endured into a sense of purpose with her inspiring book, *Freedom from Shame: Trauma, Forgiveness and Healing from Sexual Abuse*, which details her remarkable healing journey with her father, as well as her recovery from childhood sexual abuse. She's also launched The Freedom Project, a unique initiative that provides support not just for survivors but also for perpetrators willing to own their behavior and make amends to those they've hurt. In the end, the authors she'd helped showed up to support Leila in ways similar to how she'd supported them; and her book is now having an impact on those who might never have heard her liberating message had she not pushed back against the inertia of her wildly untrue source fracture story.

Let's now discover those magical words that can wake you up from the trance of old trauma and liberate you to start creating your life beyond it. Waking up to a new sense of self is not the same

> Waking up to a new sense of self is not the same as having insight into what caused an impaired identity to begin with. Rather, we look for an energetic shift—a body-based release of fear, sorrow, or shame. An untethering from the untrue, toxic *I am* or *I am not* false sense of self, and an awareness of an entirely new narrative that unleashes brand-new possibilities and potentials.

as having insight into what caused you to adopt an impaired identity to begin with. Rather, we are looking for an energetic shift—a body-based release of the low-grade fever of fear, sorrow, or shame that's been sitting in your solar plexus all these years. An untethering from the untrue, toxic *I am* or *I am not* false sense of self, and an awareness of an entirely new narrative that unleashes brand-new possibilities and potentials into your life.

Step 3 Practice: Create a Power Statement to Wake Up to the True You

Read through the following practice two or three times before engaging in it, as it is a closed-eyes exercise where your primary attention is on yourself. If you prefer, you can download free audio and/or video of me guiding you through this practice at katherinewoodwardthomas.com /trueyoubonuses.

1. **Center yourself.**

   Close your eyes and take a deep breath, as though you could breathe all the way down into your hips.

   Move into a place of deep listening and receptivity.

   Drop your awareness down into your body.

   Notice all of the feelings and sensations in your body and let go of any tension you find.

2. **Connect with your adult wise self and anchor your energy down into your body and beyond.**

   Become aware of your adult wise self—the part of you that's resourceful, resilient, capable, strong, and already shining in another area of your life. This is the "you" that easily shows up as a successful professional, a powerful leader, a loving friend, and/or a wise and caring parent. Breathe the energy of your adult wise self down into your hips, down through your legs, out the bottoms of your feet, and down into the earth. From here, extend your energy out to the edges of the room and beyond.

3. **Become aware of where you feel your source fracture story in your body and send love to this part of you from your adult wise self.**

   Consider your intention. Notice the source fracture story that has been getting in the way of you manifesting that positive, possible future and has you feeling so resigned about ever realizing your dream.

   Notice where in your body you're holding the feelings of your source fracture story, and from your adult wise self, send unconditional love and compassion to this part of you.

   You may feel the feelings associated with your story in more than one place—your throat, your heart, your belly. Look for the lowest area in your body where these painful feelings reside and lovingly place your hand there. Rather than try to get rid of these feelings, simply welcome them without judgment and without trying to fix or change anything.

   Note: If your feelings are overwhelming, stop and engage the Self-love Power Practice, beginning on page 58, before proceeding. Ask yourself, *Sweetheart, what are you feeling?* And mirror back the response. Ask, *Sweetheart, what do you need?* Again, mirror back the response until you feel more emotionally balanced, contained, and able to hold your big feelings from a deeper center within you.

4. **Acknowledge the self-defeating ways you've been mistreating yourself that have validated and perpetuated your source fracture story.**

   Notice if you've been in the habit of treating yourself in ways that have validated and perpetuated your source fracture story. For example, inside of an "I'm alone" belief, you may have the habit of self-abandoning to try to please others. Or inside of an "I'm invisible" belief, you may have a tendency to minimize or even ignore your own feelings to care for the feelings of others.

Ask yourself:

> *How have I been mistreating myself in ways that have validated and perpetuated my source fracture story?*

Once you see this clearly, speak words of acknowledgment and repentance to yourself, apologizing for keeping your source fracture story alive and well inside of your own relationship with yourself, and vowing to do things differently moving forward. For example, you might say to yourself, *I apologize for dismissing your feelings to care for the feelings of others. Please forgive me. I promise that from this moment on, I will begin listening to and honoring your feelings.*

5. **Push back against the certainty of your old belief about yourself and mentor the younger you to a more true and empowering perspective.**
   From your adult wise self, challenge the "I am" or "I am not" belief in your body and assert a deeper truth.
   Ask yourself:

> *As it relates to my old false belief about myself, what's really true about who I am and who I have the potential to become?*

For example: *It is not my fate to be alone. I came here to love and be loved, and I have the power to learn how to create loving, healthy relationships that deepen over time.*
Make sure that your answer addresses and deconstructs your specific source fracture story belief about yourself.

6. **Push back against the certainty of your old belief about others and mentor the younger you to a more true and empowering perspective.**
   From your adult wise self, challenge your assumptions about how others will feel about you and/or treat you and assert a deeper truth.
   Ask yourself:

As it relates to my old false belief about others, what's really true about how others will feel about me and/or treat me?

For example: *Others will tend to show up for me to the extent that I invite them in by taking the risk to be vulnerable.*

Make sure that your answer addresses and deconstructs your specific source fracture story belief about others.

7. **Push back against the certainty of your old belief about life and mentor the younger you to a more true and empowering perspective.**

   From your adult wise self, challenge your assumptions about your relationship with life and assert a deeper truth.

   Ask yourself:

   > *As it relates to my old false belief about life,*
   > *what's really true about my relationship with life*
   > *and the possibilities I hold for fulfillment?*

   For example: *I am a part of all that is and deeply connected to all living beings.*

   Make sure that your answer addresses and deconstructs your specific source fracture story belief about life.

8. **Weave it all together in a way that wakes you up from your source fracture story and somatically anchors you in your power center.**

   Look back at your answers to numbers four, five, and six. Your answers to those questions can now become your power statements. Statements that assert a new narrative of who you are and what is possible for you to have and create. Feel the truth of these statements in your body, and begin walking through the world from what we call your power center—that holistic place within you that is holding an expanded sense of possibility and purpose to become who you feel called to be.

Memorize your power statements and use them to push back and wake yourself up whenever you notice that you've collapsed back into an old, untrue story.*

POWER STATEMENTS SHARE THREE KEY QUALITIES

1. **They deconstruct a specific and disempowering false belief.** Unlike affirmations, which might best be described as a generic positive thought to replace a negative one, power statements are created in response to a very particular false belief. They have the sole intention of waking you up from the narrow confines of your previous disempowering narrative to a broader, more true perspective. For example, in response to the belief "I am invisible," you might assert, *I came here to be seen, and it is my job to assert myself to make myself visible wherever I go.*

2. **They declare a powerful truth you can feel in your body, more deeply than where your false story has been living.** Power statements must be experienced first and foremost as *true*, and in a way that inspires a somatic surrender to a new, more empowering perspective. For example, in response to the false belief "I am not enough," you might assert, *I am more than worthy of love just as I am.*

3. **They can be generative of the future you are standing for.** Power statements can also be generative of your desired future. For example, in response to an unfulfilled longing for a loving relationship, you might assert, *It is my destiny to have great love in my life, and I open myself to becoming who I will need to be to manifest and sustain deep happiness in love.*

    As you move through life, be vigilant against the false center and fierce in your determination to not allow your life to be used in service

---

*If you're needing help in clarifying your power statements, feel free to peek at the True You Breakthrough Blueprint in part two. Yet I encourage you to stay with the steps of part one and only use part two to supplement what you are already discovering about yourself.

to a lie. As though you were a mother lioness protecting her cubs, be diligent in your efforts to live from truth and not old trauma. In each moment, be mindful of what you are assuming is true. With every fork in the road, ask yourself, *Am I sourcing who I'm being from truth or from old trauma?* Choose wisely. For each will generate an entirely different future—either entrapping you further in more of the same or liberating you to evolve beyond your old life forever.

BONUS: STEP 3 PRACTICE IN ACTION

What is my intention?

EXAMPLES:

→ My intention is to sell my first film script by the end of this year for six figures or more.

→ My intention is to become a first-time parent within two years.

What is the source fracture story that has been getting in my way?

EXAMPLES:

→ I'm not good enough, other writers are better than me, I don't have enough time to get it done.

→ I'm alone, no one will be there for me, and I never get what I need to be happy in life.

Where does that source fracture story live in my body?

EXAMPLES:

→ In my stomach.

→ In my womb.

How have I been mistreating myself in ways that have validated and perpetuated this story?

EXAMPLE:

→ I fail to give myself enough support or structure to accomplish my dream.
→ I don't take proper care of my health.

What's really true about who I am and who I have the potential to become?

EXAMPLES:

→ I am a talented and visionary writer who's destined to have my work produced on the big screen.
→ I am a powerful manifester and am already showing up as the loving parent of the beautiful soul who's soon to join our family.

What's really true about how others will treat me and/or feel about me?

EXAMPLES:

→ Others recognize my talents and potential and happily invest in their partnership with me.
→ The soul I am calling into my life is filled with gratitude and joy that I will soon be their parent.

What's really true about my relationship with life/the Universe and the possibilities I hold for fulfillment?

EXAMPLES:

→ Life is filling me with inspired script ideas to bring forth in unique and creative ways.
→ Life is magically supporting me to become a loving parent in beautiful and unforeseen ways.

Step 4:
See Yourself as Source

⁓

Responsibility . . . begins with the willingness
to experience yourself as the generator of what
you do, what you have and what you are . . . [It] is
. . . a place to stand . . . a grace you give yourself—
an empowering context that leaves
you with a say in the matter of life.

—WERNER ERHARD

Few of us want to be thought of as victims, yet all of us understand victimization intimately. For the one thing we all have in common is that we've had to deal with people, places, and things that seem hell-bent on holding us back in life. These experiences tend to activate our own reactive, disempowering ways of responding to whatever is, or is not, occurring. It happens as quickly as an in-breath; someone or something puts you down, shuts you out, locks you in, takes what's yours, makes you wrong, or steals your thunder.

Let's get one thing out of the way right now. You have been victimized. Other people have behaved badly; they've likely been narcissistic, manipulative, mean-spirited, insensitive, dishonest, or just plain thoughtless. Maybe even all of the above. The situation you're in might also be unfair. The world's weird hierarchical systems of racism, sexism, ageism, classism, ableism, sizeism, and all other oppressive *-isms* make no sense to the rational mind, and yet they continue to exist. So, when engaging in

To not be overwhelmed by obstacles. . . . This is something that few of us are able to do. But after . . . you can see objectively and stand steadily, the next step becomes possible; a mental flip, so you're looking not at the obstacle but at the opportunity within it.

—RYAN HOLIDAY

a conversation about seeing yourself as the source of your experience, we're not denying how victimized you've been, and perhaps still are at this very moment. Yet we are engaging in a conversation about how you can shift from a place of powerlessness and reactivity—which will only create more of what you already know—and into a place of power and generativity, which will enable you to cause the positive, possible future you're standing for.

Let me give you a crucial heads-up. Disappointment will be your biggest trigger into a false center and a fast pass straight to the core of victimization. If you fail to stay conscious and act from this center, you are most assured to mindlessly create more evidence for an unwanted story. For your nature is that you are a cocreator with life, and wherever you are centered at the level of identity will soon be made evident in your experience.

Let me give you an example of this from my own life. The first time I understood the power of taking full responsibility for myself as the source of my experience was soon after my first book became a national bestseller. To accomplish this, I'd had to work extensively to combat an old source fracture story that I was not good enough to accomplish such a wonderful thing. Triumphant, I was excited to share the news with my family at my next visit to see them. I was particularly looking forward to sharing it with my older cousin, whom I'd be staying with on this visit and who I'd always felt looked down on me. As though she did not understand the years I'd devoted to personal and spiritual development, believing it to be an inferior pursuit to building financial wealth. For years I'd felt the humiliation of my own accomplishments going unrecognized, while the more material accomplishments of other members of our family were valued and celebrated.

Upon my arrival at my cousin's house, I eagerly made my way to the kitchen where I found her making dinner for the family. I was bursting to tell her about my accomplishment, yet waited patiently for the moment when she'd finally ask me what was new in my life. As she stood over the stove stirring the soup, she finally casually asked me how I was. In response, I poured out the good news, fully expecting to finally be validated as a person of value and intelligence in her eyes. Instead, she responded with a rather unimpressed "Huh," followed by "Do you want peas or carrots for dinner?" I was devastated, and immediately internally collapsed into a deeply resigned and ancient feeling of invisibility. *I am invisible, no one here cares about me, and what's the use in even trying?* A familiar narrative of mine when it came to my family.

"Peas," I responded quietly.

All through dinner I was polite and quiet, feigning fatigue, as I'd just traveled across the country to visit her and our family. Excusing myself soon after the meal was over, I lugged my suitcase up the stairs to the guest room, where I picked up a novel I'd been reading to try to calm myself. Yet my mind was racing, half of my attention on the novel and half on processing my feelings of hurt and disappointment. Though part of me was busy chattering away internally, confirming the many judgments I'd had about my cousin over the years—that she was a bona fide narcissist, self-involved, competitive, uncaring, unkind, and coldhearted—there was also a part of me that was curious as to what my part in all of this might be, if anything. As I began turning my attention toward seeing myself as the source of what had happened, I put down my book, suddenly realizing that in response to her lack of enthusiasm, I'd immediately collapsed into a story of invisibility and promptly disappeared. Almost like a little roly-poly pill bug, I'd quickly withdrawn my energy and curled up in a ball of self-protection, failing to assert how important this was to me, or how much I wanted her to celebrate with me. Worse than that, I then carried my collapse into dinner with other family members, and failed to even mention my accomplishment to those who may very well have celebrated if I'd given them the chance. At that moment, I mentored myself by saying something that has become a guiding principle of my life ever since. "Katherine," I said, "you can never give someone with a lesser consciousness the power to determine who you are going to be." And with that, I imagined my energy extending beyond my body and filling up the entire house. I then peacefully turned out the lights and went to sleep.

The next morning, I woke up feeling refreshed and enthusiastic about the day. I bounded down the stairs and headed to the kitchen to make a morning cup of coffee. My cousin, who was sitting at the kitchen table, looked up and smiled broadly. "What would you like to do today?" she asked happily. She then proceeded to organize her entire day around what I wanted, acutely aware of my feelings and needs in a way I'd never experienced from her before. As wonderful as this was, it was a huge wake-up call and made me wonder who I had been "being" all of those years that had been impacting the dismissive way she'd chronically treated me. Was it really all her? Or was her behavior informed, and perhaps even evoked, by my own tendency to protect myself by energetically erasing myself from the room?

Many of us now accept that our beliefs create our reality. Yet it's more accurate to say that it's how we interpret and then respond to life from those beliefs that is generating our experience. Inside of being swallowed up by the knee-jerk assumption that I was unseen and unsupported by my cousin, I made an automatic move to protect myself, inadvertently becoming the creator of my own invisibility by the subtle choice to withdraw my energy and disappear. Thereby becoming the source of my own experience. Though I did not do this consciously, the impact was there, just the same. My initial way of dealing with my disappointment was to judge her as uncaring and selfish. When that brought little relief, I started analyzing why I felt so chronically devalued by my own family, and what in the world I should do about it. Yet neither of these ways of processing my pain were powerful enough to change anything. I simply dug myself deeper into the despair of that story. It wasn't until I looked to see myself as the source of my suffering—and identified the specific actions I'd

> It wasn't until I saw myself as the source of my suffering—by identifying the specific choices I was unconsciously making that were generating the very thing I was unhappy with—that I was able to overcome it.

taken and choices I'd made in response to feeling disappointed—that I was able to overcome it completely.

Disappearing the story rather than disappearing myself.

Realizing the fulfillment of your intention will require you to claim your personal power in any and all situations. Particularly those situations where you've felt trapped by an unwanted pattern that insistently shows up again and again. While many of us blame our parents and early caregivers for the patterns we still struggle with today, most of us are now victimized by our own unconscious and the imprinting we received in our childhood that's keeping us tethered to an unwanted past, chronically causing us to fall short of the lives we yearn to be living.

The ability to notice and challenge any feeling of powerlessness is the direction we must take if we ever hope to be free. Doing so will require you to step back and become an almost existential detective into your own experience, as you look to discover all of the clandestine ways that you are now the source of what is, or is not, happening. It's the cultivation of a superpower whereby you can suddenly see all that has been in the dark. Recognizing with a jolt the very specific and subtle choices you are making, and the covert actions you are taking, that are keeping the past alive and well in your present.

You may already know what you're doing that is keeping you stuck and have rationalized your behavior by telling yourself that it's how your tender, younger self is trying to feel safe in the world. On the surface, your behavior may look justified, logical, and even quite harmless. Yet it is anything but. For without claiming complete authorship over your own story and holding

To change ourselves effectively, we first [have] to change our perceptions.

—STEPHEN R. COVEY

My therapists were in my corner on every single issue. Every doubt was reassured. In every conflict I faced involving colleagues, friends, family and romantic partners I felt wronged by, they sided with me. They were my best cheerleaders, my biggest fans. Which is why I fired them.

—FOSTER KAMER

yourself accountable to start showing up in alignment with who you came here to be and what you came here to create, you will not access the power you'll need to overcome your old story. All you will be left with when leaving this world is an explanation for why you never actualized your one beautiful life.

The Power of Yourself as Source

It's easy to hold others hostage by expecting them to accommodate our unhealthy, often hurtful ways of relating simply because we can explain where they come from. Yet the key that fast-tracks our freedom is to see our frustrating patterns from a volitional perspective rather than a purely psychological one. Instead of saying, "I'm this way because my mother raged at me all the time, so now I *can't* stand up for myself," you want to be able to take responsibility for your choices by saying, "I'm this way because my mother raged at me all the time, and now I *won't* stand up for myself because I'm unwilling to risk someone being mad at me." It's not only more honest; it's also more liberating. Because it's not until you can name your automatic behavior as a choice you're making that the possibility of making a new and better choice appears. By expanding our efforts to heal the past to include owning our choices and actions in the here and now, we are finally free to evolve. We recognize that our self-defeating patterns are our *decisions* and not our destiny.

> Our self-defeating patterns are our *decisions*, not our destiny.

I'm embarrassed to admit that in my early years of private practice as a psychotherapist, I rarely leaned on my clients to take responsibility for themselves as the source of their experience. So concerned was I not to break the therapeutic bond, I hesitated to ask questions that might have made them feel that I was not on their side or empathetic to their point of view. Yet I've come to understand that I did them no favors. For the only way to outgrow unhealthy patterns is to take responsibility for the many ways that we ourselves are perpetuating them.

Our early efforts to heal past wounds must explore the mistakes and misdeeds of our initial caregivers, to help us make sense of our experience and reclaim lost parts of ourselves that have been frozen in past trauma. Yet without graduating to a more sophisticated conversation as to how we are now the source of our patterns, we will never outgrow them. For a large part of why patterns repeat has to do with the habitual ways of relating to ourselves, others, and life that are reactive, subtle, and insidious. For example, in response to feeling alone as a child, you may have landed on the source fracture story of "I'm alone, no one is there for me, and I can never get my needs met." To survive this experience, you may then have learned to cultivate self-sufficiency to the extreme, so as to not need anyone too much. Yet here you are now as an adult, confused and saddened as to why you are always so alone in life. All the while sending out covert and constant signals to others that you don't really need them for anything and making it hard for them to find their way into your world. Another example might be that you never felt good enough as a child, forming a source fracture story of "I'm not enough, others don't value me, and I have to do twice as much for half the reward." Inside of this, you may have developed the habit of overgiving and overdoing to try to prove your value. As an adult, this way of relating covertly communicates to others that your time and energy are less valuable than theirs. They will come to feel entitled to you overfunctioning, enabling them to underfunction, which then provides constant relational mirroring of your old, impaired sense of self. Both are examples of the ways we unknowingly set others up to play out their roles in our story of self. We can fault them for their behavior, and we can give them labels until we're blue in the face, yet nothing will change until we ourselves begin to source how we are showing up from the truth of who we are and start consciously developing into who we came here to be. Once we do, it's often shocking how quickly things can change.

> The only way to outgrow unhealthy patterns is to take full responsibility for the many ways that we ourselves perpetuate them.

Malcolm had a rocky start in life with a volatile mother who had little patience for parenting a small child and a negligent father who failed to protect him from her. In response to Malcolm's refusal to get in the car one day at the age of three, his mother became so angry that she backed out of the driveway while he was standing there, running him over in the process. While he survived, the internal scarring from this experience showed up in the unstable, explosive women he got involved with as an adult. It's not surprising to learn that he married a woman who also had frequent intense emotional outbursts, and who could be quite abusive and mean when she was not getting her way. By the time they sought the help of a therapist, the relationship was in bad shape and looked as though it might be over. After only one session, where Malcolm's wife dominated the conversation by sharing everything that she felt was wrong with him, she quit.

To his credit, Malcolm returned on his own, hopeful he could find a way through this unbearable situation with the therapist's help. Fortunately, the therapist had studied to become a Future Forward Therapist with me, and she understood that in addition to connecting the dots between what had happened to Malcolm as a child and the volatile dynamic he was now experiencing with his wife, Malcolm also needed to discover himself as the source of what was happening in the relationship in order to turn things in a more positive direction. It was obvious to them both that Malcolm's constant and urgent need to protect himself could be traced back to growing up with two very dangerous and negligent parents. Inside of that family, Malcolm had become a fierce fighter out of necessity. Yet since fighters need someone to fight with, he admitted that he'd chosen to marry another fierce fighter, a woman who had also been abused in childhood and who shared a similar source fracture story of "I'm not safe, others have ill intent, and it's dangerous to let down your guard." He saw that, from this center, he was frequently on the defensive, which brought out the worst in his wife, as she was frequently on the offensive—highly aggressive and attacking. Both of them chronically, constantly, relentlessly put self-protection above the good of the relationship. Malcolm had a choice to make. Would he stay and try to improve the marriage or would he simply end it? A justifiable choice, given his wife's lack of interest in doing counseling. Yet the latter was not as easy as it seemed, for they shared a four-year-old daughter whom Malcolm adored. While his wife also loved their child and had never physically harmed her, her constant emotional meltdowns had Malcolm on high alert, as he feared for his daughter's emotional safety and mental health. For this reason, he preferred staying in the marriage, so that he'd be there to protect his daughter if and when things got out of hand.

He admitted, however, that this was no way to live, as the tension between himself and his wife festered in their home, creating a combative and highly charged atmosphere that was causing their daughter to become increasingly anxious. Even her preschool teacher had commented on it. When the therapist pointed out the obvious—that they seemed to be passing along their own internal lack of safety to their daughter— Malcolm became willing to do whatever it took to liberate them all from this toxic situation.

He began by setting an intention to create a safer, healthier home life. Owning himself as the source of safety, Malcolm began a journey of personal development to learn how he could manage his explosive feelings without going to war, turning his attention toward who he would need to become to steer the dynamic between himself and his wife in a healthier direction. Rather than react to his wife's nasty criticism and blame, as he'd so often done in the past, he learned to hold and contain his own larger-than-life feelings from a deeper center within. This allowed him to respond to his wife in ways that

> *If you own this story,*
> *you get to write the ending.*
> —BRENÉ BROWN

defused her anger and created greater cooperation and understanding between them. In this way, Malcolm became willing to be the leader of health in their connection, and his wife's hard edges began softening as she started feeling safe enough to drop some of her aggression and guardedness. By showing up in ways that were generative of the future he was standing for, the atmosphere in their home calmed significantly and life became more balanced and even somewhat pleasant and normal. Yet the best part was that his good efforts were soon rewarded by seeing his daughter begin to show up as the carefree, happy child he'd always hoped she'd be.

Mirror, Mirror on the Wall

Beliefs at the level of identity are relational. They were formed in relationship with others, and they can only be transformed in relationship with others. As much as we in the Western world love to think of ourselves as fiercely autonomous creatures, we are anything but. You are not a solo self. You are a relational self and therefore vulnerable to how others feel about you and treat you. Which is why it's critical to begin by becoming conscious of, and accountable for, the many ways you have been unknowingly baiting others to see you as less than who you are.

If you're like most people, you think of yourself as a noun—a solo self with a unique set of qualities and characteristics that make you *you*. Yet I invite you to consider that who you are is more of an emergent and ever-evolving verb rather than a noun. An unfolding experience of engagement with the world around you that is either reinforcing or redefining who you know yourself to be. That your narrative self is in a continual process of co-construction with others who mirror you back to yourself in myriad ways throughout your day. Either validating that you belong or that you don't. That you're good enough or sadly not. We often feel victimized by the ways that others see and treat us—particularly when rubbing up against an old source fracture story and validating an unwanted story of self. Oblivious to the specific ways that we ourselves are showing up that are evoking their insulting behavior. Perhaps even egging it on. It feels as though it's just happening *to* us against our will when it's actually happening *through* us. Seeing this clearly changes everything, as we suddenly realize that it's not who we are but something we are *doing* that's causing us to re-create validation of an unwanted story of self.

To help you see how insidious this is, let me tell you about a recent occurrence with an old family friend. Bryce is super fun to have around— the kind of person who knows how to turn a simple gathering into a festive party. Just the person you'd want at your Thanksgiving dinner table or on Christmas morning as presents are being opened. Yet as jovial as she is, Bryce is also haunted by a deep and pervasive sorrow that will occasionally swallow her whole. It's not hard to see where her sadness comes from. Her history is gnarly: Her father died of an overdose when she was just a toddler, and she grew up with a mentally ill mother who resented having to care for her and a critical stepfather who abused her for years. When she left home at fifteen, she was hoping to stay connected with her aunts and uncles and their families. But over the years, as Bryce's talents and beauty developed, her cousins became jealous of her. They dealt with their feelings by shutting her out; she became the outcast and black sheep of the family. She was rarely invited to family celebrations, most noticeably during the holidays, which she often spent alone, eating fast food and curled up in bed watching old movies.

It's easy to see where Bryce's "I'm not wanted" story came from. What was more difficult to see was how she herself was covertly enrolling others into that story and setting them up to validate it. Once my family understood how alone she was during the holidays, we began inviting Bryce to our home to share them with us. She always accepted gratefully. Yet I soon began to notice a pattern. About every other time she was expected, she would send a text at the very last minute letting us know she was not coming. On one occasion, she didn't even do that. She just didn't show up. You can imagine how disappointed we felt to have an empty place at our table rather than see our friend sitting there. Or how disheartening it was to have unopened Christmas presents under the tree, reminding us all of her absence. After this happened several times, I noticed I no longer wanted to invite her to join us, for fear of being disappointed when she failed to show up. This is how I became enrolled into Byrce's story. Becoming just one more person on her long list of those who did not want to invite her to their home for the holidays.

Luckily, I am aware of the ways we pull on each other to validate our source fracture stories, and so I picked up the phone to share what I was noticing. To her credit, she got it. She sheepishly admitted that she hadn't even questioned the certainty of her assumption that she wasn't really wanted, in spite of being invited. From this perspective, it hadn't even occurred to her that we might actually be disappointed if she failed to show up. The realization that we did really care brought tears to her eyes. It was the first time she was able to step outside of her own story and see it for what it was: an emotionally based belief informed by old trauma, and not at all the truth. We made a pact that I would indeed keep inviting her to our home for the holidays as long as she stayed conscious of her tendency to act out her old wounding and was committed to doing things differently with us.

Unearth Your Unwholesome Motives

Don't mistake my insistence that you take responsibility for yourself as the source of your patterns as a lack of compassion for all of the hardships you've had to endure. I mean, who could blame you for chronically underpresenting yourself once you explain that you grew up with a vain and narcissistic mother who competed with you and who punished you for daring to upstage her? Yet beware the tendency to avoid actually changing by endlessly explaining your unhealthy behavior from a psychological point of view. If you're serious about creating a future that's radically different from your past, you're going to have to become willing to own up to the part of you that's actually hell-bent on staying the same.

What are you getting out of your self-defeating ways of relating? Maybe you're underpresenting yourself because you're sourcing your value by how much you give. Or maybe you're avoiding being responsible for the positive changes

What do I get to not face, not feel, not experience or avoid by staying stuck here?
—TERRI COLE

you know, deep down, you're here to make in the world. Or perhaps it's because you get to punish your mother by not succeeding in life. Whichever one makes you a little sick to your stomach is probably a more honest explanation for why you've been unable to get beyond it. To be liberated to live a deeply fulfilling life, you're going to have to admit to the unflattering truth of what's been motivating you to be so shackled to the past.

What we're looking for is the payoff—what you actually get by showing up this way. For example, you get to be right, make someone wrong, or feel superior to someone. Maybe you're avoiding being dominated or you don't want to be financially responsible for yourself or perhaps you're unwilling to risk being hurt. As uncomfortable as it is to admit our hidden motives, if we want to be free, we'll have to confess the covert reasons why we're perpetuating unwanted patterns and identify what we're now willing to give up in order to manifest what we feel called to create. Though humbling, it's also hopeful. For when we take 100 percent responsibility for our own choices and actions, the resignation that this pattern could never change just up and disappears, and an energizing sense of expansion and possibility opens up instead. By finally seeing that you're the one creating your story, you also recognize that you're the one holding the power to give it a radical plot twist.

When I was first creating the Calling in "The One" process to help me outgrow my own unhealthy patterns in love, I looked for the unwholesome motives beneath my tenacious tendency to attract unavailable men. Psychologically, this predictable and painful pattern made sense. Look no further than my father marrying a woman who forbade me to be a part of their family, ensuring the likelihood that I'd pine after married men later in life. Yet, while the explanation was accurate enough, it gave me no power to do things any differently. In fact, it only made me more

frustrated to find that I was still victimized by the immaturity of my father's second wife, decades after the fact. What
finally graduated me was the question
What am I getting out of this?

Only then—when I asked that
question—did I see that by setting up
my intimate relationships with a limit on

> By seeing that you're
> the one creating your
> story, you also recognize
> that you're the one holding
> the power to give it a
> radical plot twist.

how far we could go, I was creating a false sense of safety against ever
again feeling as crushed as I'd felt as a young girl when my father suddenly exited my life, not to be seen or heard from again until I was an
adult. Once I saw this clearly, I could extend unconditional love to my
younger self and explain to her that while I understood why she'd do
this—acknowledging how clever she was to have figured out how to keep
me safe from having my heart truly broken again—it was costing us love,
and that was too high a price to pay. I reminded her that I was grown
now, and had a lot more resources to ensure that my relationships would
go well, or to make sure I'd be okay if they didn't. Inside of a kind and
compassionate mentoring dialogue with my tender, younger traumatized
self, she surrendered. Within months, I was engaged to a lovely, very
available man, and married the following year.

Cultivate a Developmental Mindset

Most of us are psychologically sophisticated enough to understand that
many of our dysfunctional ways of relating have diagnostic names: codependence, low self-esteem, social anxiety, or an anxious or avoidant attachment style. Yet all too often, these labels live for us like tattoos—neuroses
seared so deeply into our psyches that they occur for us as a life sentence.
But are we really just stuck with them? Will we forever be defined by
missing development born of an imperfect past? Or are we more mallea-
ble than we've given ourselves credit for?

Let's imagine that you grew up in a home where there was intermittent violence between your parents. Inside of this tense, walking-on-eggshells atmosphere, you may have learned at a very young age to create safety for yourself by taking up as little space as humanly possible. Becoming an almost ghostlike figure in your own home: polite, accommodating, and chameleonlike. This clever plan did indeed keep you from getting caught in the cross fire. Well done, you. Yet your victory came at a cost. For in a healthy home, you would have learned—both through the modeling of respectful interactions between the grown-ups in your household as well as your own engagement with other family members—how to identify your feelings and needs and share them with others in ways that created mutuality, safety, and love. Yet due to the unhealthy environment in which you were raised, this developmental milestone went by the wayside. It might not even be on your radar that these specific skills of (1) knowing what you feel and need and (2) making your feelings and needs visible to others are now actually missing and wreaking havoc on your life. Particularly since your heroic attempts to heal have largely been focused on looking backward to try to resolve the frozen, scary feelings of the past rather than also consciously developing specific skills and capacities that will allow you to fulfill the future you feel called to create.

Who you want to be in the future is more important than who you are now, and should actually inform who you are now. Your intended future self should direct your current identity and personality far more than your former self does.
—BENJAMIN HARDY

Without naming your own missing development and turning your full attention to now mastering the skills that will allow you to create a future better than your past, you will forever be stuck duplicating old patterns simply because you lack the ability to do it any differently. In spite of all your efforts to better your life and outgrow the invisibility of your childhood, you will find yourself a perfect match in self-involved, narcissistic people who are incapable of giving you what you most want—which is simply to be truly seen, considered, and loved for who you actually are.

Questions That Feed You Power

Most of us recognize the skill of self-reflection as key to living an empowered life. Yet, until we understand exactly *how* to self-reflect, our efforts to evolve could actually disempower us, and be the very practice that is keeping us stuck. For any kind of shame or blame stunts development, serving as a big red stop sign on the pathway to personal growth. If we're not careful, the inquiry I'm encouraging us to engage with in this chapter, *How am I the source of my experience?*, can lead us to self-reflect in a way that could have us floundering in a cesspool of humiliation, frustration, resignation, and guilt. If in response to that question you start to ask yourself why, as in, *Why am I this way?* or *Why do I always do this?*, you could easily find yourself sliding down the slippery slope of victimization, as once again, you begin recounting what was done to you that made you who you are today—your brother abused you, your teacher humiliated you, and on and on. The other wrong-turn inquiry so many of us make is the collapse into an uninspired *What's wrong with me?* Leading you to become victimized by your own unconscious. So, before we even engage the inquiry about how you are the source of your experience, let's now do a practice that ensures you will know how to self-reflect in a way that feeds you the power to actually transform your life in the most beautiful of ways.

> Without naming your own missing development, and turning your attention to mastering the skills that will allow you to create a future better than your past, you'll be stuck duplicating old patterns simply because you lack the ability to do it any differently.

Step 4 Practice: Empowered Self-Reflection

This practice is to help you become aware of the automatic questions you ask yourself when you look to see yourself as the source of your experience. It will help you discover an inquiry that can lead you to grow and develop beyond who you have known yourself to be. Read through the following practice two or three times before engaging in it, as it is a closed-eyes exercise where your primary attention is on yourself. If you prefer, you can download free audio and/or video of me guiding you through this practice at katherinewoodwardthomas.com/trueyoubonuses.

1. **Identify the pattern you're committed to transform.**

    Consider your intention, and the unwanted pattern you wish to transform. What dynamic happens that is thwarting the fulfillment of your intention and that you've felt powerless to change?

    For example: *I constantly earn less money than I need* or *I get right to the door of success and then I do something to sabotage my chances for advancement.*

2. **Notice where in your body you hold the emotions.**

    Close your eyes and drop your awareness down into your body. Notice where you feel your upset about this pattern most acutely in your body. Focus on the lowest place in your body where you can feel the energy of the emotion you hold around this pattern.

    For example: *I feel anxiety in my stomach* or *I feel a heaviness on my heart.*

3. **Make the automatic questions you are asking conscious.**

    Breathe deeply into this part of your body. Notice the automatic inner conversation you find yourself engaging around this situation over and over again.

    For example: *What's wrong with me?* or *Why can't I ever get what I want?* or *How can I be so stupid?*

Notice the lack of room for true evolution and growth in these disempowering questions.

4. **Create an empowering question that leads to growth and evolution.**

Stepping back from this automatic inner dialogue, come up with a
new question that inspires growth and development in the area of your
intention.

For example: *What have I been getting out of this pattern?* or *What do
I get to avoid by having this pattern?* or *Who, if anyone, might I be attached to making wrong by having this pattern?*

Notice how choice opens up the moment you ask a question that
points to self-responsibility.

Step 4 Practice: See Yourself as Source

You're now ready to take it even deeper by identifying the specific ways
you are showing up (or not showing up) that have been creating more of
the same. Read through the following practice two or three times before
engaging in it, as it is a closed-eyes exercise where your primary attention
is on yourself. If you prefer, you can download free audio and/or video of
me guiding you through this practice at katherinewoodwardthomas.com
/trueyoubonuses.

Let's have you again consider your intention, and the unwanted pattern you wish to transform—something that occurs for you as though it's
just happening to you, without your consent, and in a way that leaves you
feeling frustrated and/or powerless to change.

1. **Send deep acceptance and unconditional love to yourself.**

Close your eyes and take a deep breath, as though you could breathe
all the way down into your hips. Notice where you're holding the emotions associated with your frustrating pattern.

Find the part of you that's able to observe your discomfort without
becoming overidentified with it. Connect with the part of you that is

capable of simply witnessing your very human choices and behaviors with an uncommon unconditional love.

2. **Become a curious observer of yourself.**

   Step back from your feelings and your circumstances and strive to be a curious and objective observer of yourself. Bring a sense of innocent inquisitiveness and interest to the observation of your own curious life. Lean in to try to see yourself as though you were observing "a distant thing," as poet Czesław Miłosz suggests.

3. **Ask yourself questions that point to self-responsibility.**

   From this deep centered place within, begin inquiring into yourself as the source of this recurring pattern.

   For example, you can ask yourself questions such as:

   → *What part of me might be invested in having this problem?*
   → *What choices am I making that are contributing to the problem?*
   → *What actions am I taking (or not) that are contributing to the problem?*
   → *Who might I be dominating?*
   → *What might I be avoiding?*
   → *Who might I be punishing?*
   → *Who or what might I be protecting?*
   → *How old is the part of me driving my choices and actions?*
   → *How might my adult self see this differently?*
   → *Who or what have I been giving my power away to?*
   → *What's been motivating me to do that?*
   → *What could I do to restore my personal power?*

4. **Identify the specific ways of relating to yourself, others, and life that are perpetuating the pattern.**

   As you deepen your inquiry to discover how you are the source of unwanted patterns, make sure you stay open and curious without making yourself bad and wrong.

Let's now make it even more specific by asking yourself the following three questions:

1) *How am I* relating *to myself in ways that are perpetuating the pattern?*

For example: *I dismiss my own feelings and needs* or *I ignore my intuition* or *I push myself hard and often to the brink.*

Consider that others may simply be mirroring the way you tend to behave toward yourself, taking their cue from you on how you should be treated.

2) *How am I relating to others in ways that are perpetuating the pattern?*

For example: *I rarely give others a chance to care for my feelings and needs because I don't express what they are* or *I train others that they matter more than I do by putting their feelings and needs first and minimizing my own* or *I overgive because I am sourcing my value from giving and leave little room for others to reciprocate.*

Consider that you are continually training others how to treat you, not by what you say but by who you are being in the connection.

3) *How am I relating to life in ways that are perpetuating the pattern?*

For example: *I have low expectations anyone would ever be there for me and continually settle for less* or *I take on too many commitments to try to prove my worth and then fail at all of them because I'm overwhelmed* or *I play small to try to stay safe, and then feel unsafe because it's not the life I was born to live.*

Consider that life can only give to you that which you're open and available to receive.*

---

*If you're needing help in clarifying the specific ways you are the source of your own experience, feel free to peek at the True You Breakthrough Blueprint in part two. Yet I encourage you to stay with the steps of part one and only use part two to supplement what you are already discovering about yourself.

5. **Give up any excuse for why you're making these choices or taking these actions.**

Take 100 percent responsibility for the choices you're making and the actions you're taking that are perpetuating the pattern, even if they're the omission of actions, such as not speaking up for yourself, not telling the truth to yourself, disconnecting from your own feelings and needs, or failing to make your needs known to others.

6. **Consider the cost of your choices and actions to yourself and others.**

Though it's hard to confront the many ways that we ourselves have caused our own suffering, it's critical to not sugarcoat it by minimizing the impact to ourselves and others.

Ask yourself:

What has it cost me to show up in these ways?

What has it cost others for me to show up in these ways?

If you're seeing yourself as the source of your old patterns clearly, then you may be feeling some regret right about now. Sadness, and maybe even a bit of shock, for all the years that you've wasted, unconsciously re-creating your old story. As well as the many ways you may have locked yourself into a lesser life due to choices made when overly identified with a lie. Please remember to be kind to yourself. I've always found that life lessons can be very expensive, and grief is the gift that can sober us up like no other. That sobriety can turn into a fierce commitment to start making amends to yourself by vowing to live in alignment with the true you. You may not yet know how to do that. But the good news is, if you're the source of your life going south, then you're also the source of it going right and of getting on track toward your North Star. You may not yet know how to get your life in alignment with the positive, possible future you're standing for. Transformation begins first

> *Trauma is hell on earth.*
> *Trauma resolved is a gift*
> *from the gods.*
> —PETER A. LEVINE

with a pledge to manifest an unreasonable and unforeseeable future. The how-to comes later. Right now, a lot is at stake. Not just for you, but for others who are looking to you for leadership, support, and guidance. Let's move forward with a fierce resolve to do it differently from now on. You can do that by first identifying and then embracing the new ways of relating that will graduate you forever from your old story and set you free to live the life you were born to live.

BONUS: STEP 4 PRACTICE IN ACTION

What is my intention?

EXAMPLES:

→ My intention is to create a healed, healthy relationship with my mother before she passes.

→ My intention is to become a seven-figure entrepreneur in a business that inspires and empowers people by the age of forty.

What pattern has been getting in my way in this area of my life?

EXAMPLES:

→ My mother and I have a long history of being critical and speaking disrespectfully to each other.

→ I get my businesses to the brink of success, then lose interest and momentum, and they end up failing.

What have I been getting out of this pattern?

EXAMPLES:

→ I've been making my mother wrong and punishing her for the mistakes she made when raising me.

→ I don't really want to be responsible for showing up as a powerful leader in the world, so I sabotage my own success.

How have I been the source of the pattern?

EXAMPLE:

→ I treat my mother the same toxic ways she treated me when I was growing up, thereby keeping the family dynamic firmly in place by being a perpetrator myself instead of showing up as a leader of greater health between us.

→ I have not given myself the supportive mentoring I would actually need to cause my own success.

What specific ways have I been relating to myself that have been perpetuating the pattern?

EXAMPLES:

→ I constantly criticize myself in ways similar to how my mother constantly criticized me when I was growing up.

→ I shame myself for thinking that I could be somebody in this world.

What specific ways have I been relating to others that have been perpetuating the pattern?

EXAMPLES:

→ I set my mother up to attack me by criticizing everything she does.

→ I underpresent myself and fail to enroll others in the value of what I'm here to create.

What specific ways have I been relating to life that have been perpetuating the pattern?

EXAMPLES:

- → I have a lot of expectations about how life should be that I'm pissed off about, but I fail to remind myself that it's up to me to create that reality.
- → I give up at the first sign of failure rather than learn from the experience and improve my offerings because of what I now know.

What has it cost me and others to show up this way?

EXAMPLES:

- → It's cost both my mom and me the love we actually have for each other.
- → It's costing me success in life, and it's costing the world the benefit of my gifts and leadership.

What amends will I now pledge to make to myself moving forward?

EXAMPLES:

- → I will learn to be kinder to myself, and to take the risk of initiating a greater sense of friendship, kindness, and tolerance between my mother and myself.
- → I will set up accountability and support structures that will allow me to go all the way and be wildly successful in the world of business.

Step 5:
Identify New Ways
of Relating

~

Every action you take is a vote for
the type of person you wish to become.

—JAMES CLEAR

Given how vulnerable we are to the mirroring we receive, how can we now stop mindlessly showing up in the subtle ways that covertly train others to validate our old identities, and instead begin to actively create new relational evidence that reinforces who we're committed to becoming? This is the part of our journey where things get a little wild and fun as I invite you to step outside of your old identity and proactively look for opportunities to pattern-interrupt who you've assumed yourself to be—shy; reserved; the brainy, smart one; the life of the party. To instead try on new, foreign ways of relating that are generative of the future you're committed to creating—ways of relating to yourself, others, and life that may look nothing like who you've known yourself to be.

To discover what these new ways of relating are, you'll want to start with your *future self* and work backward from there. Much like I did when I walked into Starbucks each day and asked myself, *How would a world-class leader of love who is having a positive impact on thousands of people order her morning coffee?* My normally quiet, shy way of speaking suddenly transformed into a confident command of exactly how I wanted my coffee made.

Most of us get tripped up because we can't see the how-to and don't have a clue what we should *do* to create the future we desire. Right now, I invite you to let go of any preoccupation with *How can I make this happen?* and instead begin living into the questions *Who would I need to be "being" for it to happen?* and *From that center, how would I be relating to myself, others, and life?* Stretching to both embody and relate from the "you" you desire to become. Walking through the world and showing up in all your affairs as though you were already living your new story. Consciously creating from the inside out, as you lean in to discover the new ways that you think, the new ways that you act, and the new ways that you feel, from the future you're committed to manifesting.

> *The greatest habit we have to break*
> *is the habit of being ourselves.*
> —JOE DISPENZA

Outgrow Your Imprinting

Many of us have been doing anything and everything we can think of to escape from the unhealthy patterns that are the residue of our unhappy childhood experiences, including forgiving our early caregivers for the mistakes they made. Yet the habitual and unconscious ways of relating that are organic to your old story—the people-pleasing, the prickly defensiveness, the hiding in the back row, or being so self-sufficient that others don't feel needed by you and consequently don't offer to support you in ways you support them—are the true culprits in keeping it alive and well in the present. Ways of relating that are insidiously, incredulously, and incessantly enrolling others in the distorted hall of mirrors of your source

> You'll now need to evoke new mirroring from others that validates not who you've been, but who you truly are, and who you're called to become.

fracture story. By now, you may have an entire community treating you as a lesser version of who you are—undervaluing you, failing to include you, minimizing your feelings and needs, or expecting more of you than they do of others, for less reward. It's like your very own Greek chorus continually commenting on, and verifying, the unwanted old story you've so diligently been trying to outgrow.

As identity is contextual, in order to evolve you'll need to evoke new mirroring from others in ways that validate not who you've been but who you truly are and who you're called to become. This is not about going out and making new friends as much as it's about showing up as the true you everywhere you go, and with everyone you're with, and giving others a chance to catch up.

Who Are You Being?

This step is about more than making a few behavioral shifts. It's a shift in who we are *being* more than in anything we're doing. The work is to, one choice at a time, shed the habits of the old self, as those are the ways of relating that have been locking in a lesser life and creating a continual stream of feedback that our old stories are true. Yet they're not. They're simply stories we created when we were too young to know better. And if we only make a few changes at the behavioral level without shifting who we are *being*, we risk not fully convincing others of our newer, truer story. We all know the experience of being with someone who's angry yet smiling and saying they're fine. Who they're *being* is "f*#% you," but what they're *doing* is being nice. That incongruence can be confusing, as who they're being is far more impactful than anything they're saying or doing.

We access the power to transform our lives when we start sourcing who we're being from our power center—that place within where we're already connected to a preconscious, unquestionable knowing of our value, creativity, and agency, and are grounded in a place of possibility. From this center, we will effortlessly start showing up differently—with a greater sense of confidence, ease, and authenticity. It's the simple exchange of showing up this way with others that provides us with a new relational context for our transformation of identity to take root. The old insecure self begins to fade away as the truth of who we are, and who we are becoming, is revealed and mirrored back to us in the eyes of others. In this way, our newer, truer identities are both validated and fortified, and the truth of who we are soon becomes our new way of knowing ourselves, and our organic internal home base.

> *Don't fake it till you make it.*
> *Fake it till you become it.*
> —AMY CUDDY

Be Specific About Your New Ways of Relating

The new ways of relating that we're talking about are organic when you're emotionally anchored in your power center. When you're energetically aligned with the truth of who you are—worthy, powerful, and more than good enough as you are—and take actions from there, you'll naturally stand up straight, speak with confidence, look others in the eye, sit in the front row, and share freely what you feel, want, and need. Yet if you're anything like me, sometimes you feel it and sometimes you don't. We don't want to rely too much on the fickleness of feelings to be empowered in life. Feelings are fluid and not always something we can control. Because of this, you'll want to identify the specific new ways of relating to yourself, others, and life that are organic to your future self for the following three reasons.

1. **To proactively break the habit of being who you've always known yourself to be.** Even the most advanced of us will sometimes start un-

consciously relating as less than who we are out of sheer habit. Our voice will suddenly become a whisper, our shoulders will droop, and our first attention will go straight to pleasing others before ourselves. This tends to happen organically in times of disappointment, or in the anticipation of it. We are all vulnerable to this. You'll want to notice when you have the impulse to collapse into an old disempowering habit and have a clear practice up your sleeve on how to show up differently from your power center in order to actively show up in alignment with what's more true about you. For example, inside of the old story "I'm alone and everyone always leaves," you might have a habit of closing your heart and putting up a wall toward someone who's hurt your feelings. Which covertly signals to them to leave or start investing less in their relationship with you. It looks like they're the one who is leaving you, when actually you left them first. Whereas a new way of relating in the moment of feeling hurt might be to pick up the phone and share that you're hurt, yet are committed to clearing the air between you, as you value your relationship. As you talk it out, you might discover how conflict can actually deepen a connection rather than damage it.

2. **To "act as if" when you find that you've collapsed into a false center.** The second reason you want to identify specific new ways of relating is that you will need to "act as if" when you find yourself triggered into a false center. It's unrealistic to think that you will only need to wake yourself up from the trance of your source fracture story once. Any disappointment, obstacle, setback, or delay has the tendency to drop us down into a false center. The trick is to notice when it happens, and rather than react from this center—for example, isolate when you're sad, blame someone else for the situation you're in, or settle for less—instead, you want to practice your new ways of relating. No matter what you're feeling. For example, reach out to get the emotional

> The reason why a lot of people won't become who they want is because they're too attached to who they've been. . . . People say, "I've always been this way." "Well, okay, if that's working for you, keep doing that."
>
> —LISA NICHOLS

support you need, take responsibility for your part, or raise your expectations and negotiate for your needs.

3. **Notice the specific skills and capacities you'll now need to grow.** The third reason to map this all out now is that you'll need to know what specific new skills and capacities to consciously develop, so that you're capable of consistently showing up this way in life. For the ways of relating that will liberate you to grow in the direction of your dreams are not necessarily things you already know how to do: regulate your emotions, set healthy boundaries, negotiate your needs, resolve conflict well, or generate your leadership in the world. Remember, fulfilling your intention is more of a developmental journey than an analytical one. Your first step in moving toward fulfillment will be to identify the new ways of relating and simply notice how you will now need to grow in order to receive and sustain the future you're standing for.

Why This Is Tricky

Initially, new ways of relating that are reflective of your value, worthiness, and power can be a bit tricky to identify. This is for two reasons. The first is that they might be completely off your radar. Maybe no one in your family has ever shown up this way, or any of those in your social circle, so you have little reference or modeling for these ways of showing up in life. Like it just never even occurred to you to navigate life this way. For all of the years I intuitively sensed my destiny to be a transformative teacher, I had no clue how it would happen or what I should do to try to make it happen. Year after year I waited, uncertain of where my big break would come from. While I did know enough to cultivate my character and consciously grow my wisdom during those years, beyond that I was at a loss. By the age of forty-three, I began questioning myself. Was I imagining myself to be more important than I am? Perhaps my "intuition" was some sort of existential defense against accepting how small and insignificant I really was. Sitting in my therapist's office one day, I confided my frustration that nothing had happened yet that would make sense of my deeper knowing that I'd one day

Act from your future, not toward it.
—RICHIE NORTON

be speaking to thousands of people. He looked at me with confusion and said what to him was obvious: "I think people do something like write a book before that can happen." It was a "duh" moment—I couldn't believe it had never occurred to me until he'd said it. I started to write *Calling in "The One"* a few days later—a book that, to date, has sold nearly half a million copies. Thousands of people indeed.

Sometimes I think we're all savants—impressively competent and put together on one hand, yet with gaping blind spots that prevent us from seeing what's right in front of our noses on the other. Inside of my "I don't belong" story, my old way of relating was that I'd been waiting—*for years*—for someone, anyone, to finally recognize my potential and invite me to the party. Not realizing that *it was me* who needed to believe in myself and actually *throw* the party. As I said, off my radar completely.

Our second challenge in identifying the specific new ways of relating that we need to cultivate is that they can be such subtle, small shifts that we can easily miss them. In his brilliant book *Atomic Habits*, James Clear reminds us that "it's easy to overestimate the importance of one defining moment and underestimate the value of making small improvements on a daily basis. . . . Improving by one percent isn't particularly notable—sometimes it isn't even noticeable—but it can be far more meaningful, especially in the long run." Small, subtle changes in how we are relating to ourselves, others, and life are the building blocks for a new tomorrow.

One of my clients, Mara, is a successful social worker in her fifties and the director of a foster care agency. When I met her, she described herself as a high-functioning codependent; a serious overfunctioner whom others had come to rely on due to her extraordinary levels of generosity, kindness, competence, and care. While these were certainly lovely things to be known for, Mara called her tendency to give, give, give until she dropped "pathological generosity." Mostly because as a trained therapist, she'd done a lot of self-examination and acknowledged that her benevolence was not always wholesomely motivated. She sheepishly admitted that she gave excessively because on a very deep and primitive level, she craved the dependence of others to help her feel more secure in life. In her mind, if people needed her, they wouldn't leave. Hence, her self-diagnosis of codependence, which basically describes care that is given in reaction to an old fear that others will abandon her. Mara's original relational trauma happened when she was a mere baby, when her mother would go off on alcoholic binges, leaving Mara alone in her crib for long stretches of time. Because this original relational trauma happened when Mara was so young, it had an urgent life-or-death quality to it. Like if others left her, she'd die. This might have been true when she was in the crib and couldn't fend for herself, but it certainly was not true now. Yet here she was, some fifty years later, still driven to do anything and everything in order to not be left. Even if "leaving" meant that someone simply disagreed with or disapproved of her. In a normal, healthy relationship, people are free to tell the truth, even if the other person doesn't like it. Yet for Mara, just the threat of losing approval was cause for alarm.

Trying to create a happy, meaningful life on top of the "I'm alone, others always leave, and I can never get what I need" story that drove her codependence, Mara was hypervigilant most of the time. Having trained herself at an early age to meet the needs of others—before they themselves even knew what they needed—she was beyond exhausted. The lack of mutuality between herself and others, coupled with her tendency to overfunction, created a situation where Mara was forever on the treadmill of having to earn every morsel of safety, support, and love she received. Yet once she became aware of the identity-based beliefs driving her compulsive caretaking behavior, Mara took steps to wake herself up from her trauma trance with the following power statements:

Even when I do nothing to try to create connection, I am already inherently deeply connected to everyone and everything.

*I have the power to learn how to create greater
health, mutuality, longevity, and authentic
care in all of my relationships.*

*To the extent that I identify and honor my own needs
and desires, others will tend to follow suit.*

She then mapped out how she was the source of her unwanted pattern of relationships being draining and fragile. Namely, the specific ways of relating that were covertly setting others up to do the very thing she dreaded most, which was to leave. First, she examined her relationship with herself, inside of the recognition that her relationship with others could never be better than her relationship with herself. How was she treating herself in ways that were perpetuating her source fracture story? Once she journaled on the following questions, the answer came quickly. Here is an excerpt from her morning pages:

How am I relating to myself in ways that are perpetuating my "I'm alone" story?

→ *I chronically self-abandon. Inside of my desperation to keep others from being unhappy with me and possibly leaving, I constantly toss my own feelings, needs, and desires aside to make sure no one is angry or unhappy with me. In this way, I'm continually leaving myself and, in the process, re-wounding myself again and again.*

She then moved on to an inquiry of how she was relating to others that was influencing them to leave her, in spite of all of her efforts to the contrary. She asked:

How am I relating to others in ways that are perpetuating my "Others always leave" story?

→ *My chronic self-abandonment makes it easy for others to leave me, since I'm being completely inauthentic in our relationship, and therefore am un-available to bond in any true or meaningful way.*

→ *Inside of my hypervigilance to create dependence as a pseudo-safety mechanism, I disempower others. I make it an almost imperative milestone for them to graduate out of our relationship if they ever hope to become autonomous, strong, and empowered in life.*

→ *I give and give and give, without leaving any space for others to give back to me, in an immature attempt to control the relationship. When others do try to give back to me, I dismiss them and refuse to receive. In this way, I literally train them to become takers in our relationship and disregard me entirely. They then continually "abandon" me by failing to consider my feelings and needs or extend true care my way.*

→ *Inside of my assumption that I can never get my needs met, I rarely let myself be vulnerable. Yet in failing to express any of my more tender needs and desires, I don't give anyone a chance to prove me wrong by at least trying to care for me.*

Finally, Mara looked at her situation from a more global perspective by asking:

How am I relating to life in ways that are perpetuating my "I can never get my needs met" story?

→ *Inside of assuming I can never get my needs met by anyone, including from a Higher Power, I isolate when I'm hurt. I contract away from life by compulsive overeating and not answering the phone, making it impossible for me to receive any comfort or support other than from sugar and fatty foods, which only make me gain weight and feel worse than I already feel.*

→ *Inside of assuming that no one is there for me, including God, I stop praying and meditating when I've been most disappointed, shutting down my ability to receive fresh perspectives, inspiration, or life lessons that could be helpful.*

Many of us stop here. So shocked are we to discover ourselves as the source of our suffering that we're tempted to go back to the drawing board and, once again, try to solve the mystery of how we became so dysfunctional in life. I'm warning you to be on the lookout for any hint of victimization, especially when you find yourself victimized by your own psychology. Yes, it happened. Yes, it matters. No, analyzing why you are the way you are will not set you free. At least not until you wake yourself up from the disempowered meaning you made and identify the new ways of relating that will graduate you from that sad story. Remember how easy it is to be seduced into avoiding true change by getting back on the insight bandwagon, and then do your best to set it aside for now. For the miracle you're hoping for is right around the corner. If you can just keep your eyes on the future you're living into, and stay with the inquiry long enough to identify the new ways of relating that can graduate you from your old story, you'll soon be granted the freedom to evolve beyond it.

You do not need to change your story as much as you need to discover the part of you already outside of it and begin sourcing your ways of relating from there. Because Mara had set an intention to manifest healthy, happy love, and was actively "calling in" a loving relationship, she was willing to take the step of identifying the new ways of relating that would be generative of that possibility. Having only been with entitled, self-serving, highly narcissistic men in the past—people who were a perfect match for her unhealthy habit of being so selfless—these new small shifts in how she would be relating from her power center were completely foreign and, at first, difficult to identify, let alone practice. It would almost have been easier to suggest she learn to speak a foreign language than begin to show up in these odd and curious new ways. Yet she stuck with them, listing them one by one in her journal as follows:

MY NEW WAYS OF RELATING TO MYSELF ARE:

→ *Stop self-abandoning* by putting my first attention on myself. *Identify and honor my own feelings, needs, and desires before rushing in to caretake the feelings, needs, and desires of others.*

→ *Learn to identify what I'm feeling and what I'm needing in any given moment rather than become preoccupied with the feelings and needs of others.*

→ *Learn to compassionately soothe my own difficult and overwhelming feelings of fear or sadness in healthy and self-loving ways.*

MY NEW WAYS OF RELATING TO OTHERS ARE:

→ *Take the risk to share my true feelings, needs, and desires with others, particularly when I feel hurt and even if I fear they will be upset with me or displeased with what I'm sharing.*

→ *Allow others the dignity of solving their own problems and support them to find their own agency, encouraging them to grow more confident, strong, and wise without relying so heavily on me.*

→ *Tolerate the discomfort of not giving to someone long enough to discover if they have the willingness and/or the capacity to reciprocate my generosity, as a way to measure how much I should invest emotionally in the relationship.*

→ *Share my authentic needs with others and learn to negotiate on behalf of my own needs.*

→ *Raise my expectations of mutuality in all of my relationships and stop settling for less than I deserve.*

MY NEW WAY OF RELATING TO LIFE IS:

→ *Remember to stay connected to my Higher Power, which is my source of wisdom and growth. Particularly when I feel most hurt and even betrayed by the inevitable ups and downs and disappointments of life.*

As Mara began making the subtle, small shifts—such as expecting more of others or breathing through the fear that came up when she was not giving, to allow for more spaciousness between herself and others so *they could give to her*—her life began to organically change for the better. After years of analyzing why she was the way she was, in the hope that one day she'd finally get to the bottom of it, she discovered how quickly life could evolve when she started showing up in ways that were consistent with the deeper truth of her worthiness, value, and power.

Because self is a contextual experi-

Don't fight back. Fight forward.

—OLA OBISANYA IN *TED LASSO*

ence and highly sensitive to the energies between ourselves and others, it is fluid in nature and relatively easy to evolve. Once Mara knew precisely what to do to break the spell of who she'd known herself to be—such as identifying her feelings and needs and then taking the risk to share them with others—she was delighted to discover that people did actually care about her. They just weren't able to show it before, as she'd never given any indication that she needed anything from them. Most people were also understanding when she began setting boundaries at work, going out of their way to support her and to honor these boundaries. As Mara took risks to show up in the new, foreign ways she'd identified, her *true self* was both validated and fortified by the mirroring she received. She even began attracting an entirely new caliber of potential partners into her life—men who had both the capacity and the good character to love another person for the long haul.

Keep the Gifts. Outgrow the Pain.

It's inspiring to notice that many of the ways that Mara suffered in her youth turned into the golden gifts she now had to give. Gifts of protection, presence, and true care that she offered countless foster children who passed through the doors of her agency over the years. Young people who were also born into situations with caregivers who were ill-equipped to provide the love and protection they needed. Every abandoned child who came to Mara for shelter was her holy battle to fight, and fight she did—helping thousands of them. For many, that made all the difference. All of our wounds come bearing the seeds of our redemption, as we find our way to transform our deepest hurts into a meaningful sense of purpose.

Yet until Mara began including herself in those she cared for so heroically, the gifts she gave were usually at her own expense. Before we met, she frequently martyred herself to care for those who so desperately

The final stage of healing is using what has happened to you to heal other people. That is healing in and of itself.
—GLORIA STEINEM

needed her, working twelve-hour shifts, forgoing vacations and holidays, and being available at all hours of the night to deal with one crisis after another. When I met her, she was burnt out and on the brink of a major depression. It didn't surprise me. It's common for us to try to fix our own past wounding by giving to others what was missing for us, subsequently re-wounding ourselves again and again in the process. In this way, we easily become our own perpetrators, keeping our old wounds alive by treating ourselves in much the same unhealthy ways we were once treated. The sweet spot we're looking for is to keep the gifts that grew from our suffering—compassion, wisdom, kindness, and love—yet outgrow the pathologies of past pain by learning to love and honor ourselves in a way that perhaps no one else has ever done. It's here that our giving becomes our victory and our joy, rather than our burden to bear.

Ask yourself:

What gifts do I now have to give because of all I've endured?

In what ways have I been giving these gifts at my own expense, if any?

How might I start giving to myself what I've so generously been giving to others?

> *You are constantly creating,*
> *whether you realize it*
> *or not. The only question is*
> *whether you are creating*
> *by design or by default.*
> —NEVILLE GODDARD

Show Up in New Ways with Others

Trauma not only alienates us from our true selves; it also alienates us from others. At this point in our journey, you're being given the tools to re-tether yourself back to the world of the living as you start showing up in all your relationships from the truth of who you are. In turn, you will begin experiencing greater levels of authentic connection and care almost immediately. As well as receive the necessary relational mirroring to encourage you to continue moving forward toward the new story you're creating.

There are always exceptions, of course. Those who've been benefiting from you showing up as a lesser version of who you are—the self-involved, weak, and insecure ones who've been either using you as narcissistic supply or enjoying that you do so much while expecting so little in return— are the ones who'll now either need to be retrained or restrained as you lead the way toward greater health and truth in your connections. Rather than blame them for the disempowering dynamic between you, it's more effective to own your part and simply put them on notice that you will no longer think so little of them as to show up as a lesser version of who you are. If you've been fearful of speaking up or setting a boundary, own your cowardice outright. Let them know you now trust them to handle it when you start showing up more authentically and powerfully. In this way, you might even enroll them in the changes you're making. If they're really not up to it and do end up leaving, be grateful. For they were serving as the scaffolding to your source fracture story, and if that building is ever to come down, they might need to go. The game is not so much to get anyone else to change. The game is about you showing up in full fidelity to the future you're standing for. That will mean living in alignment with the truth of your power, your value, and your worthiness, no matter what. Others will either catch up or fall by the wayside. While I don't believe people are disposable, I do advocate for making some of our connections less central to our lives. Particularly those people who aren't mature or well enough to be supportive of our callings, dreams, and desires.

> The game isn't about getting anyone else to change. The game is about you showing up in full fidelity to the future you're standing for.

Step 5 Practice: Identify New Ways of Relating

Many of your old ways of relating are subtle, insidious, and outside of conscious awareness. They've become so normal to how you show up in life that you now just assume this is how you were born—*I'm a loner, I'm conflict avoidant because I'm a peacemaker and I don't like fighting, I'm fiercely independent*—as though these ways of being are coded into your DNA. They've become such an integral part of who you know yourself to be that you now have the well-informed habit of "you." And you don't yet know the new habits that would begin to tell a different story.

Most of the unconscious, habitual ways of relating are being sourced from your old, compromised false sense of self, and so it's critical that you take the time to identify the new ways of relating that would be reflective of the truth of your worthiness, value, and power. If you're really naming the new ways of relating well, they will not only be out of your comfort zone but will also feel completely foreign and unfamiliar—as though they are not "you." If this happens to you, that's a good thing! Because it means you're finally evolving beyond who you've known yourself to be and opening up the possibility of showing up in ways more aligned with the future you are called to.

In mapping out these new ways of relating to yourself, others, and life, look for small shifts that will make all the difference. Shifts such as speaking kindly to yourself after making a mistake or taking the risk to be more transparent and vulnerable with others or making the slight but significant adjustment of holding and containing your big energy so as to create more room for others to come forward in the conversation. A big clue to help you see these new ways of relating more clearly is to look back at the work you did in step 4 and identify the exact opposite ways of relating. For example, if you noticed that you tend to turn away from your own intuitive knowing, your new way of re-

The self doesn't change when we grit our teeth and decide to be different, but when other people see us [and] recognize who we are . . .

—ALISSA WILKINSON

lating might be to listen for and honor your intuition. If you saw that your old way of relating was to defer to others to keep the peace, the new way might be to take the risk to be more upfront about your feelings and needs. If your old way was to lower your expectations and settle for less, the new way would be to raise your expectations and stay generative of the highest and best for yourself and others.

So let's have you take your journal and answer the following questions:

→ *What is my intention?*

→ *What is my source fracture story that's been sabotaging my life in this area and how old is this part of me?*

→ *What's really true about myself, others, and life?*

→ *How have I been relating to myself in ways that have perpetuated my source fracture story?*

→ *How have I been relating to others in ways that have perpetuated my source fracture story?*

→ *How have I been relating to life in ways that have perpetuated my source fracture story?*

→ *What new way(s) of relating to myself would be reflective of who I truly am and who I am becoming?*

→ *What new way(s) of relating to others would be reflective of who I truly am and who I am becoming?*

→ *What new way(s) of relating to life would be reflective of who I truly am and who I am becoming?*

You will not yet know how to show up this way. That's okay. For now, we are simply discovering the ways you will need to grow to prepare yourself to receive the future you're committed to creating.

The future is not someplace
we are going to, but one
we are creating. The paths to it
are not found but created,
and the activity of creating them
changes both the maker
and the destination.

—JOHN SCHAAR

Step 5 Practice:
Rehearsal of the "You" You Are Becoming

Mental rehearsal is a practice used often by athletes, musicians, dancers, and actors to improve their performance. In study after study, this simple technique of mentally rehearsing oneself fulfilling a desired outcome has been shown to enhance performance significantly. It's basically what it sounds like—a mental and emotional walk-through of how you want your future to go that you can do while taking a walk, before falling asleep, or while sitting on your meditation cushion. Internally practicing your equivalent of the perfect pirouette, the big scene, the mind-blowing riff, or the out-of-the-ballpark home run. Going over it again and again in your mind's eye as a way to train your brain and your body to start showing up as your most brilliant and successful possible self. To notice what you are thinking, how you are behaving, and what you are feeling as that version of yourself.

Read through the following practice two or three times before engaging in it, as it is a closed-eyes exercise where your primary attention is on yourself. If you prefer, you can download free audio and/or video of me guiding you through this practice at katherinewoodwardthomas.com /trueyoubonuses.

1. **Center yourself.**

    Close your eyes and take a deep breath, as though you could breathe all the way down into your hips.

    Move into a place of deep listening and receptivity.

    Drop your awareness down into your body.

Notice all of the feelings and sensations in your body and let go of any tension that you find.

2. Imagine yourself living your desired future.

Imagine that life is on your side and has already given you all you desire in the area of your intention. Allow yourself to feel nourished and satisfied as you let your creativity soar.

Ask yourself:

What does it look like to be living the fulfillment of this future?

What does it feel like? Sound like? Taste like? Smell like?

Allow yourself to play with slivers of images in your mind's eye and sensations in your body of this future already fulfilled.

3. Notice what you are thinking, doing, and feeling.

As you try on the possible self of your future, notice what you are thinking, doing, and feeling as you mentally walk through a day in the life of your new story.

Ask yourself:

What am I thinking?

For example: *I am thinking about what I wish to do with all of the abundance coming my way.*

Imagine yourself thinking the thoughts you will be thinking in your future fulfilled as though it's happening now.

Ask yourself:

What am I doing?

For example: *I am freely sharing my creative ideas with others with an organic sense of confidence.*

Imagine yourself doing what you'll be doing in your future fulfilled as though it's happening now.

Ask yourself:

What am I feeling?

For example: *I'm feeling excited to continue expressing my ideas and plans to others, and grateful to be so well received and respected by those that I respect.*

Imagine yourself feeling what you'll be feeling in your future fulfilled as though it's happening now.

4. **Notice how you are relating to yourself, others, and life.**

   Mentally rehearse the new ways of relating to yourself, others, and life.

   Ask yourself:

How am I relating to myself?

For example: *I am compassionate, kind, and self-soothing, particularly when I've been disappointed.*

Imagine yourself relating to yourself in these new ways as though your desired future is happening now.

Ask yourself:

How am I relating to others?

For example: *I am straightforward about what I want and need and I negotiate with others for my wants and needs when necessary.*

Imagine yourself relating to others in these new ways as though your desired future is happening now.

Ask yourself:

How am I relating to life?

For example: *I make empowered meaning of disappointments, setbacks, and delays, and use these experiences to become a more mature and wise person.*

Imagine yourself relating to life in these new ways as though your desired future is happening now.

5. **Make a pledge to show up in these new ways.**

Put your hand on your heart and make a promise to yourself to begin showing up in these new ways and to live in alignment with the positive, possible future you're standing for to the best of your ability.

> *I prayed for freedom*
> *for twenty years but*
> *received no answer*
> *until I prayed with my legs.*
> —FREDERICK DOUGLASS

Show Up with Ferocity

Until you actively begin causing the positive, possible future by showing up in ways that are outside of your default ways of relating, you can expect your past to keep popping up in your present. Patterns are sneaky little buggers and endlessly tenacious. Think of patterns like rivers. They endlessly and predictably flow in only one direction until something deliberately diverts their pathway. Your intention and actions to cocreate that positive, possible future is the diversion you need to reroute the energies in the direction of your desired future.

Though you may not yet know how to show up in the new ways you've identified—such as having good boundaries or engaging with conflict in healthy and productive ways or taking risks to be visible in the world— right now what's most needed is your fidelity to the future that's calling you, and the willingness to put one foot in front of the other in the direction of your dreams. That's going to require ferocity on your part. An intense pushing back against the lies of the false stories that you've been capti-vated by. A planting of your stake into the ground; an assertion of *"This shall be so!"* against all odds. And a willingness to move yourself forward by learning the skills and capacities you did not learn in your childhood, which will equip you to fulfill your dreams and desires. The truth is, in spite of our insecurities and fears, we're fully capable of learning new things and developing new pathways in our brains throughout our lives. While you may not have learned certain skills in your formative years that would have set you up for success later in life, you're certainly able to learn them now. With so much at stake, it's critical to keep your eyes on the prize, and actively lean in to grow yourself into the version of "you" that is capable of fulfilling your potential. For more on this, let's move on to the next leg of our journey—*embrace a growth mindset.*

BONUS: STEP 5 PRACTICE IN ACTION

What is my intention?

EXAMPLES:

→ My intention is to manifest a happy, healthy, loving relationship by my fortieth birthday.

→ My intention is to write and record my first CD as a singer/songwriter by the fall.

What is my source fracture story that's been sabotaging my life in this area, and how old is this part of me?

EXAMPLES:

→ I'm not chosen. The people I like always reject me and choose some-one else. There will be no love for me in this lifetime. She's four.

→ I'm not good enough. Other singer/songwriters are better than me. There are already too many CDs out there and there's not enough room for all of us. She's seven.

What's really true about myself, others, and life?

EXAMPLES:

→ I am deeply worthy of the love I desire. The person who is my highest and best partner possible is looking for me right now. Life is supporting us to find each other and to form a happy, healthy, and loving bond that will last a lifetime.

→ I am an artist who is destined for greatness. Other successful musicians would love to collaborate with me to realize my creative potential. Life is magically making a way for me and providing all I need to get my gifts out into the world in a big way.

How have I been relating to myself in ways that have perpetuated my source fracture story?

EXAMPLES:

→ I reject my own feelings, needs, and desires as undesirable.

→ Instead of trusting the process of creating a song, I judge everything I'm coming up with as not good enough, paralyzing myself in the process.

How have I been relating to others in ways that have perpetuated my source fracture story?

EXAMPLES:

→ In anticipation that others won't like me enough to choose me, I do a preemptive strike: I fail to choose myself by constantly acting like I don't like them. In this way, they feel unwanted and unchosen by me.

I also don't signal to them that it's safe to approach me, and, therefore, they don't.

→ I underpresent myself like I'm just a beginner and express a lot of self-doubt and insecurity, thereby talking others out of wanting to play music with me.

How have I been relating to life in ways that have perpetuated my source fracture story?

EXAMPLES:

→ I have such low expectations that anyone would ever want me enough to choose me that I don't even bother putting myself out there.

→ I rarely take the risk to play my music in public inside of a fear that I'll be judged as being not good enough.

What new way(s) of relating to myself would be reflective of who I truly am and who I am becoming?

EXAMPLES:

→ I "choose" myself by turning toward and honoring my own feelings, needs, and desires, as if I were worthy of my own care and attention.

→ I value and love my own unique sound and developing style.

What new way(s) of relating to others would be reflective of who I truly am and who I am becoming?

EXAMPLES:

→ I let others know when I find them attractive by taking the risk to smile and engage them in a warm, friendly, and undefended way.

→ I present myself as the seasoned artist that I am and generate opportunities to collaborate with others I respect who can help me create a great CD.

What new way(s) of relating to life would be reflective of who I truly am and who I am becoming?

EXAMPLES:

→ I am open to myriad possibilities present for authentic connection and communion wherever I am and whoever I'm with.

→ As they say in AA, suit up and show up! Get myself and my music out there whenever and wherever I can, trusting that it's my destiny to bring my music to the world.

Step 6:
Embrace a Growth Mindset

~

In a growth mindset, challenges are exciting rather than threatening. Rather than thinking, "Oh, I'm going to reveal my weaknesses," you say, "Wow, here's a chance to grow."

—CAROL S. DWECK

G rowth must now be the context of your life, and the new North Star to which you aspire. For you're not yet who you will need to be to step fully into the future you are calling into your life. This is not a bad thing. In fact, it's pretty exciting as you focus your attention on developing in the direction of your dreams. Like the actor who risks it all by quitting their nine-to-five and moving to New York City with just a vision and a prayer of one day being on Broadway, life becomes lit up with possibilities as you grow yourself—one day at a time— into the "you" that you'll need to be to receive that thrilling future into your life. This is where you want to be right now—on the edge of your seat, waiting with bated breath for the next challenge that will provide you with the golden opportunity to develop your character, refine your skills, and grow your capacities. Your version of an exciting stream of dance, singing, and acting classes, and auditions to step-by-step bring you closer to the fulfillment of your destiny.

In her groundbreaking book *Mindset: The New Psychology of Success*, Carol Dweck of Stanford University distinguishes between a fixed mindset and a growth mindset. A growth mindset is the assumption that our intelligence and personality are flexible, fluid, and open to new learning. In this context, failure and shortcomings become opportunities for growth and expansion. Yet when one is anchored in a fixed mindset, one relates to life's difficulties and breakdowns as a threat. For a fixed mindset assumes that our personalities and intelligence are permanent and unchangeable. In this context, our shortcomings are a source of shame—something we are stuck with and therefore must either hide or try to compensate for. Putting us forever on the treadmill of trying to avoid being exposed and continually charged with the task of proving ourselves worthy, important, or good enough, while deep down anchored in a consciousness that we're anything but.

We will learn that though we think big, we must act and live small in order to accomplish what we seek. Because we will be action and education focused, and forgo validation and status, our ambition will not be grandiose but iterative—one foot in front of the other, learning and growing and putting in the time.

—RYAN HOLIDAY

All false centers are reflective of a fixed mindset, and many a beautiful dream has died on the vine due to an untrue narrative that somehow managed to take the lead. Thirty years ago, in response to my own raging "I'm not good enough" story, born from being raised in an atmosphere more prone to criticism than praise, I stopped doing the thing I loved the most—singing. For twelve years before that, I'd poured everything into my cabaret career, having performed in the nightclubs of New York and Los Angeles on a regular basis. It was both a struggle and a sacrifice, yet I so loved what I was doing that I was happy to pay the price. But I let it all go one bleak, gray day while pulled over on the side of the road in my old beat-up Toyota. Tears streaming down my face, I was convinced I wasn't talented enough to continue pursuing my dream. The night before, I'd auditioned at a jazz club when the owner—a man I'd never met before—thought he'd set me straight. Maybe he was trying to be helpful.

Or maybe he was just a sadist. Who knows? But after I sang, he beckoned me over to the bar, looked me straight in the eye, and told me in no uncertain terms that I just wasn't good enough to make it as a singer.

So I quit.

Just like that, I gave my power to a stranger and allowed his overly simplistic assessment of my talent (or lack thereof) to define my life moving forward. In looking back on this soul-crushing decision, it's clear that if I hadn't already been anchored in a story of inferiority, I likely would have shrugged it off as a bad night. But in saying it out loud, that man validated my worst fear, and I internally collapsed into the story of self-doubt that had secretly haunted me for years.

For decades after, my love for singing sat dormant like a knot in the center of my solar plexus. Though along the way I'd managed to cowrite and coproduce an album, *Lucky in Love*, with my brilliant and beloved friends the brothers Isaac and Thorald Koren, it was only when leading a class on setting intentions in my True You membership program that I decided to walk my talk by committing to reclaiming the art form of cabaret. Working with my partner, Michael, as my producer-director, we began developing a show. Immediately I was confronted with the question of who I would need to be to stand on a stage again and connect deeply with a live audience through song. Clearly, I'd need to be confident enough in my instrument to take people on a musical journey. Which is what inspired me to track down the renowned singing teacher Joan Lader, after reading about her in *The New York Times*. Joan has a long list of clients most teachers can only dream of—Paul Simon, Hugh Jackman, Cynthia Erivo, Betty Buckley, Sting, Billy Porter, and more. Patti LuPone credits her with saving her career. Well, I thought, if Joan could do that for Patti, maybe she could do it for me, too.

Some people believe in the story of the past, rather than the possibilities of their future. Yet it's so much more important to romance your future rather than romance your past.

—JOE DISPENZA

Truth be told, I never thought I'd get in to see her. Yet see me she did, though making it clear it was just for one lesson. As I stood at her piano for my first voice lesson in over thirty years, I was shaking. When she ran me through a series of vocal exercises, I did my best, but it was clear that I was horribly out of shape. At the end of the lesson, I humbly acknowledged she was used to working with much more advanced students than me, fully expecting her to not take me on. Yet it was then that she said the magic words that washed away my old fixed identity in one fell swoop, like water down a drain: "Well," she said, "you have a voice! You just haven't been using it." She took me on as a student and just like that, I woke up from the trance of the old story. I figured if one of the greatest voice teachers in the world found me worthy of her time and attention, then I must be good enough. Good thing, too. Because in the weeks that followed, Joan worked me! If I'd been attending those lessons with anything other than a growth mindset—open to learning from my shortcomings, failures, and mistakes, I likely would have quit. But centered in the awareness of my inherent talent and value, my ego wasn't so fragile, and I was able to take Joan's corrections without making it mean anything about me. In no longer having to prove myself, I was finally free to *im*prove myself by leaps and bounds.

Identify Your Missing Development Versus Analyze Your Past

Never underestimate the power of a fixed mindset to keep painful patterns firmly in place. Most of us assume we're repeating unwanted patterns—such as finding ourselves, *once again*, in a relationship with a controlling, manipulative narcissist—because we've not yet healed our past, causing us to go back to the drawing board of analyzing what happened to us way back when. Yet in addition to healing the past, it's critical that we identify the skills and capacities never learned in our youth—the missing development that can safeguard our relationships from toxicity moving forward and keep all our connections on the straight and narrow path of mutual respect and health.

When our false centers were first created—for example, the moment

> In addition to healing the past, it's critical that we identify the skills never learned in our youth—the missing development that can safeguard our relationships from toxicity and keep our connections on the path of mutual respect and health.

we landed on an "I'm invisible" story at the tender age of four in response to our narcissistic mother's inability to recognize us as a separate person from her— we failed to learn what we ideally would have learned at that stage of our lives. Skills like the ability to recognize our own emotions and needs and express them freely to another, or capacities like holding our own by speaking up for our needs when someone else is minimizing or dismissing them. Skills that would support us to relate in ways that would prevent us from winding up as someone else's doormat some twenty, thirty, forty years down the line. To generate a future unlike your past, you'll need to identify and address your own missing development in order to graduate from your old story.

If you have a hard time sustaining a belief in your ability to fulfill your intention, it's likely due to your own missing development. You intuitively know you're not yet capable of showing up as who you'd need to be to manifest that possibility. Yet in naming the specific skills and capacities you will now need to grow, and becoming willing to take on learning the basics of healthy relating, you begin to build credibility with yourself. You demonstrate that you are indeed becoming the version of yourself that you will need to be to master the fulfillment of the future you're committed to creating.

Identity-based beliefs are formed at a time in life when the brain lacks the capacity to process whatever's happening with any level of nuance or sophistication. We simply aren't capable of holding the complexities of the human experience when in the playpen, on the playground, or when trying out for the high school play. As identity is forming all the way through our early to mid-twenties, any occurrence that is deeply disappointing, hurtful, humiliating, or frightening has the capacity to lodge as a supposed truth that can stunt our growth, and therefore our potential. It might have been an acute trauma, like someone leaving or dying, that froze us in a story of powerlessness and alienation. Or it might have been what psychologists call a developmental trauma—the habitual wounding over time of never feeling safe in your home or being chronically neglected and left alone for hours at a time during your formative years. Experiences that prevented us from growing skills like how to express difficult emotions to those who matter, how to set healthy boundaries with ourselves and others, or how to assess probabilities in a way that would allow us to take calculated risks later in life. Skills and capacities that would equip us to live happy, healthy lives, and to outgrow unwanted patterns born from the hurts of the past.

If you grew up in a home where you were loved conditionally due to the narcissism of your mother—a woman who was only capable of extending approval and care when you were being who she wanted you to be—then you may have formed a sense of yourself as invisible. In feeling that your authentic self was not welcome by others, you likely came to the conclusion that no one really cared about your true feelings and needs. Inside of this story, you never bothered to learn how to express your feelings and needs to others. Why would you? If no one cared about them, it would only lead to greater pain. Yet now as an adult, you not only have the habit of disappearing your feelings and needs but you are also missing the development required to communicate what you feel and what you need to others in ways they can hear and respond to appropriately.

I recall one afternoon years ago standing in the kitchen engaged in a lively conversation with a friend. As I reached for a glass of water, she suddenly and quite unexpectedly snapped at me, saying, "I want a glass of water, too, you know!" I stopped and looked at her, surprised by her intensity. Frankly, she, too, was a bit shocked by the hostility in her voice. As we unpacked it together, she acknowledged that she often felt invisible and assumed that no one cared about her feelings and needs. The hostility did not belong to me but was historically based inside of a deep-seated assumption that others were selfish and only concerned with themselves. When speaking from her false center, all she could do was ask for what she wanted in a way that might alienate me and cause me to not give her what she wanted by saying something like, "Well, get it yourself!" This is yet another example of how we are now the source of our own ongoing re-wounding experiences. In not feeling cared for by her caregivers as a child, she'd silenced her needs. Now, as an adult, she lacked the skill of how to ask for what she wanted in a way that would inspire someone to provide it.

It's not what happened to you forty years ago, when your mother disapproved because you said something contrary to what she wanted to hear, that's causing your current pattern of attracting narcissists into your life. It's the way that forty minutes ago you so seamlessly morphed into who you thought someone else wanted you to be, and disappeared yourself from the conversation, that is causing you to fall into that trap again. However, in finally seeing your own missing development clearly, the possibility of doing it differently opens up! The biggest challenge you have now, however, is that you don't actually know *how* to show up differently. In this case, to identify what you're feeling or needing, as you've had the unhealthy habit of putting your first attention on the feelings and needs of others and minimizing your own. With the limited amount of time and energy you have to devote to personal development, I'd rather you start investing the majority of your efforts in growing yourself toward the future you yearn for instead of simply bemoaning an unhappy past.

Cultivate Beginner's Mind

In many areas of life, you likely show up as a strong, competent, and capable adult. You've probably done some pretty amazing things in life—built a career, raised children, gotten a graduate degree, organized teams, volunteered for nonprofits, or raised funds for good

> With the limited amount of time you have to devote to your personal development, I'd rather you invest your efforts in growing toward the future you desire rather than continually bemoaning an unhappy past.

causes. Yet at the same time, you might not know exactly what you're feeling. Or how to ask for what you need. Or how to recognize red flags and engage them in a way

In the beginner's mind there are many possibilities; but in the expert's there are few.
—SHUNRYU SUZUKI

that keeps you safe from harm. Maybe if you'd grown up with caregivers who were a little less damaged themselves, these are things you would have learned along the way. But here you are, having arrived at adulthood with empty suitcases by your side. Suitcases that ideally would be filled with critical life skills that would have set you up for success. And so, we roll up our shirtsleeves and get to work. Putting our full attention now on identifying your missing skills and capacities and looking for resources to help you move beyond wherever you've felt stuck in life.

The frame of mind we want to be in is what Buddhists call shoshin, or what is commonly known as beginner's mind. Beginner's mind refers to an attitude of curiosity, enthusiasm, and openness to seeing ourselves and the world through fresh eyes. It's the willingness to drop the illusion of certainty, and along with it, our preconceived perspectives, opinions, and judgments. Instead, we willingly enter into a well of uncertainty and take on the innocence of not knowing. What don't you yet know that would make all the difference? Maybe how to set a boundary or how to resolve a conflict with someone who matters. Inside of your old way of doing things, you might put up a wall to compensate for not knowing how to set a boundary, thereby cutting off the possibility of growth in the connection. Or you may dig your heels in and try to win an argument, which could cost a deepening of understanding between yourself and another. To simply be in the awareness that you don't yet know how to do it differently and reach out for help, or to honestly share with another your confusion and desire to learn so that you might increase affinity between you, can begin a profound and beautiful journey of growth. In the home you grew up in, it may have been unsafe to be so open and vulnerable. Yet now it's your only safe space.

The goal is not to be better than
the other man, but your previous self.
—HIS HOLINESS THE DALAI LAMA

Step 6 Practice: Identify How You'll Need to Grow

When it comes to outgrowing your old patterns and navigating life from the truth of your worthiness and power, we want to deepen your ability to identify those skills and capacities you'll now need to grow to prepare for the future ahead. To do this, we want to focus our attention on three areas. The first is your relationship with yourself—growing that which we call your intrapersonal skills. These include skills like the ability to identify your feelings, assess your needs, self-regulate when reactive, or shift centers when you find yourself overly identified with an old, untrue narrative. The second is your relationship with others. Your interpersonal skills. Commanding an audience, inspiring and enrolling others to join you in your vision, setting boundaries that protect the integrity of your connections, navigating conflict in ways that deepen love rather than destroy it, for example. The final area we want to look at is your relationship with life itself—such as responding to disappointments in generative and creative ways, raising your expectations of success, growing your capacity to have faith in the face of no evidence, or cultivating a trustworthy relationship with your intuitive guidance.

To support you in identifying the skills most likely to liberate you from your past and set you up for success, I offer the following lists.* Note those skills that resonate with you as weak or missing in your own development and remind yourself that you are a good student and fully capable of learning new things.

---

*The first two lists are reprinted from my book *Calling in "The One,"* courtesy of Harmony Books.

EXAMPLES OF INTRAPERSONAL SKILLS AND CAPACITIES

These are some ways you may now need to grow your relationship with yourself to be ready to step fully into the future you're standing for.

The ability to:

→ **Be aware of your feelings:** This is where you can identify whatever you're feeling in any given moment. Where you can differentiate between your thoughts and your feelings. For example, if I ask you how you feel, you might answer that you feel sad or hurt rather than saying, "I feel like he's being an idiot."

→ **Be aware of your needs:** This is where you are able to name, witness, and value what you need to be well, safe, and happy. Where you can distinguish between a healthy need and an unhealthy need that's coming from an unhealed younger place within you. For example, a healthy need might be "I need my values to be respected" or "I need to know the truth." An unhealthy need might be "I need to be the center of attention all the time" or "I need you to never care about anyone else other than me."

→ **Be aware of your own consciousness:** This is where you can examine your own assumptions and beliefs that are informing your feelings and needs. Where you can discern the lens through which you are perceiving and interpreting your experience and what's driving you to take the actions you are considering taking and make the choices you are considering making. For example, through the assumption "I am alone" you might feel depressed and then isolate from others.

→ **Be aware of and in charge of your energy:** This is where you can assess the energy you are putting out there and make conscious choices to expand or contract it, depending on what it is you're wanting to accomplish. If you have a pattern of overwhelming others, you may consciously choose to contain your energy more. If you have a tendency to disappear yourself, you may choose to expand your energy to be more visible to others.

→ **Self-define:** You are the one who has the final say to define who you are. If someone is projecting negative qualities onto you—criticizing you as bad or treating you as though you are inferior or unworthy—you are open to considering who you've been being that would give them that impression. Yet ultimately, you are the authority on you, and you are not defined by anyone's perspectives, choices, or actions other than your own. Remember, just because someone shames you does not mean you have anything to be ashamed of.

→ **Self-discipline:** The capacity and commitment to keep your word to yourself. To do what you promise you will do, and by when, as a priority in your life. For example, committing to meditating each day or eating more fruits and vegetables.

→ **Self-mentor:** This is about your ability to engage a growth-oriented dialogue with yourself that is kind and encouraging, and in ways that can help you make empowered meaning of whatever is happening. For example, in the aftermath of a mistake, instead of asking, *What's wrong with me?*, you might ask more growth-oriented questions, such as, *How did I give my power away and what can I do to restore it?* This skill also includes the ability to lovingly re-parent yourself in ways that help you to learn difficult lessons, where you offer correction, wisdom, power, and perspective to the part of you that's upset.

→ **Self-motivate:** The ability to inspire yourself to become all that you have the potential to be. When you notice yourself in a place of non-possibility or resignation in response to a disappointment, give yourself a little pep talk, reminding yourself that sometimes life is hard for us all, but it doesn't mean that we ultimately won't prevail.

→ **Self-reflect:** The ability to take responsibility for yourself and reflect on yourself as the source of your experience without shaming or blaming yourself. To admit your mistakes, unwholesome motivations, and faults honestly, while maintaining an underlying unconditional sense of respect, love, and high regard for yourself.

→ **Self-soothe:** This is your ability to de-escalate the intense emotions you're experiencing when triggered or upset. So that the actions you take and the choices you make can be made from the more rational, contained, and balanced part of yourself that has access to wisdom and maturity and can see what's occurring from a larger perspective.

→ **Shift centers:** This is the internal ability to "unblend" and/or disidentify with the younger, tender self when you are triggered, and emotionally shift into identifying with the more holistic, mature, wise, and well part of yourself in order to respond to whatever is happening in generative and healthy ways.

→ **Tolerate difficult emotions:** This is the capacity to hold whatever you're feeling from a deeper, wider center within you. When you can simply breathe through difficult feelings without automatically turning to numbing yourself or acting out. To tolerate disappointing others or being disappointed by others without going into a panic that you're now going to lose the relationship.

EXAMPLES OF INTERPERSONAL SKILLS AND CAPACITIES

These are some ways you may now need to grow your relationship with others, to be ready to step fully into the future you're standing for.

The ability to:

→ **Engage in active listing:** Mirroring back what others are saying in ways that reassure them that you get them and understand what they are trying to communicate to you.

→ **Communicate your feelings and needs:** To articulate your own inner experience in ways that allow others to find their way into your world. This includes making sure your facial expression and tone of voice match what you're really feeling. It also includes asking for what you want and need in ways that assume the best in others and offers them the chance to care for your feelings, and to either meet or negotiate your needs.

→ **Resolve conflict:** Learning to fight fair and in ways that can deepen love rather than damage it, using disagreements and differences to grow understanding and build bridges between yourself and others.

→ **Listen empathetically:** To listen to what someone is saying outside of your own agenda, as a good friend might. Growing your capacity to read social cues in order to hear what's not being said, as well as what is being said, by reading body language and attuning to the emotional tone of the communication being offered.

→ **Set healthy boundaries:** Setting limits that support you to maintain your personal integrity while staying close to and connected with others.

→ **Negotiate your needs:** Advocating for your own needs in ways that are a win-win for yourself and others. To take into account that others have different reference points and agendas, and to stay open to hearing all sides before determining the terms of the relationship.

→ **Repair relationships:** Recognizing the impact your behavior has had on another, intended or not, and discovering the art of making amends in ways that can grow trust between you. Going beyond an apology by also making things right between you.

→ **Respect differences:** Realizing that, while our shared humanity ensures many similarities, there are about as many ways to be human as there are people on the planet. We want to cultivate the capacity to not only tolerate differences but also to be open, inquisitive, and reflective about our differing worldviews, values, and visions, coming to appreciate the diversity between us.

EXAMPLES OF LIFE SKILLS AND CAPACITIES

These are some ways you may now need to grow your relationship with life. To generate a fruitful future that is unlike anything you've known before, you must now develop certain capacities to stay true to your intention, particularly when the going gets tough. Skills such as staying generative of a positive, possible future when presented with a setback, obstacle, or delay; growing your ability to make empowered meaning of a disappointment; keeping the faith in the face of evidence to the contrary; recognizing the positive possibilities present in any given moment;

and/or taking risks to follow your intuitive knowing, even when it's scary, are going to be critical to your success.

The ability to:

→ **Hold fast your faith in the face of no evidence:** Living with a sense of purpose and partnership with the Greater Field of Life, assuming that life always has your back. A deep-seated trust that you are known, supported, and loved, and that everything that happens *to* you is ultimately happening *for* you.

→ **Listen to and act upon your intuitive knowing:** To let go of needing to know the entire plan of exactly how and when things will happen before taking action in the direction of your dreams. And to instead live from a place of deep listening and inner receptivity to your own internal guidance system. As though you were partnering with the creative energies of life to bring forth the future you are standing for, even when your mind is telling you otherwise. Going within to listen for guidance on your next steps before mindlessly doing what you think you should do. Once you have a sense of your next step, to not overthink it too much. Cultivating the courage to take risks to move yourself forward inside of a commitment to manifest the miraculous.

→ **Make empowered meaning of disappointment:** Staying resilient and resourceful in the face of the disappointments, obstacles, setbacks, and delays of life; using these experiences to learn your lessons, develop your character, expand your depth, grow your strength, and deepen your wisdom.

→ **See the potential and possibilities present:** To walk through the world open and available to the limitless field of possibilities present. To raise your expectations that life is indeed supporting you to manifest the future you're standing for. To look for and act upon the openings to cocreate that positive, possible future.

→ **Stay generative in response to breakdown:** Rather than collapse into victimization and non-possibility, to stay solution-oriented, creative, and resourceful in the face of any and all breakdowns. To discover the art of bouncing forward rather than back. Normalizing breakdowns as a part of any journey worth taking and welcoming challenges as opportunities to become who you will need to be to manifest and sustain the future you're standing for.

→ **Live from the future backward.** To live from vision as opposed to your current circumstances. To unleash your imagination in service of finding your way to an unprecedented, unpredictable future that is not likely to happen unless you cause it to be so. To strive to embody your future self and make choices and take actions that are in alignment with and generative of the positive possibilities you are standing for.

Now let's have you take out your journal. Choose three to five skills you've identified as missing and that have been troublesome for you. If you've discovered a missing skill or capacity not listed in the examples above, feel free to include it here.

For each missing skill, journal on what your limitations have been up until now. For example, when you've failed at something, you've tended to beat yourself up rather than learn from the experience and encourage yourself to keep going and not give up.

Next, write about how you've been hiding, compensating for, or tap dancing around this particular deficit. For example, to avoid the possibility of failure, you've kept your life small and predictable.

And finally, explore what it's cost you in life to be missing this skill or capacity. For example, in organizing your life around the avoidance of failure, you've paid the price of your own true self-expression and the contribution you feel destined to make.

Now use your imagination to journal on what the future is like once you've mastered each of these skills, trying on the self of your future, where you are already showing up in these new, more empowering ways. For example: *Having mastered my ability to grow from my mistakes, I am free to learn from what doesn't work just as much, and even*

Become the person who would not have created the problem or in the presence of whom the problem dissolves.

—MARIANNE WILLIAMSON

more, than I do from what does work. My creativity is unleashed and I am joyfully venturing into the unknown, doing work that I love to do. I see myself making meaningful contributions to others, winning awards, speaking to large groups of people, and being deeply loved and appreciated for the gifts that I give.

Once you've identified the ways you'll now need to grow, look for resources that can support you to begin moving in that direction, such as a book, a class, or a video tutorial.

BONUS: STEP 6 PRACTICE IN ACTION

In my relationship with myself, what missing skill or capacity has been the most troublesome for me?

EXAMPLE:

→ I'm missing the ability to self-regulate. I'm very reactive and have a hard time calming myself down and responding like an adult when I'm triggered.

→ I lack awareness of my own feelings and needs and have a hard time figuring out what I'm feeling and needing in the moment.

What has this cost me in life?

EXAMPLE:

→ My relationships tend to be unstable and unsafe.

→ I sometimes end relationships prematurely because I'm hurt or angry but have no way of processing those feelings or getting what I need from the other person.

What resource can I now provide for myself to help me master this skill?

EXAMPLE:

→ Doing the Step 2 Practice: Self-love Power Practice can help me learn to soothe myself when I'm upset and show up as more balanced and less reactive.

→ A feelings and needs chart, which I found for free online, that I can refer to when I can't quite figure out what's going on inside of me.

In my relationships with others, what missing skill or capacity has been most troublesome for me?

EXAMPLE:

→ I don't resolve conflict well and therefore just avoid it by giving in to what others want, even if I'm uncomfortable.

→ I rarely share my needs, let alone negotiate for them. Instead, I just pretend to not have any needs.

What has this cost me in life?

EXAMPLE:

→ My relationships tend to get toxic because I feel taken advantage of, and I eventually just leave. So this missing skill has cost me love that lasts.

→ It's cost me happiness in my relationships as it's always about me fulfilling someone else's needs at the expense of my own.

What resource can I now provide for myself to help me master this skill?

EXAMPLE:

→ I can take a nonviolent communication course.

→ I can read a book that teaches me how to express my feelings and needs.

In my relationship with life, what missing skill or capacity has been most troublesome for me?

EXAMPLE:

→ The missing skill is listening to my intuition. Right now I talk myself out of my intuition pretty consistently, and I let my mind override my deeper knowing.

→ I'm not at all generative in the face of breakdowns. Instead, I indulge in negativity and pessimism when a breakdown occurs.

What has this cost me in life?

EXAMPLE:

→ I wind up feeling stifled and bored, like my life is too small and uninspiring.

→ I give up on my dreams when things get hard. I just stop pursuing them and fall back into old habits that are comforting but depressing.

What resource can I now provide for myself to help me master this skill?

→ I can learn to meditate at my local meditation center to connect more deeply with my own inner life.

→ I can join the True You membership community to give myself a structure of support to keep possibility alive in my life, particularly in the aftermath of a disappointment or breakdown.

Step 7:
Make New Choices, Take New Actions

~

Choice is your greatest power. It is
an even greater power than love, because
you must first choose to be a loving person.

—CAROLINE MYSS

I f you only understood the benefits of a workout routine intellectually, it would make little difference to your health. So, too, this
teaching must be a living daily practice if you hope to change your
life in any meaningful way. While it's a smart teaching, it's also a practical
one. One that can easily be boiled down to two simple words: *choice*
points. Living from the true you requires fundamental shifts in the
choices you are making on a daily basis, with every choice point serving
as a fork in the road. With each choice you make and each action you
take, you must ask yourself: *Is this choice expanding my life or contracting*
it? Am I moving into the future I desire or becoming even more embedded
in my past?

This step is where the rubber meets the road. It's where the teachings
become both real and relevant. Where it stops being just another thing
you know intellectually, and comes radically alive in your lived experience as you make the following six choice points your daily practice. For

your freedom from the story you've been stuck in is in the next choice that you make.

Choice Point 1: Show Up in New Ways

When you commit yourself to creating a future that has been, until now, outside of your identity to be and to have, you will be required to step out of your comfort zone on an almost daily basis. To take the risk of showing up in unfamiliar, new ways that are consistent with the future you're committed to causing. The game right now is to actively seek out each fork in the road and to take the least comfortable one before you. For example, in response to feeling hurt, you might pick up the phone to work it out rather than close your heart as you've done countless times before. Or in a moment of disappointment, you might make the subtle gesture of giving someone the benefit of the doubt rather than just assuming the worst as you would've normally done. Or you might take the risk to make your presence felt in a room full of strangers instead of hiding out in the back of the room. Or to hold and contain your big emotions to make room for someone else to have feelings, too. Or to look for the ways that you yourself might be responsible for a breakdown before automatically blaming another.

When deconstructing old habits in how you relate to yourself, others, and life, it's not just about understanding your old behaviors but consciously choosing new, healthier, and largely foreign behaviors. Be aware of your need to grow in order to show up in these new ways. For example, if you've traditionally put up a wall due to an "I'm not safe, others will hurt me, love is dangerous" source fracture story, we don't want you suddenly tearing it down and opening yourself up to anyone and everyone. Why? Because the wall has served to keep you safe. It's been a primitive defense that's been costing you closeness, yes, but it's also been serving a purpose. When creating

[A person] does not simply exist but always decides what . . . [they] will become the next moment . . . every human being has the freedom to change at any instant.

—VIKTOR FRANKL

your new story where it's safe to open your heart to others, you must look for the ways you'll now need to develop to create healthy protection for you.

If I asked you, "Is it safe to cross the road?," the answer is not a clear yes or no. Because it's only safe to cross the road if you know to look left and right before you start walking. Yet if you don't know to look left and right, then it's clearly not safe to cross the road and you'd best stay on the sidewalk! As you discovered in step 5, these new, healthier ways of relating are not skills you learned in your youth—how to have strong yet fluid boundaries, how to pace intimacy, how to assess a person's character and capacity before opening your heart, or how to negotiate for your needs. It's a version of you that you don't yet know, and it will require a growth mindset as you master the new skills and capacities you identified in step 6. If you're doing this well, you might find yourself feeling uncertain and confused as you begin making choices that are outside who you've known yourself to be. If so, that's a good thing. It means you're moving in the right direction. All of these new ways of creating well-being are now yours to practice as you choose to evolve who you've known yourself to be, one choice at a time.

Choice Point 2: Evolve Your Story

Waking up from the trance of who you *believe* yourself to be includes becoming aware that your story about what went down in your childhood is not as certain as you've assumed. We tend to relate to our histories as factual when, in reality, all of them are subjective in nature, and only partially true. For they were created by us at a time when we lacked the capacity to see things from a multitude of perspectives. Those of us who tend to believe everything we feel might have a hard time relating to the memory of our past as anything but 100 percent true. My mother *was* selfish and mean. My father *did* reject and abandon me. My brother *was* loved more than I was. Anyone who challenges that narrative risks getting their head chopped off and I'm afraid I was no exception.

I recall being in my mid-twenties and at the beginning of my own healing journey, attending therapy for the first time and joining a twelve-step program to try to get a handle on my very destructive food addiction. I was at the stage when the caterpillar turns into a mushy mess in its cocoon, unable to conceive of ever becoming a butterfly. The feeling that had lodged in the center of my soul as a child, and which remained in me well into my adulthood, was that I was an orphan. Now, I wasn't technically an orphan, but it's how I felt. During the early years of my healing journey, I frequently listened to Mahalia Jackson singing "Sometimes I Feel Like a Motherless Child," tears streaming down my face, grieving a past where I'd felt unloved, unwanted, and uncared for.

I got a lot of validation for this story from many compassionate friends, sponsors, healers, coaches, and therapists. I'm grateful I did, for their kindness helped me process the pain I was in. Yet once I began taking responsibility for myself as the source of my experience, I began to question my certainty about how things went down. It began one day when I overheard my mother telling a neighbor that when I left home at the age of eighteen, it broke her heart. Now, that surprised me because my recollection was that I was thrown out of the house because I refused to go to college. In fact, being a "throwaway" was an integral part of my story, and I'd been wearing it like a badge of honor for years. Yet my mother's version of the story, and the sincerity with which she told it, made me question my own, and wear it more loosely.

Inside of the story that I was an emotional orphan I felt a deep and pervasive sense of aloneness in life. While I stayed in contact with my parents in a polite sort of way—exchanging Christmas gifts through the mail, sending birthday cards, and taking the occasional trip across the country for a brief visit, I don't believe I ever felt very connected or cared for even as an adult. That sense of alienation from my roots created a feeling of being lost in the world, as though I didn't quite belong anywhere or to anyone. It wasn't until many years later when I challenged the certainty of that false center story that my relationship with my parents began to change. I'd always assumed that they were the source of the story, that it was true I wasn't loved or wanted. Yet in stepping outside of my orphan identity and no longer generating my relationship with them from that center, I discovered just the opposite—that they were actually eager to know, include, and care for me. It was confusing at first, because I'd been so sure that the story was grounded in fact, when actually I saw that I myself had been generating our estrangement in a thousand little ways—by being guarded and defensive when we spoke, rarely asking for their support, failing to invite them to attend the important events of my life, or covertly judging them for the choices they'd made in their lives. The list goes on and on. The choice to start showing up in ways that consciously created the possibility of greater connection, rather than continue indulging the habit of distance between us, made all the difference. Now we are all quite close and loving, and no one who sees us together would ever believe we spent decades feeling disconnected from one another. That's the power of releasing the certainty of our victimization and making the choice to create a new story.

Executive coach Deanna Moffitt tells a similar story. I met Deanna when she attended a recent online True You Awakening course, where she generously shared about her strained and emotionally challenging relationship with her aging mother—a woman she resented strongly, in spite of the years she'd spent working on their relationship. Deanna's main complaint was that she continually felt invisible, particularly when trying to share about childhood experiences she was hoping to heal. In response to sharing her feelings, her mother would become prickly and defensive, as if her memory of herself as a good and loving mother was suddenly under attack. As Deanna had been adopted at birth, she felt the double unfairness of a birth mother who'd rejected her and an adoptive mother who refused to see and hear her.

We have the power to choose who and how we want to be in the world each and every moment, regardless of what external circumstances we find ourselves in.

—JILL BOLTE TAYLOR

I told Deanna she had what I call an upside-down hierarchy. Meaning that the one with the least amount of psychological and emotional development was the person in charge of the dynamic between them. As Deanna had been working on herself for years, she was actually the one who needed to be the leader of their connection and not the other way around.

After taking that in, Deanna could see that by continually pulling on her mother to validate her experience—a capacity her mother clearly did not possess—she was reinforcing her "I'm invisible, no one cares about my feelings and needs, and it's dangerous to reveal my true self" story, setting herself up to be re-wounded again and again. Yet by choosing to be the leader of love in their relationship—generating love, as opposed to trying constantly to get it—Deanna could develop compassion for her mother's inability to see her, recognizing it as an indication of her mother's own need to be seen as she wanted to be seen.

As Deanna worked to accept her mother for who she was, and who she wasn't, she found herself enjoying her mother's company. As fate would have it, her mother became ill soon after, and Deanna was able to show up in a loving and supportive way to care for her. Eventually, the two women became so close that her mother confessed that Deanna was her best friend in all the world. They now talk daily, not out of obligation, but simply because the love between them is so strong.

This is what it is to be a creator of life rather than stuck in reaction to life. Have others behaved badly over the years? Most certainly they have. Have you yourself made terrible mistakes, the consequences of which you're still living with today? Probably, yes. Has life itself been difficult, unfair, and even unkind? For many of us, yes it has. We can stay mad at our parents, at our teachers, at our older siblings, at the circumstances of life that originally caused us to drop into that false center. We can feel victimized. But until you recognize that you yourself are now the one who is perpetuating the story inside of habitual ways of relating, you will not graduate from that story. I don't care how much you understand it. I don't care how much you've grieved your past. You are the creator of your experience—and you are generating your experience continually. The choice to stay generative of a positive, possible future in the face of all of life's challenges is what it is to be a mature force for love in this world.

The choice to be a person who lives from creativity, from wisdom, and from goodness in the face of all of this, and who continues to act in alignment with a positive, possible future—that's what it is to begin to really step into your power as a creator of life. Deanna chose to be a force for love in her relationship with her mother, and that made all the difference.

Choice Point 3: Expand Your Circle of Care

Ultimately, life has a way of bringing all of us to our knees and waking us up to the importance of surrendering to life on life's terms. At the end of the day, all we really have is who we choose to be in the face of life's challenges. Challenges that can occur as deeply disheartening and profoundly unfair.

By my mid-thirties, I'd accomplished little. I'd failed at creating an acting career in spite of graduating from one of the top acting schools in the country. I was struggling as a singer in spite of putting years into mastering the Great American Songbook. I was barely making ends meet by doing odd temp jobs here and there in spite of having a quality (and very expensive) education. I was still unhappy with my weight in spite of being on a diet for decades. And my love life was a complete and utter disaster. At the time, I was living in Los Angeles—the land of beautiful, successful people all doing fabulous things with their lives—and I was feeling like a complete failure. Fortunately, I was also tired of feeling sorry for myself. One day while driving toward the freeway, I made a choice that I now believe to be one of the best decisions I've ever made, though I did not know it at the time. I decided that if love wasn't coming to me, I was going to bring love to others. I simply refused to live a loveless life.

How's that for an unprecedented future? My motive was simple. Since I knew firsthand the heartbreak of not getting what I wanted in life, I wanted to alleviate that suffering for others. Yet who could I make a difference for? I had

> I decided that if love wasn't coming to me, I was going to bring love to others. I simply refused to live a loveless life.

zero credentials. This was years before I became a therapist. The only thing I'd ever really done professionally was wait tables, do temp work, and sing in nightclubs. As I pondered this question, I passed some homeless people on the freeway on-ramp begging for pocket change. I found myself wondering how I might bring love to these poor people—those who were even worse off than I was. Soon after, *In Harmony With the Homeless* was born. It started as a simple idea to create a CD with songs written by people who were homeless, telling their stories through song and giving them a voice. Yet just by putting one foot in front of the other, it eventually became a project that spanned the next five years and involved over a thousand volunteers from the Los Angeles songwriting community, helped over a hundred men and women leave street life behind for good, and was featured in a televised episode of *ABC in Concert* to coincide with the release of a CD featuring songs cowritten with some of the best songwriters in LA, and with star recording artists like Mavis Staples, Brenda Russell, and Richie Havens performing.

It seemed like such a small, simple choice at the time—to help a few people who were hurting more than I was by giving them some dignity and hope using whatever tools I had available to me at the time. Yet it ended up changing the trajectory of my entire life. While I didn't create that project to get anything in return, as the saying goes, I ended up receiving so much more than I gave. For one, it expanded my vision of what was possible for my own life beyond myself. Because of it, I ended up in graduate school to become a therapist. And it was the beginning of my teaching career, which to date has touched hundreds of thousands of lives over the past two decades. Writing that still brings tears to my eyes. I don't think I'll ever quite get over the miracle of it after such a discouraging start in life. It also helped me to grow my confidence and leadership skills. Which was no small matter as, for a long time, I'd whisper what I wanted to say into the ears of my very extroverted cofounder as we stood in front of a room filled with folks eager to participate in the project. I don't think anyone even knew what my voice sounded like for two whole years before I finally found the courage to get up and speak what was in my heart to say. It also turned my run of bad luck around. Within a relatively short period of time, so much of what I'd been trying to create in my own life came to fruition with little effort, and as if by magic. A happy marriage to a lovely man, becoming a first-time mother at the age of forty-three, increasing my income tenfold doing what I loved, buying my dream home, and getting a book deal with virtually no writing experience or platform to speak of—*Calling in "The One,"* which became a national bestseller within four months of publication even though I had no idea what I was doing and few resources to launch a book into the world. I now know firsthand that when it looks like there's no way out and no hope for a better future, the best thing we can do is to look for and make the choice to expand our circle of care to include others who are suffering, too. In her book *Living a Committed Life*, Lynne Twist, co-founder of Pachamama Alliance, puts it perfectly: "A commitment larger than your own wants and needs lifts you out of the landscape of your circumstances and personal desires. It lifts you out of day-to-day moods, irritations, and upsets about things not going your way. It pulls you out of that smallness and elevates you to a place where you find the strength and courage to generate your life out of possibility and generosity."

> *It is our choices, Harry,*
> *that show what we truly are,*
> *far more than our abilities.*
>
> —DUMBLEDORE IN *HARRY POTTER*
> *AND THE CHAMBER OF SECRETS*

Choice Point 4: Make Empowered Meaning of Disappointment

Your ability to make empowered meaning of disappointment is one of the most important skills you will ever develop. Yet my own recognition of the value of this skill came through my dismal failure to do so. When I was eighteen, I defied my family's wishes to get a good education at a known university, and instead enrolled in a small run-down Bible school where the people were sweet and the teachings sincere. Doing so strained my relationship with my mother and stepfather almost to the breaking point, and we were completely estranged for the year that followed, plunging me into near impoverishment. Feeling alone and undersupported, I was determined to pursue the necessary training to become a minister even without their approval. For months, my diligence could be seen in my many hours spent alone in the cavernous bright-red-carpeted chapel attached to the school. Head bowed, on my knees, I asked God again and again to use my life for good, offering myself to be of service in the highest and best way possible. During these months, I fully anticipated a joy-filled future serving those in need, and assumed doors would soon open for me to begin my good work in the world. Yet it did not turn out as I'd hoped. While I excelled academically, on a personal level, my life was falling apart at the seams. My boyfriend from high school broke my heart by marrying someone else. My sugar addiction went full blown and I rapidly gained an obscene amount of weight. I was making $3.25 an hour working in a day-care center and could barely afford to feed and clothe myself, let alone put a roof over my head. And on top of all this, my best friend turned against me and took all of our friends with her, leaving me completely friendless in addition to being ostracized from my family. Talk about the disappointments of life. It was all too much to bear, and outside of the conscious choice to do so, I found myself making *disempowered* meaning of my experience. Indulging in a deep resentment toward God for allowing all this to happen and tethering me further to an old false center story of aloneness, I assumed that God the Father had abandoned me, much like my own biological father had done. And so, I quit Bible school, stopped going to church, and refused to pray for the next seven years.

It was only upon joining Overeaters Anonymous for my raging food addiction that I had to confront the chip on my shoulder. Backed into a corner by my complete inability to function in life, I was forced to "turn my will and my life over to the care of God, as I understand God." Ugh. My first prayer wasn't pretty. (Cover your ears, children.) "F*&% you," I said begrudgingly. At least it got us speaking again. When it came time to list those I had to forgive, God was right up at the top. Yet little by little, I crept my way there. Thankfully God didn't seem too offended, for it was the beginning of my much-needed recovery from compulsive overeating—a journey that took another twelve years to complete as day after day, week after week, month after month, and year after year I made choices and took actions in the direction of a positive, possible future where I wasn't constantly thinking about what I was going to eat next. Instead, I started dealing with the deeper issues, such as what I wanted to do with my one precious life besides anesthetize myself.

Fast-forward to that day in the car, driving by those less fortunate than me. By then, my overeating was under control. I felt grateful to have some semblance of a normal life, even though it wasn't actually the life I'd been hoping for, and my impulse to make a difference for others was in part motivated by a desire to offer a gift of gratitude to God for liberating me from the addiction. Although I had no idea how I should go about creating a CD with homeless people, I followed my intuition and put one foot in front of the other, eventually landing at a meeting with the directors of the Los Angeles Mission and pitching my idea to run songwriting workshops with their residents. To my surprise, they said yes. We set dates for a series of meetings with eighteen people who'd been living at the mission and were in recovery from all manner of darkness, despair, and acute difficulties that had landed them in their current situation.

Our first meeting went well enough, with everyone introducing themselves and participating in a writing exercise that I'd made up a few days earlier. I invited them to write a letter to someone they cared about who was still out on the streets, sharing the experience, strength, and hope they'd gained in their time at the mission. As they read what they'd written out loud at the end of the meeting, a sense of camaraderie grew and hearts softened as they recognized how far they'd already come in their recovery, and how much they had in common. The following week, everyone came on time, eager for their next experience. As we opened the circle with sharing, one participant after the other expressed how much that exercise had changed their perspective about themselves and given them hope for the future. It was

Failure is often nothing more than good luck in disguise.
—VISHEN LAKHIANI

then that it dawned on me, like a gasp. By descending into the hellscape of addiction, poverty, failure, alienation, abandonment, and anxiety, and spending years working on myself to crawl out of the ditch, I intuitively knew how to help others heal and find hope from the direst of circumstances. I suddenly saw that when my life fell apart after all of those hours spent on my knees at the tender age of eighteen, that the darkness that took over and swallowed me whole in the years that followed was actually answered prayer. I assumed that God had abandoned me, but, in fact, God had taken me seriously enough to put me on a path that would eventually lead me to be of service in the highest and best way possible. That realization made my cheeks flush with the shame of my disbelief. Since then, I've done my best to hold fast the faith that all challenges, obstacles, setbacks, and delays are happening *for* me, rather than just *to* me.

Becoming who you will need to be to fulfill the intentions you set will likely require more of you than you initially considered or even think is fair. If that happens, don't pull back. Instead, choose to align with the overall goodness of life and make empowered meaning of whatever happens. Choose to stay generative of the future you desire, and to look for ways to use what's happening to grow your courage, capacities, and resilience. Ryan Holiday, the author of *The Obstacle Is the Way*, reminds us that setbacks are always expected, yet never permanent. That each massive breakdown before us comes bearing the opportunity to practice some virtue that's critical to the realization of our full potential: courage, patience, humility, resourcefulness, creativity, justice, or love. He encourages us to relate to obstacles as mere launching pads, and to look for ways to "steal good fortune from misfortune." The moral of the story is that we all want to lean into, and listen for, how life is trying to grow us in any given moment, and to welcome all opportunities to become stronger, wiser, and more equipped to hit it out of the ballpark in our lifetime.

What stands in the way
becomes the way.
—MARCUS AURELIUS

Choice Point 5: Live in Integrity with Your Future Self

Integrity is not about right, wrong, good, or bad—integrity is about power. As much as possible, strive to live in integrity with the future you're committed to creating. For each time you make a choice that is out of alignment with your intended future, you'll feel a loss of possibility and power. Possibility is a fluid thing, and it easily disappears when our actions are at odds with our intentions. Yet when making choices that are generative of the future you're standing for, you'll feel more hopeful and inspired. No matter if you're still stuck at a job you hate and can't yet figure out what to do next, as soon as you make the choice to do something as small as update your résumé and get it to where you want it to be, you'll begin to transcend resignation and feed energy to the dream of what can, and what *will*, be.

When we make the choice to act in integrity with the future we're claiming, we activate our power to create it. Yet the transformational leader Werner Erhard warned us not to hope for absolute integrity, calling integrity "a mountain with no top." Meaning that in aspiring toward integrity, we're continually reaching for an ideal that's slightly out of reach. That's important to remember when you're striving to learn new ways of relating that you don't quite have a handle on yet. This isn't about being perfect. Integrity is a daily practice. You'll be continually challenged to clean up inconsistencies between who you claim you wish to become and how you're showing up in this moment, right now. For example, when you say you want to be a successful entrepreneur but then sleep in until noon every day and fail to answer your email. Or you say you're ready to bring in a loving relationship but you're showing up on dates in a way that's defensive and overly self-protective and shutting others out right from the start. Integrity is about having the courage, tenacity, and spiritual strength to continually choose your intended future, even when you're frightened or you've fallen short and evidence to the contrary is showing up yet again.

Choice Point 6: Speak Your Future into Existence

Words hold frequency. If you tune into the energies of the words you speak, you'll soon begin to notice subtleties in how energy either rises or drains away, according to the words that you choose. Are there certain words you tend to use often that drain you of your personal power? The top one for me is *can't*. As in "I *can't* do that." Another might be "Well, I *have* to do that." These words hold the frequency of victimization. What words might you want to retire from your vocabulary? How about the word *should*? As in "I *should* do that." What words might you consider using more frequently? How about the word *responsibility*? As in "What's *my responsibility* in this situation?" What words will you choose to speak more often to yourself? Words of encouragement like "I *can* do this." What words might you begin to speak to others in a way that's generative? How about *believe*? As in "I *believe* in you."

Be mindful of the stories you tell, for when we continue telling our tales of victimization and sorrow, we add to the sorrows of the world. Instead, we want to turn everything that's happening to us, both the good and the bad, into wisdom, depth, inspiration, and lessons learned that feed energy into the field. We want to add to the uplift of the world with the words we choose to speak, and get into the habit of telling our stories from the perspective of where we're going and how we're transforming what's occurring into goodness, beauty, and love.

I invite you to begin relating to language as a tool of creation rather than just a passive descriptor. To develop the habit of speaking in a way that is generative and

> These choice points may seem like tiny changes, yet when implemented consistently with courage and faith, they can and will create an entirely new life.

highly inventive of the future you wish to create. Even though you have no evidence for this future, begin by speaking it into existence.

These choice points may seem like tiny, somewhat insignificant changes, yet when implemented consistently with courage and faith, they can and will create an entirely new life. One that is generative of who you have the potential to become and what you hold the possibility of creating.

Step 7 Practice: Activate the Six Key Choice Points

You will need to demonstrate fidelity to the future you are committed to creating by making new choices and taking new actions that are aligned with that possible future. In this practice, you are invited to notice the specific, subtle choice points that can lead you to your new life. And to begin to make choices that are both in integrity with that possibility as well as generative of it.

CHOICE POINT 1: SHOW UP IN NEW WAYS

Let's begin by having you review the old ways you've related to yourself, to others, and to life from step 5, which you now understand were covertly re-creating unwanted patterns in the area of your intention and validating your source fracture story.

Let's also have you review the new ways of relating that would begin to evolve your story forward and liberate you from duplicating past wounds. What new ways of relating did you identify as more consistent with the truth of who you are and what you came here to create?

Now let's have you take out your journal.

Write about some of the biggest challenges you're facing in your life today.

For each challenge, identify how you might deal with it in a generative way by making a new choice and/or taking a new action.

For example, with my mother, rather than dismiss what she's saying about my behavior, I could try listening to what she's saying like it's a contribution. Or with my boss, I could look at the feedback he's giving less defensively and see it as him investing in my growth as a leader in the company.

Identify what you might have to let go of to make this choice/take this action. For example, being right about everything, or making sure someone isn't angry with me, or holding on to the illusion of self-protection.

CHOICE POINT 2: EVOLVE YOUR STORY

Think of a recent time you felt victimized by someone's behavior.

Ask yourself: *Who wronged me?*

For example, my sister, or my boyfriend.

Validate your feelings of hurt, frustration, fear, and/or anger. Offer unconditional love and compassion to yourself for having to deal with this and notice the meaning you've been making of it.

Again, let's have you take out your journal. See if you can shift your perspective by journaling on the following questions:

→ *What specific choices have I made or actions have I taken that may have contributed to this situation? In other words, how might I be the source of this situation?* For example: *I never told my sister what I wanted and just expected her to know.*

→ *And who will I choose to be in the face of it?* For example: *I am going to be compassionate, knowing that my boyfriend is struggling with how to share his feelings. I'm going to relate to this as an opportunity to share the impact of his words in a way that could actually bring us closer.*

CHOICE POINT 3: EXPAND YOUR CIRCLE OF CARE

Consider the pain you've suffered in the area of your intention: the unfairness, humiliation, and heartbreak of it. With compassion for yourself, recognize what it's cost you to suffer this way.

Now consider that there are millions of others who are also suffering with this very painful experience at this very moment. Extend a sense of love and compassion to them in your heart. Feel yourself connected to them, as though you have a destiny to heal, elevate, and liberate all beings with your own hero's journey.

Notice that when you bring in the light of love, compassion, healing, and transformation into your own life, they, too, are lifted and unburdened. That your choice to transform your own pain lessens theirs.

Relate to your personal journey impersonally, and recognize that your experiencing is reflective of the experience that many people are having. You belong to the whole of life and I encourage you to see yourself as a healer and master practitioner of light and love.

In your journal, explore the following questions:

→ *Who else might be suffering in ways similar to how I've suffered?* For example: *In dealing with my own failure, I now know the heartbreak and humiliation of not getting what you want in life. I recognize that millions of people are also suffering in this same way and feeling like a failure in life.*

→ *What commitment could I make to the world that would provide a larger context to my own personal journey?* For example: *I see that young people need to know how to use failure to learn valuable lessons that set them up for success in life. I am committed to sponsoring young people's greatness by teaching them how to befriend failure and make it their ally in becoming their most successful selves.*

→ *How does this now change my relationship to the challenges I'm facing?* For example: *I can bear the humiliation because I now know that this experience is necessary for me to come into the fullness of my contribution to the world.*

CHOICE POINT 4: MAKE EMPOWERED MEANING
OF DISAPPOINTMENT

Consider a recent disappointment you experienced. From the part of you holding wisdom, maturity, and strength, extend love to the part of you that is suffering and making disempowering meaning in response to this experience.

In your journal, answer the following questions:

→ *Where do I feel this disappointment in my body, and what are the specific emotions I am experiencing?* For example: *My heart feels heavy. I feel hurt, confused, and endlessly sad.*

→ *What's the meaning I'm making of this disappointment? What's the "I am" or "I am not" story I've dropped down into? How old is this part of me? And how big is the energy being held in this center?* For example: *I'm not loved. I'm six years old and the energy is all around me, like a bubble of despair that covers me from head to toe.*

→ *What's really true about this idea that "I am" or "I am not"?* For example: *I am loved by several people who I love in return and I have mountains of evidence of how deeply others care for me.*

→ *What is the opportunity of this disappointment? How might I use it to grow myself beyond the patterns of my past?* For example: *I now have the opportunity to practice creating love when love is missing.*

→ *What power statement can wake me up to the part of myself able to stay generative of the future I'm standing for in the face of this breakdown?* For example: *I am the source of love and held in a field of unconditional care and compassion always.*

CHOICE POINT 5: LIVE IN INTEGRITY
WITH YOUR FUTURE SELF

Let's have you take out your journal again. Think about your intention and the future you are committed to causing, then answer the following questions:

→ *What promises have I made to myself that I'm not keeping?*
→ *How can I clean this up and get back into integrity with my word?*
→ *Where am I living out of alignment with my own values?*

→ *How can I clean this up and get into integrity with myself?*

→ *What promises have I made to others that I'm not keeping?*
→ *How can I clean this up and get back into integrity with my word?*
→ *Who else do I have unfinished business with that needs cleaning up?*
→ *How can I clean this up and get back into integrity with others?*

→ *How could I begin showing up in ways that are in integrity with the future I'm committed to creating?*

CHOICE POINT 6: SPEAK YOUR FUTURE INTO EXISTENCE

Think of something that you're going through right now that's really challenging and notice how you've been sharing about this experience with others.

Now close your eyes for a moment, take a deep breath, and imagine communicating with someone you're close to in a more generative way. See if you can find a way to tell the story of what you're enduring with humility, hope, wisdom, maturity, and depth.

Imagine describing your experience by answering the following questions.

→ In the context of your desired future, how might this be happening *for* you rather than just *to* you?
→ What wisdom are you gaining by what you're currently experiencing?
→ What gifts are you being given that you hope to one day pay forward to others?
→ What strengths are you cultivating to overcome what you must now overcome?

Expand this practice by becoming aware of how generative your words are everywhere you go and with everyone you meet. Choose to increase your personal power to manifest the miracles you're standing for by honoring your word in all situations. Do what you say you're going to do, when you say you're going to do it. Either that or renegotiate your word when necessary. Be conscious of the impact of your words and begin training the Universe that if you speak it, it shall be so! Recognize that when you do so, life will begin moving mountains in your favor.

Creating the Future of Our World

~

Deep down we know that what matters
in this life is much more than winning for ourselves.
What really matters is helping others win, too.

—FRED ROGERS

I t's one thing to pray for a world filled with goodness and hope, yet another entirely to make a decision *to become the source* of that goodness and hope.

At this point in our collective journey, we must recognize that the goal of personal development is not simply self-actualization but the actualization of all of humanity. We must be ambitious for more than just ourselves. We must be ambitious for the whole human race and be driven to elevate the quality of life for all beings everywhere.

> We must recognize that the goal of personal development is not simply self-actualization but the actualization of all of humanity. We must be ambitious for more than just ourselves. We must be ambitious for the whole human race.

For it's only when we expand our sense of self to include who we are for others that life begins to make sense, as we awaken to ourselves as an unstoppable force of nature.

If you only woke up to your power to manifest the miraculous for you and you alone, it would be as if Thomas Edison invented the lightbulb simply to read a good book by the fire in his own living room. You did not come here for yourself alone. You are here for a higher purpose. And that purpose will always point to who you came here to be for others. How can you spin the straw of your own suffering into golden gifts of wisdom, kindness, creativity, hope, and love that you can now offer others? Not in spite of what you've been through. But, actually, *because* of it.

You were not born just for you. You belong to the whole of life. And you will not know yourself until you claim the larger story of who you are for others.

One of the great losses of our time was the early death of Abraham Maslow. Most of us know Maslow as the creator of the iconic hierarchy of needs, which ranks our needs in order, starting with our basic requirement of food and water and progressing upward through safety, love and belonging, and esteem toward that which is often considered the pinnacle of our evolution—self-actualization. The ultimate fulfillment of our potential. You may know his theory as a color-coded pyramid, as it's one of the most enduring psychological symbols of our day. Yet before he died, Maslow came to question his theory. In fact, he was grieved that he'd popularized his ideas before they were ripe and ready to share, as by his late fifties he no longer believed self-actualization to be the end of our striving, but a mere stepping-stone to the next and most important stage of our development—the stage of self-transcendence.

Self-transcendence is the expansion of our circle of care and contribution beyond ourselves, and for the benefit of others. Yet Maslow's unexpected passing from a heart attack at age sixty-two prevented him from popularizing this critical evolution of his work, leaving it to you and me to carry on and build upon his legacy.

> Self-transcendence is the expansion of our circle of care and contribution beyond ourselves and for the benefit of others.

Whether or not you have an identity as a leader, I assure you that if you are here at this time, it is your destiny to become one. You need not wait for someone to recognize your talents and invite you to the party before claiming this title as your own. You must be self-authorized and make the decision to be the one to throw the party and invite others to attend. To take a stand for a world of safety, fairness, respect, and justice for all, visioning it daily, and allowing this possibility to inform—and *transform*—who you are and how you show up each day.

Though Hollywood and ultrareligious circles have filled our minds with images of a dystopian future, with global annihilation nipping at our heels, the truth is that while things are indeed getting worse in the world, things are also getting better. As the late professor Hans Rosling put it in his refreshing book *Factfulness*, "Things can be both bad and better." He encouraged us to hold complexity when it comes to the state of our world, recognizing our tendency to become preoccupied with a negative bias, as the media relies on the drama of bad news to grab and keep our attention. Yet in stepping back to see things from a more holistic perspective, we also recognize that in the past fifty years, stunning progress has been made in creating renewable energy, educating girls, elevating the status of women, eliminating unnecessary illnesses, treating cancer, reducing the child mortality rate, and expanding life expectancies worldwide. So while things seem dire, they're also extremely promising.

Yet that promise can only be fulfilled by those of us willing to take a bold stand for an unreasonable, unpredictable future, and to show up in generative ways that can begin to turn the tides in that direction.

> The promise of a more beautiful future can only be fulfilled by those of us willing to take a bold stand for an unreasonable, unpredictable future, and show up in ways that can turn the tides in that direction.

The call to leadership is rarely convenient, as none of us have had it easy in this lifetime. And those of us called to a larger purpose were likely given an extra dose of painful challenges to help grow our strength, courage, power, and creativity. We remember Dr. Martin Luther King Jr. for his extraordinary accomplishment of advancing freedom and equality in our world. Yet few of us are aware of how deeply he suffered from depression

throughout his childhood or that he was beaten by his father until he was a teenager. Or that for years, he was fiercely resentful of white people for the humiliation and oppression he and his loved ones endured at their hands. Yet rather than stew in victimization, he transformed his experience into vision, and that decision changed the trajectory of our world.

In her delightful book *Big Magic*, Elizabeth Gilbert paraphrases the poet Jack Gilbert: "He told [his students] that they must live their most creative lives as a means of fighting back against the ruthless furnace of this world." Many of us are empaths and deeply sensitive to the massive amounts of injustice and suffering we witness in our world each day. Yet rather than contract away from the world in times of trouble, we must lean in and expand our commitment to consciously create greater goodness, fairness, light, and love on a daily basis. To combat what Jack Gilbert terms the ruthless furnace and embrace the call to pay forward all we have learned about transformation—up-leveling our devotion to heal, to teach, to care for, to create, to elevate, and to inspire.

The world will change when we're more focused on creating the world we really want.
—MARIANNE WILLIAMSON

Given that we now know that the future is fluid and not fixed like it initially appeared, and now that we're awake to our ability to consciously create that which we're willing to stand for, each of us must ask ourselves . . .

What's the future I desire for us all?

and

Who will I need to be to initiate that possibility in the world?

For years, we've been able to do our personal development work divorced from who we came here to be and what we came here to cause for

Hope is a passion
for what is possible.

—SØREN KIERKEGAARD,
TRANSLATED BY ALASTAIR
HANNAY

others. Yet, that time has now passed. We each have a significant role to play in consciously cocreating the future of our world. It is my deepest desire that this book has unleashed in you the ability to hold space for the unimagined and to live into a future that is worthy of you. That it has planted seeds within your heart that will soon bloom into the bright and beautiful future we all hope to leave to the children of our world.

Part Two

TRUE YOU
BREAKTHROUGH
BLUEPRINT

How to Use This Breakthrough Blueprint

⁓

Infuse your life with action. Don't wait for it to happen . . .
Make your own future. Make your own hope. . . .
whatever your beliefs, honor your creator, not by
passively waiting for grace to come down from upon high,
but by doing what you can to make grace happen—
yourself, right now, right down here on Earth.

—BRADLEY WHITFORD

The twenty-two belief breakdowns offered in this portion of the book are a guide to help you discover your path to freedom beyond your old story. Inside of your intention to manifest and sustain the future you're committed to, you may now be eager to clarify the specific, subtle ways you've been relating to yourself, others, and life that have covertly been keeping you stuck. In particular, you're likely even more excited to learn the new ways of relating that will liberate you to start showing up in ways that are consistent with, and even generative of, the intention you've set.

When reading through the breakdown of the following identity-based beliefs, keep in mind that the lists below are both imperfect and incomplete. Imperfect in that they may not take into account the variation on a theme that is you. While each breakdown includes the most common ways of relating that have been generating an unwanted pattern, you will not necessarily identify with each one. The breakdowns are also incomplete in the sense that you might have ways of relating that have been generating evidence for an old story that aren't even mentioned yet, which are valid and appropriate to include in your own belief breakdown. Your story may also be described to a T in one of the breakdowns included, or you might not find it listed in these pages at all. If that's so for you, trust yourself and use the blueprint as a model for how to work to deconstruct your own beliefs. All of this is to say, you'll need to do your own deep dive to unpack how your particular story has been playing out in ways that are unique to you. For these reasons, you're invited to treat this blueprint as a guide and solid starting point that can help inform your own liberation from the trance of your old story.

I encourage you to also remember that beliefs cannot be transformed by insight alone. You might have a sophisticated cognitive understanding of your issues and believe that you already know the stories that have been keeping you stuck. Yet your body might actually be holding a different narrative than your mind. The identity-based stories we formed about who we are, and what is or is not possible for us—worldviews that covertly drive our choices and eventually become self-fulfilling prophecies—were formed long ago. Sometimes before we even had language. As such, they are more likely to exist as an energy that arises in your body in response to a disappointment rather than as a fully formed thought that occurs in your brain. Because of this, they can only be transformed by relating to the somatically centered part of you still stuck in that story.

While this blueprint offers many good suggestions about how your story is happening *through* you and not just *to* you, it's the narrative *that feels most alive in your body at this very moment* that you'll want to be listening for. The bottom line is to stay true to your own lived experience by working with the energy of your false center as it lives in your body at the time it's happening—occurring as a heaviness in your heart, a tightening of your throat, a knot in your neck, or a sick feeling in your belly. As Bessel van der Kolk reminds us, "The body keeps the score," and it's this somatic self you want to connect with directly and deconstruct in order to finally graduate from the endless stream of evidence you've created for your story thus far.

I also want to give you a heads-up that if you're like most people, you will identify with more than one identity-based belief listed here. The majority of us have a cocktail of false centers. False beliefs tend to reinforce one another. The belief "I am invisible" may have initially formed in response to how desperately you needed to make yourself small to try to protect yourself from a habitually angry parent. Meaning that the core of it may actually be an "I am not safe" story. Or the belief that "I am not wanted" may initially present as an "I am alone." As being all by yourself in the world may be the outcome of being so chronically rejected and unwelcomed by others.

Instead of saying, "I'm damaged, I'm broken, I have trust issues," I say "I'm healing, I'm rediscovering myself, I'm starting over."
—HORACIO JONES

Discovering which source fracture story brings tears to your eyes when you finally name it is a subjective experience and not a perfect science. So when deciding which one to work with, go for the one that makes you wince. The one that feels most energized in your body when you say it, as though you finally hit that ugly spot of shame that's been locked inside; the one you've desperately been trying to get rid of, compensate for, or hide from others for a very long time. In finally naming it accurately, you're now free to deconstruct it as *it* no longer has *you*, but *you* now have *it*.

It's also important to recognize that we have different false centers for different areas of life. You may feel perfectly confident professionally yet be a ball of insecurity when it comes to manifesting a loving partner in life. You may have a loving relationship with your physical self yet constantly struggle to make ends meet financially. You may easily enroll others in the grand vision of whatever it is you're up to in life yet be all over the map when it comes to managing your own home, which is so cluttered that you'd be horrified if someone actually showed up at your front door. Because of this, I suggest you initially look up the identity closest to the source fracture story you named in step 2 and see if any of the suggestions below offer further clarification. I also encourage you to read through the following pages with the intention of deconstructing and re-creating that one area of life that you are committed to changing via this book. You can, of course, return to this blueprint many times in the future to apply it to other areas of your life when you're ready to do so.

Ultimately, the way to best work with this blueprint is to relate to it as a master map that lays out a path to align your life with the true you and to bring your behaviors and self-development efforts into integrity with who you really are and who you are called to become. Graduating you from the life you've known and liberating you to manifest and sustain the life you are consciously choosing to create instead.

I Am Alone

Source Fracture Story

ABOUT YOURSELF

→ *I am alone.*

→ *I am on my own.*

→ *I am a loner.*

→ *I am an orphan.*

ABOUT OTHERS

→ *Others always leave.*

→ *No one is ever here for me.*

ABOUT LIFE

→ *I can never get what I need from others.*

Yourself as Source

WITH YOURSELF, YOU:

→ Disregard your feelings and needs to do whatever is necessary to try to prevent others from leaving you, including the withdrawal of their love, support, and approval.

→ Are disconnected from your own deeper feelings and needs, as your attention is largely outside of yourself to caretake the feelings and needs of others.

→ Run yourself into the ground trying to do everything on your own, exhausted by how much you have to do and how little support you have.

→ Assume you'll never get your needs for love met, so you struggle with chronic low-grade depression, which lies below the surface and causes you to isolate and/or stay in a relationship where your needs are not being met.

WITH OTHERS, YOU:

→ Work alone from home or in a profession where you're exceedingly independent.

→ Are self-sufficient to the extreme, priding yourself on your lone wolf ability to not need anything from others.

→ Rarely ask for support, ask in ways others can't hear (i.e., drop hints or subtly imply), or in ways that alienate others (i.e., you're demanding or whiny).

→ Stay too long in unhealthy relationships you know are not good for you or that have no future.

→ Rarely take risks to be vulnerable as you are more comfortable being the giver than the receiver.

→ Pursue unavailable or love-avoidant people or get entangled with "impossible loves."

→ Isolate when you feel sad.

→ Cut people off or close your heart when they disappoint you, destabilizing your connections in the process.

→ Avoid conflict inside of assuming disagreements to be the beginning of the end. However, in failing to engage conflict directly, you don't give your relationships a chance to bond, making them easy to leave.

→ Give your power away for fear that if you tell the truth, raise your expectations, and/or set boundaries, others will leave.

WITH LIFE, YOU:

→ Settle for less inside of having low expectations that your needs will ever be met.

→ Are disconnected from your intuitive knowing and on your own to figure out the best way forward.

Others May Experience You As:

→ Not needing anything from them because it seems like you have it all together.

→ Unapproachable, prickly, or off-putting.

→ Hard to support, even when they suspect you need it and they want to help.

→ Judgmental and intimidating.

True You Power Statements

→ *I was not born to be alone. I came here to love and be loved, and I have the power to learn how to have more meaningful and loving connections that can deepen and grow over time.*

→ *I am a part of all that is and am deeply connected to all of life.*

→ *Others will be there for me to the extent that I let them into my life by taking the risk to be vulnerable.*

New Ways of Relating

WITH YOURSELF, YOU:

→ Are aware of your own feelings and needs and always able to acknowledge what they are with self-compassion and care.

→ Prioritize self-care over caring for others, barring a true emergency.

→ Are loyal to yourself, first and foremost, before mindlessly being loyal to others.

WITH OTHERS, YOU:

→ Put the growth of the relationship above any impulse to protect yourself by shutting down and pushing others away when your feelings are hurt.

→ Engage in conflict directly and fairly with those who matter.

→ Share your feelings and needs vulnerably, so that others can find their way into your inner world.

→ Ask for support in ways that allow them to give you what you need.

→ Are open to receiving support from them in the ways they're able to give it.

→ Let go of your wall of self-sufficiency by taking on activities and projects you cannot do alone and by giving up doing what needs to be done all by yourself.

→ Leave (or lessen your investment in or expectations of) relationships when you're being treated poorly and/or if the other person fails to adjust their behavior once you've addressed it clearly and directly.

WITH LIFE, YOU:

→ Raise your expectations that your needs are appropriate and should be considered and honored by others you let into your life.

→ Connect with your intuitive knowing, particularly when confronted with choices that will determine the direction of your life.

Skills and Capacities to Learn

→ Identify and validate what you are feeling at any given moment.

→ Identify and validate what you need at any given moment.

→ Differentiate between your unhealthy needs and your healthy needs. For example: *I need to be the center of attention at all times* versus *I need to be heard by those who matter.*

→ Tolerate disappointing others, so that you can set healthy boundaries to stay true to yourself.

→ Grow object constancy* so that even when you're upset with someone, or they with you, you can still feel emotionally connected to them.

---

*According to attachment theory, *object constancy* refers to the ability to maintain a positive emotional connection to someone even when they're absent or when you are experiencing negative feelings toward them such as confusion, anger, or disappointment.

→ Engage in conflict in healthy ways that can deepen your connection rather than damage it.

→ Share your feelings and needs in nondefensive ways that invite others to be there for you.

→ Negotiate your needs with those who matter.

→ Have faith in the overall goodness of life when taking a risk to let someone go or to lessen your investment in the connection when others are not treating you well and/or not responding to your requests that they change.

→ Expand your healthy sense of entitlement to have your needs met or at least considered by those you let into your life.

→ Hear and trust your intuition, listening for wisdom and guidance when needed.

Gifts

→ You are exceptionally competent and resourceful.

→ You are fiercely loyal and deeply committed to others.

→ You are wonderfully independent, self-motivated, and self-sufficient.

I Am Bad

~

Source Fracture Story

ABOUT YOURSELF

- → *I am bad.*
- → *I am selfish.*
- → *I am evil.*
- → *It's all my fault.*

ABOUT OTHERS

- → *Others are always mad at me.*

ABOUT LIFE

- → *Life is punishing me.*
- → *Life will punish me if I'm not good.*

Yourself as Source

WITH YOURSELF, YOU:

- → Beat yourself up, speaking harshly and punitively to yourself and overtly blaming and punishing yourself when you make a mistake or fail at something.
- → Frequently break your word to yourself, undermining your confidence.

WITH OTHERS, YOU:

- → Give your power away to others to determine whether you are a good or bad person, and are highly sensitive to whether or not they approve of you.
- → Are overly responsible for the bad behavior of others, often assuming responsibility for the mistakes and misdeeds that are not your fault.
- → Play the hero by overpromising or overcommitting, yet eventually let others down and set them up to be irritated with you.
- → Frequently fail to keep your word, causing others to be angry and lose confidence in you, and resulting in a profound loss of power in your relationships.
- → Have a lot of *should*s for yourself and others, and see things in black or white, right or wrong terms, often cutting off deeper and more subtle levels of inquiry and self-reflection in the process.
- → Are late for most of your appointments, which sets others up to be irritated with you.
- → Defend against owning your part in breakdowns due to an overwhelming sense of shame and your confusion between being responsible and being to blame.
- → Overcompensate by being good to the extreme, relentlessly engaging in subservient service.

WITH LIFE, YOU:

- → Are compelled to act out in destructive, contrarian, and rebellious ways.
- → Stop being generative when things don't go your way because you assume life is punishing you.

Others May Experience You As:

- → Their scapegoat—the one they can always fault due to your willingness to be overly responsible for their bad behavior. They are more than happy to let you take the blame, as it lets them off the hook.
- → Someone they need to try to manage, like a child or teenager.

→ Frequently on their bad side.

→ Not someone they can count on.

True You Power Statements

→ *I humbly acknowledge my mistakes, failures, and shortcomings without shame, and recognize them as opportunities to learn and to grow.*

→ *Other adults are fully capable of taking responsibility for their choices and actions and owning the impact and consequences of their behavior.*

→ *I no longer give my power away to others to determine whether I am a good and worthwhile person. I humbly and honestly assess my own motives, behaviors, and choices.*

→ *The measure of my goodness lies in my willingness to learn from my mistakes and to make amends whenever possible.*

→ *I choose to be a good person and I align my choices and actions with this decision.*

→ *I strive to honor my word and grow my ability to show up as someone who others can trust and count on.*

New Ways of Relating

WITH YOURSELF, YOU:

→ Speak to yourself in ways that are kind, self-compassionate, and self-encouraging in the aftermath of a mistake or failure, so that you're able to grow and learn from the experience rather than get stuck in shame.

→ Keep your word to yourself. Do what you say you are going to do and by when. If you can't, then you honor your word by acknowledging this to yourself and renegotiating it.

→ Are clear about your own values, recognizing that you're only accountable to live in alignment with *your* values, and not the values that others try to impose on you.

WITH OTHERS, YOU:

→ Are open to feedback and thoughtfully consider what might be true about the negative feedback you receive, even if offered unskillfully. Ultimately, you and you alone are the authority on your own life.

→ Keep your word. If you can't, then you honor your word by acknowledging that and renegotiating it.

→ Set realistic expectations of what you will and will not do and by when, and communicate these limits clearly so that you're not constantly falling short or failing to fulfill the expectations that others have of you.

→ Let others know that you're no longer willing to be overly responsible for their behavior or to protect them from the consequences of their choices and actions.

WITH LIFE, YOU:

→ Assume that life is delighted with you and happy that you're open to learning lessons that can make you wiser, stronger, more caring, and more creative.

→ Hold greater complexity regarding your own humanity, recognizing that we all have a capacity for both good and evil. Choose to create goodness because it's your privilege to do so and not because you're somehow in trouble with life.

Skills and Capacities to Learn

→ Self-soothe in the aftermath of making a mistake or failing to fulfill your goals.

→ Self-reflect—without moving into shaming or blaming yourself—to take full responsibility for how you are the source of your failures and breakdowns in a way that will allow you to grow.

→ Identify and make amends to yourself for your mistakes by implementing lessons learned straightaway.

→ Accept all parts of yourself as worthy of being loved, even when you don't live up to the expectations of who you or others think you "should" be.

→ Discern the amends you can make to others to clear the field between you in the aftermath of hurt feelings, mis-attunements, and misunderstandings.

→ Discern what's yours versus what belongs to others and give back responsibility to others for their own choices and behaviors.

→ Assess and communicate clearly what you can or cannot do, in order to set reasonable expectations that others should have of you.

→ Recognize and care about the impact your choices and behaviors have on others.

→ Hold others accountable for their choices and behaviors in healthy, honest ways that are factual and not shame-based.

Gifts

→ You care about being a good person and are often the source of great goodness in the world.

→ You're able to shoulder a great deal of responsibility.

→ You're fearless and take big risks in life that can lead to great success.

→ You have compassion for those who've made mistakes and are gifted at helping others become better people because of it.

I Don't Belong

Source Fracture Story

ABOUT YOURSELF
- → *I don't belong.*
- → *I am lost.*

ABOUT OTHERS
- → *Others don't see or value my gifts or potential.*
- → *Others know more than I do.*

ABOUT LIFE
- → *I'm always on the outside looking in.*
- → *I have no reference points for who or where I am.*

Yourself as Source

WITH YOURSELF, YOU:
- → Hop from one area of expertise to another, without sticking to them long enough to firmly establish yourself as a true expert in any of them.
- → Hurl yourself into new situations and have high and unrealistic expectations that you'll navigate them well without any orientation to what might be required or expected of you.

→ Hop around between various teachings and philosophies without ever truly claiming one as your own to anchor your life in one meaningful direction.

WITH OTHERS, YOU:

→ Fail to ask questions or do the research that would orient you to your environment. This leaves you out of sync and confused as to the context, frames of reference, and/or rules of your environment, and baffled by how others seem to know what's going on when you don't. For example, you don't know the point of the meeting or are constantly confused about the logistics of the class.

→ Allow your attention to wander in social situations, such that you lose track of what's happening around you without admitting it to others. This keeps you on the sidelines, lest your wandering attention be revealed.

→ Stay on the periphery of groups and communities.

→ Only create community on your own terms—usually as the leader and not as a member.

→ Don't share your talents with the communities you find yourself in, keeping your brilliance inside of you as though it were inconsequential or unneeded.

→ Don't bother learning the names of those in your communities, somehow dismissing the importance of getting to know people, because in your mind, your connection will only be temporary.

→ Throw away connections easily, failing to invest in relationships you've spent time and energy creating, as though they were not important.

→ Leave communities without proper closure, creating a chronic sense of loss, alienation, and disconnection for yourself and others.

→ Long for a place to belong, patiently hoping and waiting for others to invite you to the party and feel confused as to why they don't.

→ Feel chronically dislocated, left out, and disconnected from communities of people and mysteriously unable to locate your place in them.

WITH LIFE, YOU:

→ March to the beat of your own drum without recognizing your role and where you fit into the community at large.

→ Are more tethered to your own inner life—your unique ideas and ideals—than you are to the people around you.

Others May Experience You As:

→ On the outside of things, assuming you know the rules of engagement and are deliberately choosing not to follow them and to stay on the sidelines.

→ Unapproachable and difficult to get to know, experiencing you as having your energy and attention elsewhere in ways that don't include them.

→ Out of sync with the world around you, which they interpret as a lack of interest in being a part of what they are up to. They would be surprised to learn how deeply you long to be invited to join them.

→ A bit spacey and clueless as to where you are and what's required of you.

True You Power Statements

→ *I am an essential member of any and all communities that I choose to belong to. My ideas and contributions are essential to the well-being of any group I am a part of.*

→ *Everyone, everywhere, belongs to me, and I to them.*

→ *I first try to understand my surroundings before I move into action.*

→ *I am responsible for generating my own belonging in any and all communities I find myself in.*

→ *I choose to bring my attention back to whatever is happening in the room, and to ask questions about what I may have missed, freely admitting that my attention wandered without judging myself.*

→ *I am fully capable of asking questions, listening, and learning all I need to know to participate fully wherever I am and whoever I'm with.*

New Ways of Relating

WITH YOURSELF, YOU:

→ Give yourself the information you need to navigate new environments well.

→ Lower your expectations that you should be able to handle any and all situations that you find yourself in without proper orientation, training, and support.

→ Believe in your gifts and talents enough to stick with them, recognizing that the fruition of your contributions may take a bit longer than you anticipated.

WITH OTHERS, YOU:

→ Throw the party you've been waiting to be invited to and recognize that belonging is something we must continually generate for ourselves and others.

→ Take care to learn the context of the groups you're in—their mission statement or the purpose of this particular meeting—and to engage inside of these frameworks.

→ Look to discover the frames of reference for all that you're up to. For example, study the syllabus of a class before it begins, look at a map of the town you're visiting, inquire about the beliefs of the church you attend, or read the instruction manual for the computer you just bought.

→ Volunteer your unique skills and talents to benefit the groups you are a part of, participating fully and giving of yourself in ways that allow others to know the real you.

→ Engage conflict directly with the intention of deepening the bond between yourself and others in ways appropriate to the context of the connection.

→ Get to know the needs and concerns of those around you with authentic interest and curiosity.

→ Pay attention to what's occurring, and when you don't understand something, are honest about that and ask for clarification.

→ Find people and projects that you can commit yourself to fully and that you can own as yours.

WITH LIFE, YOU:

→ Open yourself to being a channel of creativity, truth, goodness, and light, recognizing that your unique way of experiencing the world, and the gifts and talents that are inherent to you, are necessary to the well-being of all.

Skills and Capacities to Learn

→ Think contextually. Get into the habit of looking for the larger cultural and/or social influences, agendas, and/or patterns of the person or group you're relating to.

→ Slow down and learn the rules and reference points of the communities you're in, recognizing that they are not yet familiar to you and that it may take time and patience to orient yourself.

→ Notice where your attention is at any given moment. When your attention has wandered, bring it back to what's happening with the people you're with and/or admit you've wandered so they can scoop you in.

→ Share yourself with others, taking the risk to be seen as you authentically are.

→ Tolerate differences without making it mean that you don't belong. Stay open, receptive, curious, and humble when learning about those who think differently than you.

→ Navigate conflict in healthy ways. Use disagreements as opportunities to deepen understanding between yourself and others.

→ Learn social skills that will allow you to create authentic connections that are nourishing to your heart and soul.

→ Clarify your core values so that you're able to align yourself with people, organizations, and projects that are meaningful to you.

Gifts

→ You enjoy a rich inner life and are profoundly creative, with fresh perspectives and unique ideas to offer.

→ You're gifted at creating a sense of belonging for others who also feel disenfranchised and on the outside of things.

→ You're a visionary trailblazer and a pioneer. You offer innovative ways of doing things that have never been done before.

I Am a Burden

Source Fracture Story

ABOUT YOURSELF

→ *I am a burden.*

→ *I am needy.*

ABOUT OTHERS

→ *Others are overwhelmed by my needs.*

ABOUT LIFE

→ *It's my job to fulfill all of the needs I notice need to be filled.*

Yourself as Source

WITH YOURSELF, YOU:

→ Minimize and dismiss your needs, and therefore have an undeveloped capacity to identify and tend to them, setting you up to be easily overwhelmed and burdened by your own needs.

→ Fail to discern between your healthy needs and your unhealthy needs, which makes it nearly impossible to advocate for your appropriate adult needs.

→ Minimize and dismiss your feelings, and therefore have an undeveloped capacity to contain your own big emotions, setting you up to be easily overwhelmed and burdened by your own feelings.

WITH OTHERS, YOU:

→ Are profoundly self-reliant and rarely ask for what you want and need to be okay, pretending you have no needs to appear "low maintenance" and not needy—inadvertently giving others the difficult task of trying to figure out what you need on their own.

→ Have close relationships with people who are less developed than you and/or who easily become overly dependent upon you, thereby frequently becoming a burden to you.

→ Have intimate relationships where you show up more like a parent than a partner, caretaking and overfunctioning and creating an imbalance where you habitually give more than you receive.

→ Date those who you hope will commit to you but who end up telling you they "admire" you but are not "in love" with you. This is due to how you present yourself as not needing anything from anyone.

→ End up in intimate relationships with people who behave like entitled teenagers, rarely rising to a more mature expression of mutual adult love.

→ Ask for what you want and need in ways that make it difficult for others to hear, often making a demand rather than a request. This causes others to react by either ignoring you, making you wrong, only giving you a small portion of what you're asking for, or leaving.

WITH LIFE, YOU:

→ Overgive everywhere as though you have to earn your keep.

→ Fail to set up structures of reciprocity to reap the rewards of your generosity, and are therefore often in deprivation.

Others May Experience You As:

→ Profoundly self-reliant, nondemanding, and "low maintenance."

→ Burdensome, because when you do ask for what you want and need, you tend to do so at inopportune times, in ways that are stressful and demanding, and/or are challenging to fulfill.

→ Burdensome, because when you express your feelings and needs, it's a violation of the unspoken contract between the two of you, which was always about you taking care of them and not the other way around.

→ Burdensome, because of your tendency to give in ways they don't really need and never asked for, and then they feel resentful and compelled to take care of you, as you are taking care of them.

→ Hard to contribute to, feeling rebuffed and shut down by you when they try to give to you.

True You Power Statements

→ *My feelings and needs are reasonable and valid, and it's essential to the well-being of my relationships that I express them in appropriate ways and at appropriate times.*

→ *When I share my feelings and needs in conscious and respectful ways, most people will be receptive and stretch to provide what I need to be well.*

→ *It is important that I respect others enough to assume them to be well enough to care for the needs of others, myself included.*

→ *It's appropriate for me to express my healthy needs openly, and with the expectation that others will do their best to address and accommodate them.*

→ *I recognize that healthy interdependence includes mutual care for the appropriate needs of all involved.*

→ *Meeting my healthy needs helps others to mature.*

New Ways of Relating

WITH YOURSELF, YOU:

→ Are aware of your own internal feelings and hold them with self-compassion and self-love.

→ Prioritize caring for your own healthy needs before caring for the perceived needs of others.

→ Honor your desires by making choices that set you up to receive what you want.

WITH OTHERS, YOU:
→ Ask for what you need when you need it and in open, vulnerable, and sensitive ways that others can hear and respond to positively.
→ Elevate your healthy sense of entitlement to reciprocity in your relationships and express your feelings, needs, and desires freely and honestly.
→ Receive the support, appreciation, and gifts that others offer without needing to immediately reciprocate or one-up them.
→ Give only when giving is needed and don't give when it's not. Wait after giving to see if your generosity is reciprocated before giving again to assess how much to invest in this particular connection.

WITH LIFE, YOU:
→ Raise your expectations of the laws of reciprocity, asking the Universe for what you need and creating space to receive support graciously.

Skills and Capacities to Learn

→ Identify and contain your own feelings, needs, and desires with self-compassion, reassuring yourself that they are not a burden to you.
→ Discern between unhealthy needs born of old wounds versus appropriate and healthy adult needs that foster well-being in your relationships.
→ Expand your capacity to receive, learning to tolerate the vulnerability of being given to without necessarily earning it or reciprocating.
→ Be sensitive to the timing of your requests, noticing the mood of the moment, the resources at hand, the capacity and character of who you are asking, and/or the circumstances you're dealing with.
→ Share what you feel and need in vulnerable ways that allow others to know you and emotionally connect with what you're needing from them.
→ Set boundaries around how much you caretake the needs of others, particularly when they are showing up from a younger, wounded part of themselves and not meeting their own needs.

→ Discern what the true needs are of those around you, making sure to not overgive and overdo, which puts them in the position of having to caretake you as you caretake them.

Gifts

→ You accomplish more than most due to your advanced capacity to hold large levels of responsibility.
→ You're independent, self-reliant, and extremely resourceful.
→ You're not intimidated by big projects and have the capacity to be hugely successful with them.
→ You provide a profound sense of well-being and nourishment for those you care for and give to.

I Am Crazy

~

Source Fracture Story

ABOUT YOURSELF
- → *I am crazy.*
- → *I am confused.*
- → *I can't trust my own perceptions.*

ABOUT OTHERS
- → *Others know what's right for me more than I do.*

ABOUT LIFE
- → *Life is overwhelming and confusing.*

Yourself as Source

WITH YOURSELF, YOU:
- → Continually second-guess your own perceptions and opinions.
- → Dismiss your intuition and take action directly opposed to the inner guidance you're receiving.
- → Are constantly stressed because you often make bad decisions, undermining your ability to feel confident in your own judgment.
- → Are chronically indecisive, which keeps you feeling stuck and debilitated from moving forward.
- → Suffer from debilitating anxiety.

WITH OTHERS, YOU:

→ Become overly dependent on outside professional advice, such as astrologers, therapists, spiritual mentors, and/or psychics.

→ Have difficulty discerning what's real from what's not, particularly as it relates to others. For example, how they feel toward you or the quality of their character. This makes you a potential target of gaslighting.

→ Are very sensitive to nonverbal cues yet uncertain about how to read them accurately.

→ Give your power away to others to tell you what to do, what to think, and what to feel before making a move.

→ Present your ideas and feelings in histrionic and overly dramatic ways.

→ Are so hyperfocused on trying to read others and discern their feelings, needs, and desires that you lose touch with your own.

→ Push others away with your lack of trust in their motives.

WITH LIFE, YOU:

→ Disempower your connection to a Higher Power by negating and dismissing your inner guidance, leaving you on your own to navigate the bigger decisions of life, such as which career to choose or who to marry.

Others May Experience You As:

→ Frustrating, because you can't make up your own mind.

→ Burdensome and irritating, due to the constant need to give you advice and the responsibility of helping you to run your own life.

→ Untrustworthy and not someone they should invest in because you make such bad decisions.

→ Confusing, as they have difficulty following your logic as you tend to think from a highly reactive, emotional, and nonlinear place.

True You Power Statements

→ *I know myself better than anyone and I am the one who is best equipped to know what's right for me.*

→ *I am highly intuitive and I can learn to trust my deeper knowing. I have the ability to discern the voice of fear from the voice of truth within me.*

→ *Just because others question or invalidate my deeper knowing does not mean that my deeper knowing is not accurate.*

→ *I have the ability to question others to get the clarity I need about their motives and intentions so I can make healthy and informed decisions about how to proceed.*

→ *When things are not lining up between what I sense to be true and what others are telling me, I have the ability to discern for myself what I will or won't believe.*

→ *I trust my own perceptions above the perceptions of others.*

→ *I value and celebrate the many ways I see the world differently than others and recognize this unique ability as a source of great creativity and power in my life.*

→ *My unique ways of perceiving the world are a refreshing gift to others.*

New Ways of Relating

WITH YOURSELF, YOU:

→ Seek counsel from your own wise self *before* seeking the counsel of others.

→ Value your own intuitive knowing.

→ Trust yourself to make your own choices. If you make a mistake, recognize that we all make bad decisions sometimes, and that's how we learn and grow.

→ Empower the decisions you've already made by letting go of worrying about paths not taken and roads not traveled.

WITH OTHERS, YOU:

→ Take the advice offered with a grain of salt.

→ Discern the motives and intentions of others before giving them the power to determine your own actions and choices.

→ Enroll them into your own unique and creative way of perceiving the world.

WITH LIFE, YOU:

→ Trust and rely upon your intuition, particularly as it relates to important decisions, and take risks to follow it.

Skills and Capacities to Learn

→ Stop overwhelming others by going to them first to make your choices for you, thereby making them overly responsible for your life. Instead, learn good decision-making strategies, such as assessing pros and cons, recognizing risk-to-reward ratios, and dialoguing with your higher self to hear inner wisdom.

→ Discern the difference between the voice of your own intuition and your more fear-based, anxious, impulsive voice to direct your actions.

→ Increase your ability to hear and trust your own inner guidance by taking risks to act upon it.

→ Appreciate your uniqueness and creativity, learning to value and internally validate your unusual ways of seeing the world.

→ Recognize your own feelings, needs, and desires about any given situation before accommodating the suggestions of others.

→ Express your intentions and visions to others and engage their support and sponsorship to get behind your unique callings and dreams.

Gifts

→ You see things in unique and creative ways.

→ You're an original thinker; a dreamer who lives in a world of positive possibilities and potentials, unconstrained by the limits of the current world in which we live.

→ You recognize possible solutions to challenges that are completely outside the box and currently undetectable to others.

→ You're likely to be artistically gifted.

→ You're highly intuitive, which allows you to know things that others don't yet know.

I Am Damaged Goods

~

Source Fracture Story

ABOUT YOURSELF
- → *I am damaged goods.*
- → *I am broken.*
- → *I am dirty.*

ABOUT OTHERS
- → *Others use and then discard me.*

ABOUT LIFE
- → *There's no hope for me.*

Yourself as Source

WITH YOURSELF, YOU:
- → Give up on yourself easily.
- → Fail to invest in your dreams, desires, and potential.
- → Speak to yourself in shame-based ways and chronically put yourself down.
- → Abuse and do damage to yourself. For example, smoke too much, drink too much, or binge eat.
- → Chronically try to fix yourself by endlessly analyzing why you are the way you are.

WITH OTHERS, YOU:

→ Get involved with unstable, volatile people with poor character and then tolerate abuse from them, often even baiting them to treat you poorly.

→ Fail to set boundaries to adequately protect yourself from being used and abused.

→ Give your power away in order to not be abandoned, which causes others to disrespect you and eventually to leave after they've gotten what they wanted.

→ Convince them that you're screwed up beyond repair and not one to invest in or count on.

→ Humiliate yourself by showing up in ways that are off-putting, needy, and repelling.

→ Reject help when it's offered, pushing it away and/or sabotaging the connection with whoever's offering it.

→ Chronically explain why you are the way you are to try to get others to understand why you do the destructive things you do.

WITH LIFE, YOU:

→ Are more apt to pull the covers over your head than you are to seek the help you need.

→ May compulsively clean your clothes and/or your environment to try to compensate for the assumption that you're dirty.

→ Don't trust the Universe enough to surrender your willfulness to a Higher Power, which would allow the light in.

Others May Experience You As:

→ Frustrating, as you are filled with so much unrealized potential and they can't understand why you are continually self-sabotaging and backsliding.

→ Untrustworthy, as one minute their efforts to help you are received with great gratitude and the next discarded as impotent.

- → A bottomless pit of neediness.
- → A prime target for their abuse.
- → Someone they can take from, then easily discard.

True You Power Statements

- → *I have the power to learn how to create a stable, healthy, successful, and fulfilling life.*
- → *Life is supporting me to fulfill my potential and providing all I need to release the past and become the healed and whole person I am called to become.*
- → *It is safe for me to set boundaries and it's necessary for me to do so for the well-being of all involved.*
- → *Every disappointment is just another helpful lesson learned. With each bump in the road, I am becoming wiser, stronger, and more equipped to live a happy and fulfilling life.*
- → *Life is supporting me to heal my heart, my psyche, and my soul. I have the ability to get the support I need to turn my old pain into a renewed sense of power and purpose.*

New Ways of Relating

WITH YOURSELF, YOU:

- → Treat yourself as though you are someone precious who you love and value.
- → Organize your life around recovery, healing, and transformation.
- → Forgive yourself for mistakes made and destructive roads traveled, keeping only the compassion and wisdom you gained from those experiences.
- → Nurture yourself and protect your well-being in healthy and appropriate ways.

WITH OTHERS, YOU:

- → Reach out for support when you need it from those who are well-equipped to provide it. For example, your therapist or a friend from your twelve-step program.

→ Let go of those who are not healthy enough to treat you well and cocreate safety in your relationship. Either that or you set clear boundaries that are designed to create safety for you both.

→ Show up with respect for yourself and others in all your relationships.

→ Tolerate, accept, and do your best to honor the boundaries that others set with you.

→ Enroll others to invest in your potential and show up in ways that demonstrate your ability to fulfill it. For example, make amends quickly after making a mistake or honor your word with others.

WITH LIFE, YOU:

→ Open yourself up to the life-affirming support that it is offering, remembering that our prayers are usually answered through other imperfect human beings. For example, join a twelve-step program or work with a Future Forward Therapist or one trained in dialectical behavior therapy.

Skills and Capacities to Learn

→ Hold and contain your larger-than-life emotions (including shame) with deep self-compassion, kindness, and love.

→ Self-soothe difficult emotions to bring you back to balance after being triggered.

→ Recognize and validate what you appreciate and love about yourself.

→ Identify all of your feelings and needs as you are experiencing them.

→ Discern your unhealthy needs from your healthy needs and grow a sense of entitlement to have your healthy needs acknowledged and considered by others.

→ Speak to yourself in kind and encouraging ways.

→ Invest in your development in the direction of your dreams.

→ Assess your mistakes and failures objectively, outside of shame and in ways that inspire you to grow.

→ Prioritize doing all you can to give yourself what you need to thrive in life.

→ Tolerate your own imperfections with compassion and without moving into shame.

→ Establish healthy boundaries designed to create well-being and safety in all your relationships.

→ Navigate relational breakdowns and challenges in a mature and contained way.

→ Share hurt feelings in a way that allows for relational repair.

→ Assess the character, capacity, and availability of others before investing too much in the relationship.

→ Create healthy external support structures that you can count on to help stabilize and balance you when you're unable to do so for yourself.

Gifts

→ You're exceptionally compassionate, generous, and kind, especially when it comes to the suffering of those less fortunate than you.

→ You have a deep capacity to feel, which also allows you to be deeply empathetic toward others.

→ You are highly resourceful and able to land on your feet no matter what.

I Am Different

~

Source Fracture Story

ABOUT YOURSELF

→ *I am different.*

→ *I am weird.*

→ *I am a freak.*

ABOUT OTHERS

→ *Others don't get me.*

ABOUT LIFE

→ *There's no place for me in this world.*

→ *I'm not from here.*

Yourself as Source

WITH YOURSELF, YOU:

→ Shame yourself for how different you are, thereby stunting your development as the creative inventor and/or artist you are.

→ Fail to recognize your own extraordinary gifts, which keeps them dormant within you.

WITH OTHERS, YOU:

→ Notice differences between yourself and others far more often than you notice similarities.

→ Flaunt your differentness in a way that's often alienating rather than share yourself in ways that would enroll others into your colorful and unique world.

→ Use your differentness as a defense against getting to know others.

→ Often keep to yourself and make it hard for others to include you.

→ Overcompensate by trying to fit in and pretend to be "normal" when clearly you aren't, which only internally alienates you further.

WITH LIFE, YOU:

→ Fail to create a place for yourself in this world by boldly sharing your unique and creative way of seeing the world.

Others May Experience You As:

→ Off-putting and hard to get to know.

→ Confusing, as they can't tell where you're coming from.

→ On the outside of things.

→ Arrogant and feeling like you're better than they are.

→ Rejecting and judgmental of them for being too normal.

True You Power Statements

→ *I am a pioneer and an innovator. Everything new has come into the world from someone who sees the world just a little bit differently.*

→ *I am refreshingly creative, and my unique ways of being in the world are a gift to all who know me.*

→ *Life uses me as a portal to wake people up to the myriad of possibilities surrounding them.*

→ *I cherish the ways in which I'm different and recognize my unique ways of being in the world as the heart of my creativity and contribution.*

New Ways of Relating

WITH YOURSELF, YOU:

→ Appreciate and accept your own uniqueness unconditionally, assuming that you are the way you are for good reason.

→ Protect and develop your own unique and innovative ideas and plans, recognizing them as a valuable resource to the community at large.

WITH OTHERS, YOU:

→ Connect through your shared humanity and are aware of the many things you do have in common.

→ Enroll others into your unique and colorful way of understanding things and recognize the relevance of your perceptions to their lives.

→ Share in openhearted and vulnerable ways that help others get to know you as a person.

→ Create context for your differences by creating plans, projects, and programs that provide an inspiring framework for others to understand and appreciate who you are.

WITH LIFE, YOU:

→ Recognize yourself as a portal for fresh and innovative ways of relating to reality, partnering with the creative energies of life to bring forth that which is new and original.

Skills and Capacities to Learn

→ Cultivate team-building and enrollment techniques to gather the support you need to birth your unique ideas out into the world.

→ Develop creative visions and frameworks for your out-of-the-box ideas, and in ways where others can find a place for themselves in your big dreams.

→ Pursue forms of artistic expression to provide playing fields for your artistry and self-expression. For example, learn to play piano or take up costume design.

Gifts

→ You're profoundly creative and coded to bring forth that which is brand-new in the world.

→ Even when others can't quite see what you're seeing, you have the fortitude to stick with it until they can.

→ You're a futurist and filled with unique and brilliant visions and dreams.

I Am Disgusting

Source Fracture Story

ABOUT YOURSELF

→ *I am disgusting.*

→ *I am ugly.*

→ *I am gross.*

ABOUT OTHERS

→ *Others are disgusted by me.*

→ *Others are grossed out by me.*

ABOUT LIFE

→ *God has forsaken me.*

→ *Everything I touch turns to sh%#.*

Yourself as Source

WITH YOURSELF, YOU:

→ Fail to take care of your things properly so that they become ratty and rundown.

→ Have basic life habits that are undisciplined and unhealthy. For example, poor eating habits or failing to clean your home on a regular basis.

→ Constantly fear you have bad breath or body odor.

→ Clutter up your work and home environments.

→ Consistently judge yourself harshly and wish you were someone else.

→ Punish and withhold love from yourself for what you consider to be your deviant behavior.

→ Are impulsive, self-indulgent, and prone to doing self-destructive things that lead to feelings of humiliation and shame.

WITH OTHERS, YOU:

→ Disregard their boundaries.

→ Say things that shock people and turn them off. For example, make crude and inappropriate comments or dress in provocative ways that are inappropriate to the situation.

→ May cross the line of your own sexual standards and what you consider to be normal sexual behavior. For example, sleep with several people in one week or fantasize about or even engage in what you consider to be a deviant sexual act.

→ Provoke bad and ugly behavior in them. For example, leading people astray or egging them on to start fighting with you.

→ Set others up to reject and dislike you by being critical of them and con-frontational.

→ Overcompensate by being excessively prudish and rejecting of any hint of intimacy with others—whether that be emotional or physical.

WITH LIFE, YOU:

→ Let opportunities pass you by and fail to follow through on your dreams and callings.

→ Give up before good things can happen.

Others May Experience You As:

→ Volatile, unpredictable, and a little bit dangerous, often in a way that's exciting.

→ A charmer and debaucher who tempts them to act out and misbehave.

→ Someone to have a good time with but not one to commit themselves to.

→ A turnoff to the point of being repulsive.

→ Rejecting and judgmental of their desire for intimacy.

True You Power Statements

→ *I am a child of God (Life, the Universe) and inherently worthy of love, appreciation, and respect.*

→ *I have a beautiful heart and soul, and I show up in ways that reflect and respect this truth.*

→ *I extend unconditional love and care for myself, the things I own, and the environments I'm in.*

→ *I have the power to learn how to hold and contain the parts of me that feel shame with deep love and self-compassion.*

→ *I forgive myself for behaving in ways I feel ashamed of and I pledge to start anew this day.*

→ *I respect others enough to adhere to their boundaries.*

New Ways of Relating

WITH YOURSELF, YOU:

→ Care well for your body, your environment, and the material things you own.

→ Clear out the clutter and create order in your schedule, your closets, your drawers, and in your home and work environments.

→ Talk yourself off the ledge when you have the impulse to do something you know is self-destructive, such as smoke or drink excessively.

→ Are kind and gentle with yourself when you fall off the wagon or make a mistake.

→ Humbly hold yourself accountable to live in integrity with the best you have within you, and to restore integrity quickly whenever you deviate from your own ideals.

WITH OTHERS, YOU:

→ Notice and respect boundaries, both stated and assumed, in order to create enough safety to be close.

→ Create a sense of well-being for yourself and others by behaving in ways appropriate to the circumstances you're in.

→ De-escalate potentially volatile situations and engage in conflict in healthy ways that can deepen the bonds between you.

→ Find healthy ways to deepen your connections, like sharing your vulnerability, listening deeply, and/or expressing your desire for greater acceptance and love.

→ Find dignified and safe ways to express your sacred sensuality and sexuality.

WITH LIFE, YOU:

→ Humbly admit the error of your ways and ask God (Life, the Universe) to forgive you, as well as to help you to live the healthy, productive life you feel called to live.

→ Reclaim your sensuality as a sacred gift.

Skills and Capacities to Learn

→ Self-soothe your big emotions by holding and containing them with kindness and love.

→ Self-mentor when your choices lead you down the wrong path and you need to learn an important life lesson in order to successfully change your ways.

→ Care well for your own basic hygiene and nutrition. For example, schedule regular dental cleanings or eat fruits and vegetables each day.

→ Care well for your own environment. For example, organize your desk so you can easily find what you need or change the sheets of your bed on a regular basis.

→ Learn executive functioning skills to help you better organize your life and your environments.

→ Recognize and create healthy boundaries to keep your relationships clean and healthy.

→ Cultivate a healthy relationship with your own sexuality.

→ Develop conflict resolution skills to de-escalate challenging situations and use differences to deepen understanding between yourself and others.

Gifts

→ You can find beauty in all people, places, and things no matter how ugly they may first appear.

→ You're a pioneer who isn't afraid to challenge the status quo, stretch boundaries, and discover new pathways.

→ You are filled with a life force that ignites and inspires others to see things in new and creative ways.

I Am Not Enough

~

Source Fracture Story

ABOUT YOURSELF

→ *I am not enough.*

→ *I'm not good enough.*

→ *I am inferior.*

→ *I am inadequate.*

ABOUT OTHERS

→ *Others don't value me.*

→ *Others are better than me.*

ABOUT LIFE

→ *I can never do enough to prove my value.*

→ *I never have enough time, money, love, etc.*

Yourself as Source

WITH YOURSELF, YOU:

→ Put yourself on a never-ending treadmill of obligations due to a feeling that you're never doing enough or that you don't yet have enough.

→ Doubt the value of what you offer, chronically feeling that what you bring to the table is lacking and less than what others expect of you.

→ Are a jack-of-all-trades, master of none.

→ Are other-directed, taking your cues from others on how you should feel about yourself.

→ Fail to celebrate your accomplishments, moving from one fulfilled goal to striving for the next without resting or acknowledging a job well done.

WITH OTHERS, YOU:

→ Overgive, overbuy, and overdo everything and with everyone.

→ Endlessly give without regard for reciprocity as a way to try to prove your value.

→ Are overly responsible for the feelings of others, continually tap dancing to try to make them happy.

→ Are excessively self-sacrificing, often martyring yourself at your own expense.

→ Speak in deprecating ways about yourself, even when people are trying to compliment you.

→ Overfunction, as you assume you have to do more to get the same amount of approval and appreciation.

→ Underpresent yourself, failing to make others aware of your unique talents and gifts.

→ Overcommit out of a sense of obligation rather than because it brings you joy.

→ Represent that you'll do more than you're equipped to do, setting others up to mirror back that you're not doing enough.

→ Settle for less than you deserve and desire, and then make others feel as though they're not good enough for you.

WITH LIFE, YOU:

→ Overschedule yourself so that you don't have enough time to fulfill all of your obligations.

→ Spend what you have, generating debt and creating a feeling of being financially indebted and enslaved.

→ Have a tendency to fill your space with too much stuff out of a fear that you won't have enough.

Others May Experience You As:

→ Someone who is always available to them, often having unhealthy expectations and demands on your time and attention.

→ Untrustworthy, as you often fail to fulfill the excessive promises you make, leaving others feeling frustrated and irritated with you much of the time.

→ Subservient, feeling entitled to have you do more for less reward.

→ Devaluing of *them*, feeling that no matter how much they do to show their love and support, it's somehow never enough.

→ Disappointed in them, as though you're settling in your relationship with them.

→ Critical of them, feeling that they are never enough for you.

True You Power Statements

→ *I am neither inferior nor superior to anyone. We are all unique expressions of Divine Love.*

→ *Others will value me to the extent that I value myself.*

→ *My very existence is more than enough to be worthy of great love and respect.*

→ *I need do nothing to prove my value.*

→ *It's not my job to make other people happy. The feelings of others are their responsibility, not mine.*

→ *The only one I need to compare myself with is my former self.*

New Ways of Relating

WITH YOURSELF, YOU:

→ Connect with your own feelings and needs to make sure you actually want to do something and have the time and energy to give, before you say yes.

→ Notice which obligations feed your energy and which ones drain it, keeping only those commitments that inspire you or that you're truly obligated to keep. For example, volunteering at your church or getting up early to take your kids to school.

WITH OTHERS, YOU:

→ Practice setting limits and saying no when you're not lit up by the requests of others or you feel deep down they are not yours to do.
→ Negotiate for what you want and need to make sure it works for you before agreeing to take something on.
→ Are realistic and pragmatic when representing what you can and cannot do with the time and resources you have.
→ Speak about yourself in ways that are self-respecting and self-honoring.
→ Present your gifts and talents accurately so that others understand the value of what you have to offer.
→ Set higher standards for those you let into your life and stop settling for less.

WITH LIFE, YOU:

→ Create more spaciousness and downtime in your schedule.
→ Practice gratitude for all that you are, all that you do, and all that you have.
→ Do less to enjoy the simple pleasures more.
→ Clear clutter from your home and work environments, keeping only what you love, need, and/or value.
→ Create fiscal well-being by appreciating what you already have, by living within your means, and by saving a portion of your income.

Skills and Capacities to Learn

→ Know what you feel at any given moment.
→ Differentiate your feelings from your thoughts in order to self-soothe difficult feelings. For example: *I feel anxious* (a feeling) versus *I feel like I should be doing more* (a thought).
→ Know what you need at any given moment and strive to honor your own needs first and foremost.

→ Tolerate the anxiety that can come up when disappointing others by saying no or setting a boundary.

→ Know your limits and communicate them effectively.

→ Set boundaries around how much you expect of yourself.

→ Set appropriate boundaries around how much others should expect of you.

→ Assess the market value of what you have to offer and create structures to be compensated accordingly.

→ Negotiate for your needs, making sure to create agreements that take your needs into account, as well as the needs of others.

→ Cultivate mutuality and reciprocity in your adult relationships.

→ Raise your healthy sense of entitlement to include other adults accommodating you in the ways you do for them.

→ Recognize how to request and receive greater support and love.

→ Declutter your environment.

→ Create fiscal health and well-being.

Gifts

→ You're profoundly generous and take pleasure in sharing freely with others.

→ You provide a sense of abundance for others.

→ You're good at many things, having cultivated many different skills and talents.

→ You're a "can-do" person who inspires others with a sense of possibility.

I Am a Failure

~

Source Fracture Story

ABOUT YOURSELF:

→ *I am a failure.*

→ *I am a loser.*

→ *I am a disappointment.*

→ *I am a screwup.*

→ *I am a mess.*

ABOUT OTHERS

→ *Others are disappointed in me.*

→ *Others are a disappointment to me.*

→ *Others look down on me.*

ABOUT LIFE

→ *Life is a disappointment.*

→ *Life lets me down.*

→ *Life sets me up to fail.*

Yourself as Source

WITH YOURSELF, YOU:

→ Hop from one thing to another and give up at the first sign of failure rather than use failure as useful feedback and a helpful learning tool.

→ Beat yourself up mercilessly when you make a mess or screw something up, which prevents you from growing from the experience.

→ Fail to give yourself the support and the structures you need to succeed in life.

→ Frequently break your word to yourself, letting yourself down time and time again.

→ Create chaos in your environment.

WITH OTHERS, YOU:

→ Let people down in key moments by not coming through for them, disappointing them time and time again, and un-enrolling them in your potential.

→ Procrastinate to the point of self-sabotage and fail to make the most of your opportunities.

→ Overpromise and underperform, setting others up to be disappointed in you.

→ Frequently break your word to people and then feel disappointed in them when they stop investing in their relationship with you.

WITH LIFE, YOU:

→ Have magical thinking and unrealistic expectations, failing to realize what it takes to build a successful life.

→ Quit or stick your head in the sand when things get difficult rather than rise to the occasion by figuring out ways to make it work.

Others May Experience You As:

→ Frustrating, because they see how successful you could be if you only tried harder.

→ A big disappointment, as you so often don't come through for them when they need you to.

→ A bad investment.

True You Power Statements

→ *What matters is not how often I make a mess and screw things up, but how often I learn from my mistakes and become a wiser, more mature person because of them.*

→ *Failing at something does not mean I'm a failure. The only failure is to not learn and grow from the experience of failing.*

→ *We learn just as much or more from our failures as we do from our successes. I am a great learner and trust myself to put what I'm learning to good use moving forward.*

→ *Just because I feel ashamed does not mean that I have anything to be ashamed of. I am a gifted, talented, intelligent person who is capable and worthy of great success.*

→ *I commit to actualizing my potential fully and am deeply devoted to manifesting the success I well deserve.*

New Ways of Relating

WITH YOURSELF, YOU:

→ Make empowered meaning of failure, recognizing it as a normal part of the learning curve when creating something new.

→ Are kind and encouraging to yourself when you make a mistake or fail to accomplish something that is important to you.

→ Set yourself up for success by creating the structures you'll need to stay on track. For example, hire a trainer or work with a business coach.

→ Hold yourself accountable to keep your word to yourself or to renegotiate it if you're unable to.

→ Create order, cleanliness, and balance in your environment.

WITH OTHERS, YOU:

→ Show up for those who matter in your life when they need you.

→ Make the most of the opportunities that come your way.

→ Set realistic expectations of what others can expect of you, and when, and execute accordingly.

→ Keep your word, and if you're unable to, let others know and renegotiate what you will or will not do and by when.

WITH LIFE, YOU:

→ Assume that life is on the side of your success and you aren't afraid to work hard and take risks to bring that success to fruition.

→ Trust in the process of life and look for the inherent potential for growth and innovation in every problem and breakdown you face.

Skills and Capacities to Learn

→ Mentor yourself with encouraging self-talk to get you through the tough times and to build your confidence, character, and enthusiasm to keep moving forward no matter what.

→ Cultivate resilience in the face of disappointments, setbacks, and delays.

→ Stay generative of the future you're committed to in response to disappointments, setbacks, and delays.

→ Learn what it takes to launch something new into the world and patiently build what you're called to create.

→ Clear the air after failing to keep your word to someone in a way that restores integrity between you.

→ Raise your expectations of what you have the power to accomplish in life.

Gifts

→ You're a dreamer with big and beautiful dreams.

→ You think outside the box and are highly imaginative.

→ You're an innovator, seeing potential and possibility that others can't yet see.

I Am Not Important

~

Source Fracture Story

ABOUT YOURSELF

→ *I am not important.*

→ *I am not heard.*

ABOUT OTHERS

→ *Others underestimate me.*

→ *Others don't hear me.*

ABOUT LIFE

→ *I have to grab attention if I want to be heard.*

Yourself as Source

WITH YOURSELF, YOU:

→ Make mountains out of molehills, getting all worked up and making a big deal out of relatively small matters. In other words, you make things more important than they actually are and then obsess about them.

WITH OTHERS, YOU:

→ Overtalk your perspective to the point of exhaustion, as you're not reading the room to notice when others have heard you and received what you're saying.

→ Take ten minutes to say something that could have been said in one.

→ Consistently fail to have the kind of impact you want to be having inside of being a one-person band and failing to collaborate well with others.

→ Need to be the most important person in the room to feel like you're a part of what's happening. For example, director of the project or leader of the group.

→ Disappear into yourself when you're not a designated important person in the group, as you feel invisible and devalued.

→ Love to be the celebrated hero who swoops in to rescue those in need.

→ Have friends in high places, surrounding yourself with "important" people who are having an impact in the world.

→ Speak your truth in ways that cause others to marginalize or dismiss you, or to stop listening entirely. For example, by rambling or issuing a command or a complaint.

→ Speak in conclusions that leave little room for negotiation, collaboration, or a deepening of understanding between yourself and others.

WITH LIFE, YOU:

→ Play too small as a way to ensure that you're the most important person in the room. For example, lead a team of two rather than join a team of two hundred.

Others May Experience You As:

→ Long-winded, often zoning out when you speak because you take so long to get to the point.

→ Exhausting, due to your constant big reactions to what, for them, occurs as small and relatively insignificant details.

→ Frustrating, because of your inability to adjust your behavior after people have given you feedback, as you are convinced that you must do things your way.

→ Non-collaborative, as you come to conclusions about how things should be done without others' input.

→ Confusing, as people have a hard time tracking what you're saying due to all of the superfluous details you include when sharing.

True You Power Statements

→ *I am a valuable and equal member of the team, with or without a designated leadership role to play.*

→ *I am open to discovering the feelings, needs, knowledge, and perspectives of others to help inform the conclusions I come to.*

→ *I am appreciated and richly rewarded for my important and meaningful contributions to others.*

→ *Collaboration with others who share a similar mission and vision increases the impact of my contributions to the world.*

→ *I can say what needs to be said in half the time by leaving out superfluous details and by focusing on the most important points I wish to convey.*

New Ways of Relating

WITH YOURSELF, YOU:

→ Calm down when you find yourself getting all worked up over relatively small matters.

→ Recognize and validate the significance of who you are and what you have to offer internally, without the constant need for external validation from others.

WITH OTHERS, YOU:

→ Are aware of your listener as you speak and notice their level of attention, understanding, and interest in what you are saying before continuing.

→ Focus on the point of what you wish to say rather than include all of the superficial details in order to be heard more clearly.

→ Speak in ways that invite input from others. For example, ask questions, make suggestions, and ask for feedback before coming to conclusions.

→ Are a good team player, comfortable being "one among many" when not the designated leader or given a clearly defined role.

→ Share leadership, aware that more than one of you gets to be the important person in the room at the same time.

→ Assess the true value of your offerings with modesty, neither overvaluing nor undervaluing your contributions.

WITH LIFE, YOU:

→ Recognize that you are inherently significant in this world and allow the creative energies of life to flow freely through you, without being overly concerned with credit or social positioning.

Skills and Capacities to Learn

→ Put things in perspective and self-soothe when you find yourself getting all worked up over small matters.

→ Communicate your feelings, needs, perspectives, and desires in ways that allow others to think with you and come to joint conclusions.

→ Communicate your point in clear, concise, and succinct ways that others can hear.

→ Listen to what's not being said, becoming more aware of the nonverbal cues that let you know when others have heard enough and are starting to zone out.

→ Be in a collaborative dialogue with others, not just the director who alone decides how things will be.

→ Share leadership without feeling diminished because you are not the only one deciding how things will be.

Gifts

→ You are gifted at highlighting the voices of those who've been marginalized and oppressed, making sure their message is heard and featured as an important part of the collective conversation.

→ You spotlight the importance of certain issues and problems that have not received the attention they deserve.

→ You make others feel important, particularly those who have felt unheard, invisible, or undervalued.

→ You are a seasoned director, creating direction and safety for others due to your clear vision and certainty of how things should go.

I Am Invisible

~

Source Fracture Story

ABOUT YOURSELF
- → *I am invisible.*
- → *I don't exist.*

ABOUT OTHERS
- → *Others don't care about me.*
- → *Others are selfish.*

ABOUT LIFE
- → *It's dangerous to be seen.*

Yourself as Source

WITH YOURSELF, YOU:
- → Dismiss and minimize your feelings, needs, and desires to the point where you don't even know what they are.
- → Second-guess and undermine your own thoughts and opinions when swayed by those with charismatic personalities.

WITH OTHERS, YOU:
- → Have your first attention on them, making their feelings and needs more important than your own and training them to be self-involved in the process.

→ Rarely share your feelings, needs, and desires even when you know what they are.

→ Deflect attention away from yourself by redirecting conversations to keep the focus off of you. For example: "Oh, I'm fine but tell me, *how are you?*"

→ Ask for what you want and need in covertly hostile ways due to the assumption that others don't care about you, which alienates them and causes them to validate your assumption.

→ Fail to support the fulfillment of your own dreams while providing excessive support to fulfill their dreams.

→ Chronically engage in selfless service to the point of exhaustion and depletion.

→ Do for them what they could and should be doing for themselves.

→ Leave the relationship when you don't get what you need, with little warning and without explanation, assuming they won't even notice when you're gone.

→ Resent them for not intuitively knowing what you feel and need, since you're so good at intuiting their feelings and needs.

→ Create relationships where there is only one of you in the room. In some relationships, you're the visible one and in others, the invisible one.

→ Misrepresent how you feel and what you think by a lack of transparency in your facial expression and body language, making it easy for others to misinterpret or miss what you're saying. For example, smile when telling someone you're upset with them or look down and speak softly when setting an important boundary.

WITH LIFE, YOU:

→ Source safety by disappearing yourself, almost as though you were a vapor or a ghost, which energetically leaves you unprotected and vulnerable to predators.

Others May Experience You As:

→ An appendage of themselves. It doesn't even occur to them to ask what you feel or need. They simply assume you'll go along with whatever they prefer.

→ Someone they love being with because they feel puffed up when they're with you—special, important, and seen.

→ Very likable, as you rarely demand that others take their attention off themselves.

→ Out of line when you do decide to ask for what you want and need, as it's a violation of the unspoken contract between you—that your relationship is about their needs, not yours.

→ Someone devoid of feelings, needs, aspirations, or desires of your own.

→ Confusing and hurtful, if and when you leave the relationship without warning or explanation.

True You Power Statements

→ *I came here to be seen. It is my destiny to be visible in the world and it is up to me to share my authentic self with others.*

→ *The more I share my feelings, needs, and desires, the more I give others a chance to demonstrate that they care about me.*

→ *The best way to assess how much others care about me is to assume they do, to share my feelings and my needs, then see how they respond.*

→ *I recognize, honor, and anticipate my own needs and create agreements, circumstances, and structures for their fulfillment.*

→ *I am here as a force of nature, destined to have an impact for good in the world around me.*

→ *I invest in the fulfillment of my own dreams and desires with as much devotion as I've invested in the dreams and desires of others.*

→ *I make sure that my body language and my facial expressions are congruent and aligned with the words I speak and what I wish to convey.*

New Ways of Relating

WITH YOURSELF, YOU:

→ Put your first attention on yourself, so that you are always aware of your own feelings, needs, preferences, and desires at any given moment.

WITH OTHERS, YOU:

→ Risk sharing your feelings, needs, and desires from the start to discern someone's capacity for mutuality and to discover which connections to invest more in and which to keep at bay.

→ Assume they are interested in knowing your feelings, needs, and desires, and share them freely, giving others a chance to demonstrate their interest and care.

→ Articulate your thoughts and preferences with everyone, even those who do not have ears to hear or eyes to see. Do this simply as an affirmation that you exist and are worthy of being heard and seen.

→ Good-naturedly make your thoughts and opinions known, particularly when they differ from the thoughts and opinions of others.

→ Anticipate your own needs and negotiate on your own behalf.

→ Ask for support to fulfill your own dreams and callings.

→ Let others know clearly what you want in return for your support, loyalty, and love.

WITH LIFE, YOU

→ Create structures that support you to fulfill your dreams and desires and to set limits on how much support you provide for others.

→ Expand your circle of care and your commitment to others in a way that inspires you to outgrow shyness or any impulse you have to hide your gifts.

Skills and Capacities to Learn

→ Identify the nuances of what you are feeling and needing such that you are able to acknowledge them to yourself at all times.

→ Assess the support and structures you'll need to fulfill your callings, creativity, and contributions, and to prioritize creating them.

→ Articulate your feelings clearly and in ways that give people a chance to know you and to see you as separate from themselves.

→ Name and negotiate your own needs with others, making them visible and clear.

→ Ask for what you want in ways that inspire others to want to give these things to you.

→ Tolerate disappointing or irritating others by saying no when no is the appropriate response.

→ Create healthy, clear boundaries that honor what you realistically have to give and what you don't.

→ Give others the benefit of the doubt when they fail to intuit what you feel and need as you so easily do for them, recognizing that your ability to do this is a special gift most people don't have.

→ Assess the capacity of others to give you what you need to thrive and be well in life, and create agreements accordingly, making sure to not overly invest in those who have little to give.

→ Practice "twoness" in your relationships, recognizing there are two of you here, each with your own distinct way of seeing and experiencing the world, which may be quite different and unique.

Gifts

→ You have an amazing capacity to read what's between the lines and to understand what's not being said.

→ You're highly creative and able to see possibilities and potentials that are not yet visible to others.

→ You possess an exceptional ability to help others due to your highly developed capacity for insight, empathy, perception, and discernment.

→ You create healing and well-being for people due to your highly developed capacity to see into and mirror them so accurately.

I Am Not Loved

~

Source Fracture Story

ABOUT YOURSELF

→ *I am not loved.*

→ *I am unlovable.*

ABOUT OTHERS

→ *Others don't care about me.*

→ *No one loves me.*

ABOUT LIFE

→ *Life is empty and devoid of comfort and care.*

Yourself as Source

WITH YOURSELF, YOU:

→ Are disconnected from what you want and need to thrive in life.

→ Deprive yourself and neglect your needs and desires. For example, forget to eat or drink water or live in a home that's furnished with hand-me-downs you don't like.

→ Fail to give love and care to yourself. For example, don't engage in self-care rituals and routines like washing your face before bedtime or speak to yourself in belittling, unkind ways when you're discouraged.

→ Don't create support structures that would help you to thrive in life. For example, don't go back to school to get the training and credentials you'd need to do your dream job.

→ Organize your days around simple survival rather than flourishing, creating a barren existence devoid of what makes life joyful and colorful. For example, fail to schedule time for fun or don't ever take vacations.

WITH OTHERS, YOU:

→ Look for love and affirmation in all the wrong places and in ways that ensure you will not get it. For example, stay in relationships with narcissistic people or tolerate being chronically taken advantage of in your job.

→ Are incredibly giving and loving, yet love is often a one-way street, as they do not necessarily give to you what you give to them.

→ Rarely ask for what you want and need to thrive in life, not knowing what that is and hoping others will just figure it out and provide it, which they rarely do.

→ Borrow against your own needs, sacrificing them for the perceived wants and needs of others.

→ Stay in relationships with people who fail to meet your needs and/or stay in deprived situations that fail to nourish and support your well-being in life.

→ Sadly wait on the sidelines for others to invite you in rather than generate your own participation and belonging in social situations.

WITH LIFE, YOU:

→ Have low expectations of what's yours to experience in life and in love.

→ Assume that God (Life, the Universe) doesn't care about or support you to fully thrive, and therefore you fail to set intentions where you go for the highest and best that life and love have to offer.

Others May Experience You As:

→ Needy, as you seem to want more from them then they're willing to give.

→ Unworthy of their time, attention, and love.

→ An afterthought; someone they can easily neglect or fail to support, even when you ask for it.

→ A bit of a doormat, as they can count on you to give love and loyalty to them even if they are not loving or loyal to you, and even when they treat you badly.

True You Power Statements

→ *I came here to love and be loved. I have the power to learn how to create loving and mutually satisfying relationships that deepen and grow over time.*

→ *I am lovable just as I am. I accept all parts of myself as worthy of love.*

→ *I choose to love myself today and make caring for myself my top priority.*

→ *I commit to giving myself the supportive structures I'll need to fully thrive in life.*

→ *I am deeply loved by God (Life, the Universe), and I open myself to receive the continual stream of love coming to me always, and in the many ways it's given.*

→ *My worthiness to receive love is inherent in who I am. I need do nothing to prove that I am worthy of love.*

New Ways of Relating

WITH YOURSELF, YOU:

→ Love and care for yourself unconditionally, acknowledging and accepting even those parts of yourself you don't particularly like.

→ Create systems and structures that support you to realize your higher potentials in life.

→ Do things to nourish your heart, body, and soul. For example, take walks in nature, read books you love, listen to music that moves you, spend time with people you like, invest in cooking nutritious and delicious meals.

WITH OTHERS, YOU:

→ Either end relationships once it's clear your healthy needs for consideration, care, and respect will not be met or lessen your investment in the connection.

→ Create structures and situations that allow you to share the big love you have in that huge heart of yours in healthy and wholesome ways. For example, become a professional healer, create a block party that brings neighbors together, or volunteer at a local food bank.

→ Receive love from others in the ways they offer it, even if it's not exactly what you were hoping for.

→ Communicate your healthy needs clearly so that others know what they can give you to feel safe, happy, and cared for.

→ Are aware of the flow between how much you give and how much you receive, to ensure healthy mutuality. If you notice you're giving more than you're receiving, you lower your investment in the connection.

WITH LIFE, YOU:

→ Raise your expectations of what's possible to have and experience in life and in love.

→ Set your sights high and go for the gold by setting powerful intentions that can pull you forward into a fruitful, happy, and productive life.

Skills and Capacities to Learn

→ Identify what you want, what you like, what brings you pleasure, and what nourishes your heart, soul, and body.

→ Identify your own feelings and needs and learn to turn toward them and tend to them on a regular basis, with deep compassion, kindness, and care.

→ Discern between your unhealthy needs that are sourced from old wounding and your healthy needs and grow a sense of entitlement to have your healthy needs considered and met. For example, "I need to be the only person you care about" versus "I need for my feelings to be taken into account and cared for."

→ Share your feelings and needs in generative ways that others can hear and positively respond to. For example, make a request versus a demand or speak about what you do want versus just voicing your complaints.

→ Tolerate the anxiety that comes up when you stop giving extra love in response to others giving too little. Just breathe through the awkward gap that can inform you how much to continue investing in this relationship.

Gifts

→ You have a huge, kind, and compassionate heart.

→ You're exceptionally generous with your love, lavishing care on others with great joy.

→ You give others a sense of being cared for and loved in ways that are deeply healing to them.

→ You inspire others to follow your lead by giving love more generously to themselves and others.

I Don't Matter

~

Source Fracture Story

ABOUT YOURSELF
- → *I don't matter.*
- → *I am nothing.*

ABOUT OTHERS
- → *Others matter more than I do.*

ABOUT LIFE
- → *My life doesn't really matter and is insignificant to the world at large.*

Yourself as Source

WITH YOURSELF, YOU:
- → Dismiss your own feelings, treating them as though they're nothing and don't matter.
- → Are unaware that you even have needs, let alone able to identify and tend to them.
- → Speak to and about yourself in diminishing and dismissive ways.
- → Downplay your accomplishments and rarely acknowledge or celebrate your successes in life.
- → Overwork, ignoring and sacrificing your own well-being in the process.

→ Neglect your own dreams as you immerse yourself in making the dreams of others come true.

WITH OTHERS, YOU:

→ Rarely share your true feelings and needs, yet you're acutely aware of and even anticipate the feelings and needs of others.

→ Fail to set boundaries that would keep you healthy, well, and safe in the relationship.

→ Compulsively provide everything others want and need to try to keep the connection, which trains people that their needs matter more than yours.

→ Underrepresent your true talents and gifts while making sure that the talents and gifts of others get lots of recognition.

→ Abdicate your power of choice by letting others choose for you.

→ Invest in relationships with people who have things happening in their lives that matter more than you.

→ Withhold your ideas and opinions in social gatherings or are the last to speak up, only to just agree with what's already been said, assuming the ideas and opinions of others matter more to the discussion.

→ Make yourself indispensable in order to prove that you matter.

→ Let them down because you fail to show up for things you've committed to inside of assuming that your presence is inconsequential and doesn't matter.

WITH LIFE, YOU:

→ Fail to do what's needed to bring your own callings to fruition inside of assuming that nothing you do will ever really matter.

Others May Experience You As:

→ Unmemorable, often forgetting to include you in things you should be included in due to how skillfully you disappear and downplay yourself.

→ Relatively easy to have around, since you're so low maintenance, with so few needs.

→ Not someone to invest too much in. For example, they don't marry you or they don't hire you as an employee.

True You Power Statements

→ *My feelings and needs matter. They matter to me, and it's appropriate for me to expect them to matter to those I'm in a relationship with.*
→ *I am here to have a significant and meaningful impact on the world. My life, and what I give myself to, matters.*
→ *Who I am being matters and impacts any and every room I enter.*
→ *Every action I take, and every choice I make, has a significant impact on others.*

New Ways of Relating

WITH YOURSELF, YOU:

→ Check in with yourself to identify and tend to your own feelings and needs first and foremost, affirming their validity and importance.
→ Speak to yourself in loving, kind, and respectful ways.
→ Celebrate your accomplishments and successes in life.
→ Take time to rest, play, and replenish your energy.
→ Prioritize your own dreams and callings and give yourself the training, resources, and support you'll need to realize them.
→ Live a life that you choose rather than a life that is expected of you.

WITH OTHERS, YOU:

→ Share your feelings and needs with a healthy sense of entitlement that they should matter to those you're in a relationship with.
→ Negotiate your needs so that your relationships are healthy and mutual and include the needs of all involved.
→ Set healthy boundaries to keep yourself happy, well, and safe in your relationships.
→ Include your needs in any negotiation of needs with others.

→ Share your gifts and talents freely, making the value of them visible to others.

→ Join in social discussions, freely sharing your ideas and opinions.

→ Show up for things you've committed to inside of assuming that your presence does indeed matter.

WITH LIFE, YOU:

→ Prioritize the pursuit of your callings and dreams, saying no to what others want and need from you when it interferes with your own agenda.

Skills and Capacities to Learn

→ Know what you're feeling at any given moment.

→ Identify and validate your healthy needs. For example, *I need my feelings and needs to matter to those I'm in a relationship with.*

→ Expand your healthy sense of entitlement to have your feelings and needs validated and honored by others.

→ Express your feelings and needs in ways that others can hear and understand.

→ Negotiate with others so that you can come to agreements that meet your respective needs.

→ Develop social skills to join in community conversations.

→ Tolerate your own anxiety when saying no and setting limits with others.

Gifts

→ You're exceedingly generous and always ready with a helping hand.

→ You're a tireless worker bee and able to accomplish massive amounts of good.

→ You're highly intuitive and sensitive to the feelings and needs of others.

→ You're humble and willing to do whatever it takes to get the job done, without needing to draw much attention to yourself.

I Am Powerless

~

Source Fracture Story

ABOUT YOURSELF

→ *I am powerless.*

→ *I am small.*

→ *I am helpless.*

ABOUT OTHERS

→ *Others are more powerful than I am.*

ABOUT LIFE

→ *Nothing I say or do holds any weight in this world.*

Yourself as Source

WITH YOURSELF, YOU:

→ Invalidate your own perspectives and opinions.

→ Devalue your own credentials and accomplishments.

→ Collapse physically and demonstrate a sense of deflation in your body language with hunched shoulders, a lack of eye contact, or a head held low.

→ Do just the opposite to compensate by buffing up at the gym or doing things like competing in triathlons.

WITH OTHERS, YOU:

→ Give your power away to others to make important decisions about your life for you.

→ Have a high tolerance for verbal and emotional abuse.

→ Accept and adopt the perspectives and preferences of others without asserting your own.

→ Ride the coattails of others, giving them responsibility for your happiness and success in life.

→ Passively wait for others to solve your problems.

→ Silently adhere to the rules that others set, even when they feel wrong to you.

→ Pretend that others have your best interests at heart, even when you suspect that they're using you to their own advantage.

→ Fail to set boundaries that might offend or upset others.

→ Complain about the situations you find yourself in, yet fail to take concrete and generative actions to change things.

→ Underpresent your intelligence, competence, accomplishments, and abilities.

WITH LIFE, YOU:

→ Resist the call to leadership, preferring to empower the leadership of others over asserting your own.

Others May Experience You As:

→ An easy target for gaslighting, as you empower their perspectives over your own.

→ A good second-in-command, as you're so trustworthy that you do their bidding without questioning their authority.

→ Excessively loyal, no matter how self-serving and/or amoral their actions may be.

→ Someone they can easily dismiss and silence if and when you do have the courage to speak up with an opinion that differs from their own.

True You Power Statements

→ *I am willing to be responsible for my own success and happiness in life.*

→ *I am responsible for my own choices and actions in life. It's my job to live in alignment with my own sense of what's right and what's wrong.*

→ *My perspectives and opinions are valid and worthy of consideration, even when others attack, dismiss, or devalue them.*

→ *My actions have agency. I have the power to impact any and all situations I find myself in for the better.*

→ *I am a leader of goodness, light, and love. It's my privilege to lead by empowering others to live happy, healthy lives and to cocreate a happier, healthier world.*

New Ways of Relating

WITH YOURSELF, YOU:

→ Take full responsibility for your own happiness and success in life.

→ Treat your feelings and needs as though they matter.

→ Validate and value your own perspectives and opinions, investing in and exploring them more deeply by researching and developing them fully.

→ Celebrate your credentials and accomplishments. For example, put your degrees up on the wall, brag about yourself in appropriate moments, and make sure to create a bio that reflects how accomplished you are.

→ Stand tall with shoulders back, look people in the eye when speaking, and hold your own physically in any and all spaces you occupy.

→ Proactively solve your own problems, showing up with agency and intentionality.

WITH OTHERS, YOU:

→ Lower your tolerance for their bad behavior and set clear boundaries and/or leave toxic situations.

→ Listen to their perspectives and preferences and assert your own as well.

→ Challenge the rules that they set when those rules seem unfair or inappropriate to you.

→ Engage your concerns about their potentially unwholesome motives directly with them.

→ Are willing to adhere to boundaries that protect your well-being and safety, even if others become angry and/or make you wrong for it.

→ Take generative actions to better any and all unhealthy or disempowering situations you find yourself in.

→ Own your intelligence, competence, accomplishments, and abilities everywhere you are and with everyone you're with.

WITH LIFE, YOU:

→ Grow your leadership abilities and are willing to lead in the ways you're called to, whether or not others sanction your leadership.

Skills and Capacities to Learn

→ Hold your own center in the face of someone else's projections, which may idealize you and/or devalue you.

→ Know yourself and your own perspectives, preferences, and opinions.

→ Hold sacred your own mission and cultivate your intuition to find your way to the fulfillment of your calling.

→ Discern abusive behavior and set firm boundaries to curb it.

→ Stay generative of a positive, possible future in the midst of breakdowns.

→ Develop strong leadership skills.

→ Engage in conflict directly and in generative and healthy ways.

→ Negotiate healthy boundaries to keep yourself and others safe.

Gifts

→ You are a powerful leader who is here to inspire and elevate the masses.

→ You understand the difference between holding power *over* others versus holding power *with* others to empower the highest and best for all involved, which makes you a trustworthy leader.

→ You have the capacity to be highly creative and generative in how you respond to breakdowns.

I Am Not Safe

~

Source Fracture Story

ABOUT YOURSELF
- → *I am not safe.*
- → *I am in danger.*

ABOUT OTHERS
- → *Others have ill intent.*
- → *Others will hurt me.*

ABOUT LIFE
- → *It's dangerous to let others get too close.*
- → *Life is unpredictable and scary.*

Yourself as Source

WITH YOURSELF, YOU:
- → Avoid taking care of yourself in ways that would ensure your well-being and safety. For example, drive an unsafe car, don't sign up for health insurance, or overspend so you are living paycheck to paycheck with no financial safety net.
- → Take huge, largely uncalculated, and often reckless risks.
- → Are highly reactive to stories you hear about trauma and violence, feeling as though what is happening to others is happening to you. For

example, can't watch the news or read a newspaper without getting emotionally upset.

→ Have your primary relationships with animals because they are so much safer than people.

WITH OTHERS, YOU:

→ Are love avoidant, as you assume that close, committed relationships will take *from* you rather than give *to* you.

→ Fail to take appropriate precautionary and protective measures before entering into agreements and/or relationships.

→ Disclose personal information before the relationship has been properly established.

→ Are overly idealistic and naive, which sets you up to feel hurt, disillusioned, and disappointed when they fail to live up to your unrealistic expectations and overly optimistic assumptions.

→ Complain to and/or attack them instead of making clear requests or setting boundaries for what you need to feel well and safe.

→ Get involved with them too quickly, without taking the time to get to know their character before becoming intimately entangled in their lives or involving them in yours.

→ Create push-pull dynamics in your intimate relationships due to your tendency to destabilize connections when others get too close.

→ Are hypervigilant and highly reactive, perceiving much of what others say as a potential threat.

→ Bring out the worst in them due to your high levels of mistrust and defensiveness, leading them to behave in ways that may be uncharacteristic of them.

→ Are a target for con artists, sociopaths, and perpetrators due to how easily you give trust before it is earned.

→ Are overly trusting and generous before they have earned your trust and generosity.

WITH LIFE, YOU:

→ Relate to obstacles, disappointments, and breakdowns as though they're evidence of how unsafe life is rather than recognizing them as here to help you grow wiser, stronger, more resilient, and more mature.

Others May Experience You As:

→ Defensive and difficult, frequently feeling attacked by your intense reactions to things that seem ordinary, routine, or even mundane to them.

→ Unapproachable and prickly, often feeling as though they are walking on eggshells around you.

→ Hyperactively reactive.

→ Volatile and unpredictable.

→ Someone they tend to hurt in ways they don't usually hurt people. For example, they fear setting you off, and so they withhold the truth even though they don't normally lie—yet you find out and feel justified and vindicated in your initial lack of trust.

→ Someone they can never win with.

True You Power Statements

→ *I have the power to learn how to keep myself and others safe. I am the source of safety.*

→ *I ask the questions I need to ask to assess the level of risk involved and to make wise and informed decisions about my own safety.*

→ *The more I am willing to set healthy, clear boundaries, the more I am able to deconstruct the walls I've built around me.*

→ *The more I recognize and negotiate for my needs, the safer it is to let others into my life.*

→ *I trust others to the extent that they demonstrate their ability to show up with integrity and to grow trust between us.*

→ *I choose to have faith in the overall goodness of life. I choose to trust that life has my back, even when I am facing uncertainty.*

New Ways of Relating

WITH YOURSELF, YOU:

→ Create safety nets for yourself. For example, take proper care of your car, make sure you're adequately insured, save a portion of your income.

→ Assess risks before jumping into things too quickly.

→ Create strong psychic boundaries so that you can stay present with what's happening in the world without taking other people's traumas into your own body.

→ Create energetic boundaries around your physical self that covertly signal others to respect your space.

→ Stay connected to your own inner experience to recognize when you feel safe and when you don't, and identify what you would need to restore a sense of safety.

WITH OTHERS, YOU:

→ Share clearly what you need to feel comfortable and safe, and you negotiate for what you know you need to be okay. For example, "I need to not rush into sex" or "I need a written agreement before loaning you money."

→ Pace yourself and take your time to get to know someone's character before becoming entangled with them financially, romantically, sexually, or legally.

→ Share intimate information about yourself only after trust has been established over a period of time.

→ Are clear about agreements and expectations, renegotiating them when necessary and cleaning up any inconsistencies that might create a lack of safety in the connection.

→ Manage your own reactivity and defensiveness to cultivate greater well-being and stability in your relationships.

→ Have balanced and realistic expectations that include both the positive and the not-so-positive behaviors you might anticipate from them.

→ Make requests and/or set healthy boundaries for what you need to feel well and safe in your relationships.

→ Pay attention to your own intuition, asking questions to clarify your gut feelings in order to accurately assess the meaning of the danger you're sensing. For example, is someone lying maliciously or perhaps just withholding information they are hoping to surprise you with for your birthday next week?

WITH LIFE, YOU:

→ Relate to obstacles, disappointments, and breakdowns as here to help you grow wiser, stronger, more resilient, and more mature.

Skills and Capacities to Learn

→ Self-soothe in ways that will allow you to respond generatively to breakdowns rather than react in destructive and potentially damaging ways.

→ Distinguish between your fear voice and your intuitive voice in order to live in sync with your own intuition.

→ Recognize your own healthy boundaries and assert them in ways that are nonthreatening and relationship enhancing.

→ Discern the level of psychological development of others to realistically assess their ability to show up in trustworthy ways before putting your full trust and faith in them.

→ Discern the character of others to realistically assess their ability to show up in trustworthy ways before putting your full trust and faith in them.

→ Assess the motives of others, both wholesome and unwholesome, in order to determine how to navigate the relationship.

→ Adequately measure risk factors before moving into action.

→ Have good energetic boundaries to not overly identify with those experiencing trauma; cultivate the ability to have compassion, yet also differentiate between yourself and others.

Gifts

→ You have a high tolerance for risk, which allows you to create enormous success for yourself and others.

→ You're a tireless fighter for the greater good.

→ You're highly perceptive, possessing an extraordinary capacity for intuitive knowing.

→ You're a master of detail and nuance.

I Am Stupid

~

Source Fracture Story

ABOUT YOURSELF
- → *I am stupid.*
- → *I am an idiot.*
- → *I am a moron.*

ABOUT OTHERS
- → *Others are smarter than me.*

ABOUT LIFE
- → *I can never figure anything out.*

Yourself as Source

WITH YOURSELF, YOU:
- → Assume your intelligence was fixed at birth rather than is ever expanding, which has you playing it safe and refusing to risk failure to avoid validating your fear that you're stupid.
- → Look for a steady stream of easy wins where you don't have to work very hard as a way to boost your self-image.
- → Undermine your own perspectives by second-guessing everything you do and say.

→ Judge yourself harshly for saying or doing something you fear others will think is stupid.

WITH OTHERS, YOU:

→ Present factual information as though it's a question and you're asking for permission or validation for even the simplest of assertions. For example, "My name is Jane?"

→ Fail to ask questions that would provide you with enough information to create more confidence in your own knowledge, for fear of being revealed for what you don't yet know.

→ Underpresent yourself, giving them the impression that you are less intelligent than you actually are.

→ Speak in a high-pitched, almost childlike, voice.

→ Try to hide by being silent and failing to speak up.

WITH LIFE, YOU:

→ Assume that life hasn't given you what you would need to be successful.

Others May Experience You As:

→ Nonthreatening.

→ Less intelligent than you actually are.

→ A target for bullying.

→ Someone they can mold to their own perspectives and use to their own advantage.

True You Power Statements

→ *I am a smart, intelligent adult and I can figure this out.*

→ *My intelligence is not fixed but continually expanding according to the courage I have to ask questions and learn new things.*

→ *It's safe for me to not know things. Curiosity is my superpower.*

→ *I value the unique ways that I'm naturally intelligent, recognizing book smarts as only one way to understand the world.*

→ *Failure is simply an opportunity to grow and to learn. It's only when I refuse to risk failure that I shrivel and stagnate.*

New Ways of Relating

WITH YOURSELF, YOU:

→ Value the various forms of intelligence that might come more naturally to you. For example, creative intelligence, musical intelligence, intuitive intelligence, or interpersonal intelligence.

→ Slow down when you don't understand something to give it greater attention and effort, leaning in to try to learn something new in the face of a challenge.

→ Engage in encouraging and optimistic self-talk, such as, *I've almost got it now*, as you stay the course to try to figure something out.

→ Relate to your failures and mistakes as learning opportunities.

WITH OTHERS, YOU:

→ Assert factual information in a matter-of-fact tone of voice rather than speak it as a question. For example, "My name is Jane."

→ Speak in your adult voice when asserting your thoughts, opinions, and ideas.

→ Ask questions when you don't quite understand what's being said.

→ Freely reveal what you don't yet know without making it mean anything about you.

WITH LIFE, YOU:

→ Look for and value the gifts you *do* have and organize your life around developing and sharing them with the world.

Skills and Capacities to Learn

→ Recognize various forms of intelligence and value them all equally.

→ Practice encouraging self-talk, particularly when you don't understand something.

→ Stay with it when you don't understand something, breaking it down into more manageable parts until it begins to make more sense to you.

→ Take up space and assert yourself honestly in social situations.

Gifts

→ You have a thirst for knowledge and the potential to become a great life-long learner.

→ You're likely gifted with one or more alternative intelligences, such as kinesthetic or spatial intelligence.

→ You have the potential to be a patient and effective teacher of young children, as you instill a love of learning in others.

I Am Too Much

~

Source Fracture Story

ABOUT YOURSELF

→ *I am too much.*

→ *I am too big.*

→ *I am too loud.*

ABOUT OTHERS

→ *Others are overwhelmed by my big energy.*

ABOUT LIFE

→ *It would be grandiose to assume that my big vision for my life is real.*

Yourself as Source

WITH YOURSELF, YOU:

→ Are oversized in almost all you do, from wearing wild, flashy colors and clothes, to talking a lot and taking up a lot of space socially, to gathering too much stuff that clutters your home.

→ Shame yourself for your large energy and huge visions and dreams and fail to take constructive actions to build a life that's big enough for you.

→ Hold yourself back with self-doubts and self-judgments, dismissing your big dreams as a form of narcissism. You then make yourself wrong for not being, doing, or having enough.

With Others, You:

→ Dim yourself to try to be acceptable, then feel stuck in relationships that are not enough for you, as though you are Alice in Wonderland spilling out of a house that's too small.

→ Choose lovers and friends who are unable to contain you and who feel overwhelmed and even threatened by your big energy. When you finally have the courage to start sharing yourself uncensored, they shame you and try to get you to dim yourself.

→ Are gregarious and loud, which evokes shaming criticism from them, as though being that way is a bad thing.

→ Have few structures for the leadership you're here to express, and frequently find yourself in situations where you're offending them by taking the lead, as you are not the designated leader. Nor have you cultivated the skills of leadership that would have it go well.

→ Try to "keep a lid on it" by pretending to be less than who you are and failing to share the magnitude of your vision with those you are close with. When you finally do, they're unable to hold your vision and covertly mock you for thinking you could do what you want to do.

WITH LIFE, YOU:

→ Fail to follow your intuition to take those actions and make those choices that would allow you to cause the big life you're here to create for the benefit of all.

Others May Experience You As:

→ Overly reactive and theatrical about every little thing.

→ Dominating and/or bossy when you start asserting your leadership without the agreements, titles, or structures that would give you that role.

→ A bit exhausting because of your incessant need to take over a room due to not having a large enough platform to express your big, creative energy.

→ Confusing, because your life seems too modest for the big, dramatic energy you have.

→ Upsetting, as after weeks of knowing you, you suddenly stop pretending to be smaller than you are and start sharing what you really feel and want, which both blindsides and overwhelms them.

→ Someone they've come to expect will overgive and overfunction on their behalf.

True You Power Statements

→ *I have been given a double dose of energy for a reason! I came here to take up a lot of space in this world for the benefit of all beings.*

→ *I own my many wonderful talents and gifts, and I make it a top priority to get the training and support I need to express them fully.*

→ *I am here as a big and brilliant light for this world and it is my privilege and great joy to shine as brightly as I can.*

→ *My big energy is a blessing to all and I am supported to live and love as large as I can!*

New Ways of Relating

WITH YOURSELF, YOU:

→ Invest in your dreams by getting the right training for the future you sense is possible.

→ Create the right platforms, structures, and systems that can support you to reach your potentials for creativity and contribution.

WITH OTHERS, YOU:

→ Share your big visions and dreams up front to discern if they're able to hold the bigness of who you are—in order to know who to try to build a close relationship with and who not to.

→ Renegotiate the terms of your current connections to align everyone with your big and bright future. If they are unable to hold that with you, lessen your investment in the relationship to be more appropriate to where you are called to go.

→ Make sure you have the alignment and agreement of the group before automatically taking on a leadership role.

→ Expand your circle of care to include people you may never meet in person, recognizing that many of your gifts are meant to be shared with the world.

WITH LIFE, YOU:

→ Organize your life around actualizing the brightest and most expanded future you feel called to create and give up trying to fit into your life as it currently is.

Skills and Capacities to Learn

→ Get the training and credentials you'll need to both develop your talents and have the frameworks necessary to start sharing them with the world.

→ Cultivate leadership skills to provide trustworthy guidance and governance.

→ Assess the capacity of others to hold big visions and dreams in order to determine the level of investment you make in each connection.

→ Enroll others in your visions in ways that allow them to locate themselves inside of what you're up to in life and take a role in helping you make it happen.

→ Create teams of people who are behind you all the way, actively supporting your efforts to give your gifts to the world.

Gifts

→ You're multitalented, with many brilliant gifts to give the world.

→ Others feel well cared for by you.

→ You're excessively generous and loving.

→ You bring delight into social situations with your over-the-top joie de vivre.

→ You're the life of the party! The fun doesn't really start until you walk into the room.

I Am Unworthy

~

Source Fracture Story

ABOUT YOURSELF
- → *I am unworthy.*
- → *I am undeserving.*
- → *I am a servant.*

ABOUT OTHERS
- → *Others can't take care of themselves and I have to sacrifice myself to do it for them.*

ABOUT LIFE
- → *I am only here to serve others.*

Yourself as Source

WITH YOURSELF, YOU:
- → Are unclear about your needs and therefore don't acknowledge or tend to your needs properly.
- → Give more than you have, leaving you feeling tired and depleted much of the time.
- → Are conflicted about having anything in life when others in the world are going without.

→ Are prone to workaholism, going from one accomplishment to the next without pausing to appreciate or celebrate your successes.

→ Experience chronic feelings of emptiness underneath the busyness of your life.

→ Are chronically in debt, never having enough to take care of yourself properly.

→ Source your value by overgiving and overdoing for others.

WITH OTHERS, YOU:

→ Play the martyr, compelled to serve their needs, usually at your own expense.

→ Are keenly aware of what they want and need, and feel compelled to provide it as quickly as possible.

→ Have difficulty receiving nourishment, even when given with no strings attached.

→ Respond to being given a gift by immediately giving the giver something of equal or greater value.

→ Have a low sense of entitlement to getting your needs met, and an even lower sense of entitlement to asking for what you want.

→ Rarely set limits or say no to requests, even when what's being asked of you is unreasonable or something others could be doing for themselves.

→ Form relationships with people who are "takers" and who feel entitled to your care.

→ Give away your time, talents, and services for less than they are worth.

→ Lose track of your valuables, either giving them away or simply losing things of value.

WITH LIFE, YOU:

→ Have low expectations of what's yours to have in this lifetime and continually settle for crumbs.

Others May Experience You As:

→ There to serve them, expecting you to do for them what they could be doing for themselves and feeling entitled to your care, even when it's clearly at your own expense.

→ Generous in ways that pull on them to become overly dependent on you and to stop generating for themselves.

→ Burdensome, as they feel covertly responsible for trying to care for you in the ways you're refusing to care for yourself.

→ A workhorse. Someone they can always count on to go the extra mile.

True You Power Statements

→ *I honor my feelings, needs, and desires as worthy of my own attention and love.*

→ *I prioritize self-care, recognizing how deserving I am of care.*

→ *I am a humanitarian lover of the world. I attend to the well-being of all living beings and include myself in my circle of care.*

→ *I gratefully receive from others and release any impulse to reciprocate from a sense of unworthiness or obligation.*

→ *I open myself to all manner of love, support, recognition, and financial reward, recognizing my deep worthiness to receive abundantly.*

→ *I live in a field of synchronicity, magic, and miracles, and allow the abundance of life to flow through me and to me.*

New Ways of Relating

WITH YOURSELF, YOU:

→ Recognize your feelings, needs, and desires, and prioritize doing what it takes to tend to them all.

→ Nurture yourself on a regular basis, discovering what brings you rest, renewal, and a sense of joy, and make these activities mandatory rather than optional.

→ Prioritize caring for yourself emotionally, physically, and financially before giving to others.

→ Own your inherent value, recognizing you need do nothing to try to prove it.

→ Celebrate your accomplishments.

WITH OTHERS, YOU:

→ Are present to their suffering without assuming it's your job to rescue, fix, or provide what you perceive to be missing.

→ Say no or negotiate just a portion of what's requested of you if and when you don't have all to give, while maintaining an openhearted connection.

→ Receive freely with gratitude and without automatically reciprocating.

→ Raise your expectations of mutuality and reciprocity, and if others are unwilling or incapable, let them go or lessen your investment in the connection.

→ Put limits on the time, energy, talents, and services you give, particularly when you're not being financially rewarded for your generosity.

WITH LIFE, YOU:

→ Raise your expectations! Assume you're here to experience the fruits of abundance in your life and stop settling for less.

Skills and Capacities to Learn

→ Identify what you are feeling and needing at any given moment.

→ Recognize the limits of what you can do for others and set clear boundaries to keep your relationships balanced and safe.

→ Receive graciously without reciprocating and with an open, humble heart.

→ Manage your tendency toward pathological generosity to ensure you have it to give before volunteering.

→ Manage your financial resources so that you always have low to no debt and money in the bank.

Gifts

→ You are profoundly generous, philanthropic, and altruistic, either giving away large sums of money and time to worthy causes or inspiring others to do so.

→ You are deeply sensitive to the suffering of others and possess a huge capacity for compassion and kindness.

→ You have an excellent work ethic and are a tireless worker for the common good.

I Am Not Valuable

~

Source Fracture Story

ABOUT YOURSELF

- → *I am not valuable.*
- → *I am worthless.*
- → *I am disposable.*
- → *I am a nobody.*

ABOUT OTHERS

- → *Others don't value me.*
- → *Others are better than me.*

ABOUT LIFE

- → *My life is worthless.*

Yourself as Source

WITH YOURSELF, YOU:

- → Underestimate and devalue your gifts, talents, and capacities.
- → Devalue your achievements.
- → Give or throw away things that are valuable to you.
- → Shop in cheap stores, filling your home with things you don't value and easily throw away.

→ Put yourself in jeopardy by giving away your money to those you think need it more than you.

→ Don't spend money on yourself even when you have it, or waste your money on things that don't really support you or bring you pleasure.

→ Feel a sense of shame and inferiority much of the time, confused about how others create successful and abundant lives when you feel so unable to do so.

WITH OTHERS, YOU:

→ Underpresent yourself and the value of what you have to offer.

→ Fail to create structures to receive money. For example, setting up an online payment system.

→ Are unclear about what to charge for your services, either undercharging or charging more than the market value. Either way, you fail to bring in the finances you need to live well.

→ Present yourself in haphazard, inconsistent, and sloppy ways that make it hard for them to see the value of what you offer.

→ Are unclear when it comes to matters of money. For example, quote one price but then charge another or forget to bill for services rendered.

→ Chronically borrow against your own well-being to ensure the well-being of others.

→ Have sex with people who don't value you and have no regard for your relationship.

→ Give away your time, energy, and services for free or for much less than their value.

→ Devalue others and therefore leave relationships easily, giving up on people prematurely. Either that or you stay too long with those who devalue you or fail to treat you with consideration and respect.

→ Self-abandon, overfunction, and overgive to try to convince others of your value, inadvertently convincing them otherwise.

→ Overcompensate by overcharging and overvaluing what you are providing.

WITH LIFE, YOU:

→ Can't get any traction and chronically feel stuck in survival mode.

Others May Experience You As:

→ Undeserving of appropriate financial remuneration. They fail to pay you what you're worth and offer less than the going rate.

→ Unworthy of their support and sponsorship to help you achieve your goals or reach your potential.

→ Someone they can easily dispose of without warning or proper closure. For example, they ghost you or fail to follow up as they said they would.

→ A person they can take from without feeling the need to reciprocate in any meaningful way.

True You Power Statements

→ *I need do nothing to prove my value. My value is simply inherent in who I am.*

→ *I am grateful for the value of all that I already am, all that I already do, and all that I already have.*

→ *I own the value of my gifts and express them in unique and purposeful ways.*

→ *I am recognized and richly rewarded for who I am and the value I provide.*

→ *Others are inspired to support and sponsor me to realize the fullness of my creative contributions.*

→ *I am capable of manifesting more than enough money to meet all of my needs and fulfill my deepest desires.*

→ *The more I value myself and what I have to offer, the more others will, too.*

→ *I value others and all they have to offer, focusing on all that they are rather than all they are not.*

New Ways of Relating

WITH YOURSELF, YOU:

→ Fill your home with what you truly need, value, and love, and let go of the rest.

→ Spend your time doing what you believe in and care about deeply.

→ Take excellent care of your possessions.

→ Pay attention to and take excellent care of your physical health.

→ Celebrate your achievements.

→ Set up structures to receive financial abundance into your life.

→ Create an abundance savings account, even if you only put in a small amount each week.

→ Set intentions and commit to visions that would create abundance and joy in all areas of your life.

WITH OTHERS, YOU:

→ Present yourself with modesty, yet make visible the value of who you are and what you have to offer.

→ Charge an appropriate amount for your offerings and services—not too much but not too little.

→ Create structures that make the value of your offerings visible to others. For example, a well-thought-out bio that inspires people to want to work with you or a website that demonstrates clearly the value of what you have to offer.

→ Create structures that give you clarity and visibility into how much money you have, how much money you need, how much money you make, and how much money you intend to make in the future.

→ Consider and communicate clearly what you need and want to create clarity and safety before becoming sexually involved with someone.

→ Value your relationships and do your best to nurture and care for them.

WITH LIFE, YOU:

→ Expect the best! Raise your expectations of what's possible and live into a future that is abundant and fulfilling.

Skills and Capacities to Learn

→ Anticipate your own needs as they relate to your time, energy, and finances.

→ Assess the appropriate value of your offerings and charge accordingly.

→ Present well professionally.

→ Create structures for money, recognition, and reward to come to you.

→ Negotiate to receive adequate compensation.

→ Discern when and how to say no and set limits while maintaining relatedness.

→ Use conflict resolution to work things through with others.

→ Expand your capacity to receive abundance. For example, buy quality clothes you love or a reliable and safe car.

→ Cultivate a sense of gratitude and appreciation for the value of what you already have.

Gifts

→ You're highly resourceful and able to make do with very little.

→ You're exceptionally creative and able to transform what appear to be scraps into unique and beautiful treasures.

→ You're a trustworthy worker and provide exceptional value to those you serve.

→ You possess a keen ability to sense and address the real needs of others rather than just the surface needs they may express.

→ You create art, projects, and programs that provide great value for others.

I Am Not Wanted

~

Source Fracture Story

ABOUT YOURSELF
- → *I am not wanted.*
- → *I am not liked.*
- → *I am not chosen.*

ABOUT OTHERS
- → *Others will reject me.*
- → *Others don't like me.*
- → *Others don't choose me.*

ABOUT LIFE
- → *The world doesn't want what I have to offer.*

Yourself as Source

WITH YOURSELF, YOU:
- → Don't want what you have and long for what you don't.
- → Reject and marginalize your own deeper feelings and needs.
- → Judge yourself harshly and are often exacerbated and frustrated by your own behavior.

WITH OTHERS, YOU:

→ Are rejection-sensitive and often protect yourself by rejecting others before they have a chance to reject you.

→ Have an assertive, and at times even aggressive, communication style that causes others to back up or push you away, which you then perceive as rejection.

→ Unconsciously violate their personal space, causing them to feel uncomfortable and push you away or withdraw.

→ Speak in a strident, disagreeable, and/or loud voice.

→ Are the last person picked for and the first kicked off the team.

→ "Cast your pearls before swine" by sharing tender parts of yourself with those who've not demonstrated they care enough about you to warrant such disclosures.

→ Try to buy people by giving them things you think they want to get them to like you and make you their friend.

→ Launch into an intense conversation without first checking in to see if this is a good time for others to engage in deep dialogue.

→ Miss important social cues. For example, someone looking at their phone or starting to gather their things. Rather than take the hint, you keep talking as though nothing is wrong and even escalate the intensity of the conversation.

→ Interrupt or intrude at inappropriate and/or inconvenient times and without noticing how your behavior impacts others.

→ Aggressively assert your opinions without being asked or invited to speak.

→ Talk beyond their capacity to listen.

→ Force things onto them rather than enroll them into what you're up to.

→ Overgive to try to convince them to choose you.

WITH LIFE, YOU:

→ Always push to try to make things happen, often before it's time.

Others May Experience You As:

→ Pushy and overbearing.

→ Intrusive, leaving them with nowhere to go but to back up, leave, or put up a wall.

→ Someone who takes hostages by talking at them rather than engaging in a mutually meaningful dialogue.

→ Someone they dread running into.

→ Someone not worth choosing.

→ Rejecting of them. They may even feel disrespected or disliked by you.

True You Power Statements

→ *When I like and accept myself, others tend to like and accept me, too.*

→ *When I stop trying so hard and just allow for a spacious back-and-forth flow to the conversation, others tend to like and come toward me.*

→ *Other people tend to like those who like them. It's safe for me to lean in and be curious and openhearted toward others.*

→ *I live in a welcoming world. My presence is welcomed and my gifts are wanted by others.*

→ *I am here for a purpose and my gifts and talents are both wanted and needed in this world.*

→ *I am worthy of being chosen, even when someone I'm choosing is not choosing me.*

New Ways of Relating

WITH YOURSELF, YOU:

→ Welcome all of your feelings and needs without judgment.

→ Want what you have. Appreciate what you already possess. And assume you have the power to create even more.

→ Are patient and kind to yourself when you're not getting the results you want.

WITH OTHERS, YOU:

→ Contain your enthusiasm and energy to make room for their energy, conscious to not just take over the conversation.

→ Allow for more physical space between yourself and them so you're not standing too close or getting "up in their face."

→ Are aware of how your words and actions are impacting them and are sensitive to their responses.

→ Check in before you launch into sharing what you want to say, to make sure that others are available to hear you at this time.

→ Are mindful of not calling or texting at inappropriate times. For example, at dinner time, midnight, or six a.m.

→ Are agreeable, collaborative, and cooperative. You work well with others.

WITH LIFE, YOU:

→ Use your big energy to push forward projects and programs that need an unstoppable energy to create great things.

Skills and Capacities to Learn

→ Feel genuine gratitude for all that you already are and all that you already have and do, cultivating the ability to love yourself and your life as it is.

→ Recognize social cues such as body language, facial expressions, and subtle hints as to what's happening for others.

→ Learn the subtle art of inspiring and enrolling others into your ideas and visions rather than pushing them to think as you do.

→ Create cohesion in a conversation so that what you're saying is related to and fits into the already existing discussion, rather than just dump your own viewpoint onto others.

→ Manage your own big energy to make room for others.

→ Listen with empathy for how others might feel and what they might need to feel safe, seen, and heard.

Gifts

→ You're unstoppable and capable of creating great success due to your highly developed ability to stay the course, even in the face of multiple rejections and disappointments.

→ You're able to achieve extraordinary results, as you're in it for the long haul; you are not a quitter.

→ You take advocacy to a whole new level, as you are able to sell almost any idea for the greater good.

I Am Wrong

~

Source Fracture Story

ABOUT YOURSELF

- → *I am wrong.*
- → *I am a mistake.*
- → *I am defective.*

ABOUT OTHERS

- → *Others know what's right for me better than I do.*

ABOUT LIFE

- → *My life is all wrong.*
- → *My life is a mistake.*

Yourself as Source

WITH YOURSELF, YOU:

- → Make more than the average number of mistakes, frequently messing things up. For example, lose keys, forget appointments, or misplace important documents.
- → Constantly judge and shame yourself for being wrong, making it difficult to grow and learn from your mistakes.
- → Are risk averse to the extreme, playing way too small a game for fear of making a mistake.

→ Take a long time to make even small choices, then undermine them by second-guessing yourself. Either that or you make ill-considered and poor decisions quickly and then beat yourself up for them.

→ Discount, dismiss, and override your intuition when trying to decipher what to do, compromising your capacity to make holistically informed decisions.

→ Berate yourself in response to making a bad decision, undermining your ability to trust yourself moving forward.

WITH OTHERS, YOU:

→ Make them wrong and stubbornly assert your need to be right to the extreme, even if it costs you love.

→ Frequently break your word due to how often you change your mind and second-guess yourself.

→ Are defensive against any suggestion that you may not have done something correctly, putting people in the oppressive position of not being able to give you any feedback unless it's positive.

WITH LIFE, YOU:

→ Fail to differentiate between taking responsibility and being to blame, which means you're both unable to learn from your mistakes and come into the fullness of your power.

Others May Experience You As:

→ The one at fault, blaming and shaming you for whatever goes wrong.

→ Irritating and frustrating due to your chronic indecisiveness.

→ Difficult to give feedback to, due to your high level of defensiveness.

→ Someone they judge more harshly than others.

True You Power Statements

→ *There are no mistakes in nature. There is nothing wrong with how the Universe made me. I embrace my flawed humanity with unconditional self-love and self-respect.*

→ *I trust my intuition and easily navigate the choices of my life in partnership with a force and field of life greater than myself.*

→ *All of my mistakes help me to learn and grow in ways that promise to make me a better person.*

→ *I accept my own flaws and imperfections and allow them to bring me closer to others, who are also flawed and imperfect.*

New Ways of Relating

WITH YOURSELF, YOU:

→ Take responsibility for your mistakes in a way that allows you to learn from them, without shaming yourself or making yourself wrong.

→ Create systems to help you better manage the details of your life. For example, put your keys in a predictable spot, set up calendar alerts, and organize your file cabinet.

→ Take greater risks, assuming that you'll make mistakes along the way that will teach you what you'll need to know to succeed.

→ Give up the fantasy that there is such a thing as a perfect decision and do the best you can to weigh and measure the choices you have.

→ Empower the choices you make by recognizing that you can never know the path not taken.

→ Listen to your intuition, paying particular attention to alternative ways of knowing, such as dreams, signs, and synchronicities, to help you make holistically informed decisions.

→ Are kind to yourself when you make a bad decision, valuing the learning opportunity it provides.

WITH OTHERS, YOU:

→ Humbly assume that they might be right and you might be wrong, without making it mean anything about either of you.

→ Honor your word by being responsible for what you've said you'd do and by when, and renegotiating your agreements if and when you change your mind.

→ Take feedback well, listening to what others have to say with an open mind yet recognizing that you are ultimately the one to decide what feedback is valuable to you and what is not.

WITH LIFE, YOU:

→ Recognize that you're here by divine design and, as such, have a responsibility to play your biggest game in life, even if that means you'll make some mistakes along the way.

Skills and Capacities to Learn

→ Practice self-soothing techniques to use in the aftermath of making a mistake.
→ Process your mistakes outside of shame with humility, curiosity, and a willingness to learn.
→ Improve executive functioning skills to help you organize your life.
→ Weigh and measure the pros, cons, and potential consequences of making any given decision.
→ Live in alignment with your own intuition.
→ Give and receive feedback with nonviolent communication skills.

Gifts

→ You are deeply compassionate and have a profound ability to accept the flawed humanity and limitations of others.
→ You are powerfully forgiving—of yourself and others.
→ You possess a sweet humility that inspires trust, deep-rooted love, and loyalty in others.

Acknowledgments

～

All of us have special ones who have loved us into being.

—FRED ROGERS

There are so many beautiful souls who've been supporting me for years as I developed the ideas contained in this book. First and foremost, gratitude goes to my loving partner, Michael Fried, who believed in this work long before I was ready to write it all down. Michael, your relentless stand for this work, and your confidence in me to bring it forth, has given me the courage and conviction to complete it. This book would not exist were it not for you. Deep thanks also go to my wonderful agent, Bonnie Solow, whose standards of excellence inspired me to strive to do my best to meet them. This book would not be what it is without your investment and thinking partnership. To my lovely editor, Amy Sun at Penguin Life, my deepest gratitude goes to you for your intelligence and wise guidance in bringing this book over the finish line. And to Claire Coghlan, who has been by my side during the entire process of writing this book, and who tirelessly made sure that the best of the True You teachings made it into these pages.

Thank you, too, to my family, who went above and beyond, each in their own way. Sandra Pullman, to whom this book is dedicated; my loving father, Bob Kersch; as well as my brothers, Todd Grupe and Scott Grupe; my daughter, Alexandria Thomas; and my goddaughter, Jennifer

ACKNOWLEDGMENTS

Morgan Eresh. A special heartfelt thank-you goes to my chosen family—my bonus daughter, LeRoya Sanford, and my dear friend Lee Sanford, for so generously and heroically supporting me to bring this project to fruition.

I also wish to thank my core team. Those who have been in the trenches for the past several years to grow our True You community—Susan Dumbarton, Jessica Yip, Kirsten Monks, Braden Ong, Jeffrey Kihn, Lindsey King, and the late Wendy Speigner. As well as our newer team members whose support allowed us to fly—Simona Ksoll, Myriam Jenni, Michael Speigner, Selin Sari, Tiffany Harnsongkram, and Salina Wittmer.

Gratitude also goes to Shelley Griswold, whose steadfast kindness and wisdom have been the ace up my sleeve. And there are no words to express my love and appreciation for my beloved circle of friends who prayerfully supported me through many wild ups and downs as I was writing—Marianne Williamson, Debra Poneman, Victoria Pearman, Tina Cameron, Genevieve Deely, Bruce Bierman, and Todd Hutcheson.

My deepest thanks also go to the nearly two thousand coaches I've had the honor of training and certifying over the years—in particular, True You Coaches Leila Reyes, Kim von Berg, Paige Ramsey Palmer, Jeanne Byrd Romero, Charmaine Heard, and Saybel Nunez, as well as those in our True You courses and membership communities for providing a vibrant and creative incubator in which to evolve this work. Gratitude also goes to my small but mighty group of Future Forward Therapists, who are pioneering a new form of psychotherapy based on the teachings of True You—in particular, Kate Wechsler, Brandyn Caires, Lori Frison, Lisa Sloane, Heide Malat, and Margot Parker.

And finally, my thanks go to you, dear reader, for taking this work to heart in your own life and for joining us as together we strive to cocreate a happy, healthy future for us all.

Note to Therapists, Counselors, and Coaches

For those of you who've been helping people to heal and find a way forward from the most dire of circumstances, I want to both acknowledge and applaud your good efforts. The hurdles, challenges, and heartbreak we sometimes experience when holding people in their pain can weigh on us, and my intention is that the True You framework provide you with a renewed sense of creativity and possibility. As the fields of psychotherapy and coaching are continually evolving, it's my hope that this book both honors the work you've been doing and also provides you with additional tools for the next steps of your professional development.

The concepts I've introduced here might be curious to some of you and confronting to others. Ideas such as that we are the source of our own experience, or that we must wake up out of victimization if we ever hope to change, or that the future is not fixed but open to our influence and intentions, or that healing is a different domain than transformation, or that beliefs are relational, *formed* in relationship with others and *only transformed* in relationship with others—these are the entry points to liberation beyond the pain of the past and the gateway toward a truly transformed future.

For those of you who'd like to enliven your own practice and learn more about how to begin implementing these Future Forward technologies into your work with clients, I've created two free introductory trainings—one for therapists and counselors and one for coaches. Both of these complementary trainings will provide you with basic Future Forward techniques based on the True You teachings, such as how you can:

→ Motivate clients to set powerful intentions that inspire them to outgrow who they've known themselves to be for the possibility of who they might become.

→ Help clients to take responsibility for themselves as the source of their experience in a way that creates hope for their future, and without moving into self-blame or shame.

→ Teach clients to mentor themselves when they're triggered in a way that helps them to regulate difficult emotions, increase a sense of self-compassion, and awaken their own inner wisdom.

→ Move clients away from endless insight and analysis as to why they are the way they are and toward the ability to live from the center of their wisdom, strength, and power.

→ Be empowered as a therapist, counselor, or coach by demonstrating how you can integrate the True You steps into all aspects of your work with clients.

To access these complementary resources, please go to katherine woodwardthomas.com/therapists-coaches.

Glossary

Adult self: The part of you that has access to the intelligence, competence, resilience, and resourcefulness of an adult. This is the "you" that's able to see any situation from a larger perspective and discern the voice of Truth with a capital *T* from the interpretive lens of past trauma. It is the "you" that has access to wisdom, power, and maturity, and that can tolerate disappointments, setbacks, and delays and stay the course in the face of them.

Blended: This term, originating with Richard C. Schwartz, PhD, describes the collapse into a false center, where you suddenly find yourself overly identified with a younger part of you and interpreting what's happening through the lens of the "you" that you created in response to past trauma.

Choice point: When committed to living from the true you, you will be required to fundamentally shift the choices you make and the actions you take, whereby each choice serves as a fork in the road, offering an opportunity to source who you're being from the future you're intending to create—such that your actions are both in integrity with that possibility as well as generative of it.

Disidentify: To be able to witness the part of you that is triggered into an old story without becoming blended with the self of that story. By disidentifying from that self, you are free to look for a more accurate and empowering narrative of who you are and who you feel called to become. By disidentifying from the wounded self, you're free to step outside of yourself enough to name and tame the inner conversation that has had you in its grip. You can wear your automatic assumptions a bit more loosely and recognize your internal dialogue not as truth but as remnants of old trauma.

Enmeshed: This is another way of naming the experience of blending, where one becomes overly identified with the younger, tender self that's holding an old, disempowering narrative at the level of identity. Seeing through the lens of that perspective, a person is then vulnerable to responding to what's happening in ways that validate and perpetuate evidence for that old story.

False center: This term is interchangeable with the term *source fracture story*. It describes the holistic narrative of self that you created in response to an old wounding. This narrative includes a belief about yourself, how others will feel about you and treat you, and your relationship with life. It was created before you had the cognitive capacity to create a more holistically informed and accurate interpretation of whatever was happening in your world at the time. This false "you" lives as a cluster of emotions and energies in your body. When you act from this center, you will tend to show up in ways that covertly generate more evidence for this perspective. No matter what you do to try to outgrow old patterns, when acting from this center, you will stay painfully stuck in them.

Future Forward technologies: The professional wing of the True You transformative teachings that trains and certifies Future Forward Therapists and True You Coaches.

Future self: This describes the "you" of your intended positive, possible future. The "you" that you are sourcing from the future you're called to create versus the "you" that you've known yourself to be.

Higher self: The part of you that is connected to a force and field of life greater than you, and which exists even beyond this lifetime. It is the part of you that is eternal, omniscient, conscious, and intelligent, and which has access to wisdom beyond your years. It is the highest and truest version of yourself.

Masterful manifester: Someone who has taken their rightful place as a creator of life and not simply a reactor to life. For many of us, this is a new way of being in relationship with life, one where you have the spiritual strength, as well as the agency, to actively generate the future you desire.

Positive, possible future: The future you hunger for. An unprecedented, unreasonable, and even irrational future that's not at all predictable when looking at your history, your circumstances, or the inadequate resources you currently have at your disposal. It is a future that's completely outside of your current identity to create. One that immediately pulls on you to redefine and recalibrate who you've known yourself to be for the possibility of who you might become. It is a possibility that infuses you with the creative energy you'll need to start sourcing how you show up in life from the "you" of the future you're committed to creating.

Possible self: The "you" of the positive, possible future fulfilled. This is the "you" that you can begin to feel in your body when setting an intention to manifest a miracle in your life. It's the "you" that is activated when you take a stand to create the future *from* the future, and begin sourcing who you are being, and how you are showing up, from that positive possibility.

Power center: That holistic, grounded place within you that's holding an expanded sense of possibility and purpose to become who you feel called to be and create what you feel called to create.

Power statement: A concise, powerful statement that acts as a conduit to deconstruct a false center and anchor you in a greater truth. Like a bull's-eye struck right at the heart of a source fracture story, a good power statement will liberate you from the false center in a way you can feel in your body. It will then begin elevating you to a higher plane in consciousness and unleash a sense of creativity and hope for a happier life moving forward. Let's call it a chiropractic adjustment to your consciousness.

Relational trauma: A traumatic experience from your past that occurred at a time when your identity was still being formed, whereby the wounding happened in relationship with others who mattered, such as your early caregivers. Because identity is formed in relationship with others, it can only be transformed in relationship as well.

Self: The word *self* with a small *s* refers to our consciousness at the level of identity and is often called the ego or the personality self.

Self-love power practice: A potent practice that can be used when you feel triggered or simply as a kind and self-caring check-in with yourself throughout your day. It's a loving practice that can be used any time you need help to hold and contain difficult feelings from a deeper, wider center within.

Shifting centers: A change in where you are centered within yourself, from being overly identified with the traumatized self in your body to being centered in the wise, more mature true you—the calm, clear, wise, and resource-ful self that lies at the core of who you are. It's stepping out of the quicksand of your false center in order to respond to whatever is happening from the truth of your value, worthiness, and power. In doing so, you grow your capac-ity to live from your power center and secure a solid, sovereign sense of self as your *primary* internal home base.

Source fracture story: An interchangeable term with *false center*, it's the story you created in response to your original attachment trauma—the original break in your heart and your initial break in belonging. It's a story about your-self, your relationship with others, and your relationship with life that lodged in your psyche as a self-defeating, shame-based sense of identity that you're vulnerable to collapsing into when you feel disappointed, threatened, or scared. It's an internal narrative—such as *I don't matter, others matter more than I do*, and *I'm insignificant and nothing I do will ever matter*—that lies at the heart of the frustrating and painful patterns you're here to outgrow.

Trauma: A distressing wounding that leaves a long-lasting negative imprint on your nervous system, body, psyche, and soul. When trauma happens dur-ing your formative years—the time when your identity is still forming—it can also leave a long-lasting negative impact on your sense of self, your assump-tions about your relationships with others, and your viewpoint of what's possi-ble for you to have and create in this world.

Traumatized self: The self you formed in response to a traumatic event or ongoing experience, or the self-sense you inherited from your lineage. The "you" that you created in response to what happened to you long ago and that lives in your body as a highly sensitive knee-jerk reaction or an automatic flight, fight, freeze, fawn, or flop response whenever you feel disappointed, threatened, or afraid. When emotionally identified with this story, you'll have a tendency to show up in ways that create more evidence for this perspective.

True self: This term is interchangeable with the term *true you*. It represents the strongest, most creative, resilient, and resourceful part of you that has ac-cess to wisdom beyond your years, as well as power, possibility, and perspec-tive. This part of you can observe whatever is happening with objectivity, compassion, and unconditional self-love.

True you: This term is interchangeable with the term *true self*. This is the part of you that's centered in a preconscious conviction of your worthiness, value, and power. The "you" that is holistically, somatically aligned with your value, your power, and your worthiness to create the future you're standing for. The "you" beyond who you assumed yourself to be in response to the wounds you experienced long ago. The "you" that will help you not just *deal* with these old hurts but will give you direct access to freedom beyond them. Awakening your power to make all of the wonderful things you want to happen in your life happen.

True You Breakthrough Blueprint: A practical and easily understood atlas of the twenty-two most common source fracture stories (aka false centers or identity-based beliefs). This blueprint provides clarity on the very specific and habitual ways you have been showing up in relationship with yourself, with others, and in life that have unconsciously generated relational evidence for your source fracture story and the exact steps you can now take to graduate from these stories such that you are finally free to generate your life outside of them.

Unreasonable intention: An unreasonable assertion to create a positive, possible future that is completely outside of your current identity, and whose fulfillment is not predictable from where you stand today. It is a powerful stand for the positive, possible future you yearn to be living.

Wise self: Your inner, resourceful, wise adult self. You might also refer to this part of you as the *adult self, higher self,* or simply *Self* with a capital *S*. It's your inner fairy godparent who is trustworthy, wise, and kind, and able to mentor you to a higher perspective. This part of you brings maturity, kindness, wisdom, and love to comfort and contain runaway feelings of shame, alienation, fear, or unworthiness that the younger you might be struggling with.

Wounded self: This term is interchangeable with the term *traumatized self.* It describes the version of "you" that was formed in response to past disappointments and/or relational traumas, whereby you're interpreting the world through the eyes of your hurt, younger self. From this center, you tend to see things in an overly simplistic, absolute, and childlike way, as you initially created this worldview at a time when you developmentally lacked the cognitive capacity to see things from a more holistic and well-rounded perspective.

Selected Bibliography

Clear, James. *Atomic Habits: An Easy and Proven Way to Build Good Habits and Break Bad Ones.* Avery, 2018.

Collins, Nathan. "Mental Rehearsal Prepares Our Minds for Real-World Action." *Stanford Medicine News Center*, February 22, 2018. med.stanford.edu.

Daniel, Andrew. *Awaken to Your True Self: Why You're Still Stuck and How to Break Through.* MetaHeal, 2022.

Dispenza, Joe. *Breaking the Habit of Being Yourself: How to Lose Your Mind and Create a New One.* Hay House Inc., 2012.

Dweck, Carol. *Mindset: The New Psychology of Success.* Ballantine Books, 2006.

Fisher, Janina. *Healing the Fragmented Selves of Trauma Survivors: Overcoming Internal Self-Alienation.* Routledge, 2017.

Gilligan, Stephen. *The Courage to Love: Principles and Practices of Self-Relations Psychotherapy.* W. W. Norton & Company, 1997.

Goddard, Neville. *The Power of Awareness.* DeVorss Publications, 1952.

Hardy, Benjamin. *Be Your Future Self Now: The Science of Intentional Transformation.* Hay House Inc., 2022.

————. *Personality Isn't Permanent: Break Free from Self-Limiting Beliefs and Rewrite Your Story.* Portfolio, 2020.

Hershfield, Hal. *Your Future Self: How to Make Tomorrow Better Today.* Little, Brown Spark, 2023.

Holiday, Ryan. *The Obstacle Is the Way: The Timeless Art of Turning Trials into Triumph.* Portfolio, 2014.

Lipton, Bruce H. *The Biology of Belief 10th Anniversary Edition: Unleashing the Power of Consciousness, Matter & Miracles.* Hay House Inc., 2016.

Madhubuti, Haki R. *Liberation Narratives: New and Collected Poems: 1966–2009.* Third World Press, 2009.

Markus, Hazel, and Paula Nurius. "Possible Selves." *American Psychologist* 41, no. 9 (1986): 954–69.

SELECTED BIBLIOGRAPHY

Maté, Gabor, and Daniel Maté. *The Myth of Normal: Trauma, Illness, and Healing in a Toxic Culture.* Avery, 2022.

Moser, Jason S., Adrienne Dougherty, Whitney I. Mattson, et al. "Third-Person Self-Talk Facilitates Emotion Regulation Without Engaging Cognitive Control: Converging Evidence from ERP and fMRI." *Scientific Reports* 7, no. 4519 (July 2017).

Murphy, Mary C. *Cultures of Growth: How the New Science of Mindset Can Transform Individuals, Teams, and Organizations.* Simon & Schuster, 2024.

Neff, Kristin. *Self-Compassion: The Proven Power of Being Kind to Yourself.* William Morrow Paperbacks, 2015.

Paris, Jennifer, Antoinette Ricardo, and Dawn Rymond. *Understanding the Whole Child: Prenatal Development Through Adolescence.* College of the Canyons, 2019.

Perry, Bruce D., and Oprah Winfrey. *What Happened to You? Conversations on Trauma, Resilience, and Healing.* Flatiron Books, 2021.

Rosling, Hans, Ola Rosling, and Anna Rosling Rönnlund. *Factfulness: Ten Reasons We're Wrong About the World—and Why Things Are Better Than You Think.* Flatiron Books, 2018.

Schwartz, Richard C. *No Bad Parts: Healing Trauma and Restoring Wholeness with the Internal Family Systems Model.* Sounds True, 2021.

Siegel, Daniel J. *IntraConnected: MWe (Me + We) as the Integration of Self, Identity, and Belonging.* W. W. Norton & Company, 2022.

Singer, Michael A. *The Untethered Soul: The Journey Beyond Yourself.* New Harbinger Publications, 2007.

Taylor, Jill Bolte. *My Stroke of Insight: A Brain Scientist's Personal Journey.* Plume, 2009.

Thomas, Katherine Woodward. *Calling in "The One": 7 Weeks to Attract the Love of Your Life*, rev. ed. Harmony, 2021.

van der Kolk, Bessel. *The Body Keeps the Score: Brain, Mind, and Body in the Healing of Trauma.* Penguin Books, 2015.

Verny, Thomas, with John Kelly. *The Secret Life of the Unborn Child: How You Can Prepare Your Unborn Baby for a Happy, Healthy Life.* Dell Publishing, 1981.

Wolinsky, Stephen. *The Dark Side of the Inner Child: The Next Step.* Bramble Books, 1994.

_____. *The Way of the Human: The False Core and the False Self.* The Quantum Psychology Notebooks, vol. 2. Quantum Institute Inc., 1999.

Wolynn, Mark. *It Didn't Start with You: How Inherited Family Trauma Shapes Who We Are and How to End the Cycle.* Viking, 2016.